Sex in Question

Sex in Question:
French materialist feminism

Edited by

Diana Leonard and Lisa Adkins

Taylor & Francis
Publishers since 1798

UK	Taylor & Francis Ltd, 1 Gunpowder Square, London, EC4A 3DE
USA	Taylor & Francis Inc., 1900 Frost Road, Suite 101, Bristol, PA 19007

First published 1996

A Catalogue Record for this book is available from the British Library

ISBN 0 7484 0293 4
ISBN 0 7484 0294 2 (pbk)

Library of Congress Cataloging-in-Publication Data are available on request

Cover design by Amanda Barragry

Typeset in 10/12 pt CG Times
by RGM, The Mews, Birkdale Village, Southport PR8 4AS, England

Printed in Great Britain by SRP, Exeter.

Contents

Acknowledgments

Publication history of the articles included in this volume:

1978

'Pratique du pouvoir et idée de Nature' ('The Practice of Power and Belief in Nature') by Colette Guillaumin was first published in *Questions féministes*, no 2, pp. 5–30 and no 3, pp. 5–28 in February and May 1978. A translation in English (by Linda Murgatroyd) was in *Feminist Issues* in Winter 1981, pp. 3–28 and Summer 1981, pp. 87–108. It was originally in two parts — '(I) L'appropriation des femmes' (Part I: The appropriation of Women) and '(II) Le discours de la Nature' (Part II: The Naturalist Discourse) — but here we include a new combined version, abridged by the author. The full version appears in her collection *Racism, Sexism, Power and Ideology* (London: Routledge), 1995.

'Nos dommages et leurs intérêts' ('Our Costs and Their Benefits') by Monique Plaza was originally published in *Questions féministes*, no 3, in 1978, and a translation was provided in *Feminist Issues*, vol 1, no 3, Summer 1981, pp. 25–35 ('Our Damages and Their Compensation. Rape: The Will Not to Know of Michel Foucault'). The version here is a new translation by Diana Leonard.

1982

'The Category of Sex' by Monique Wittig was first published in *Feminist Issues* in 1982 (but dated as written in 1976), vol. 2, no. 2, Fall, pp. 63–68, and later included in her collection *The Straight Mind and Other Essays* (Boston: Beacon Press and Hemel Hempstead: Harvester Wheatsheaf) in 1992.

1985

'Fertilité naturelle, reproduction forcée' ('Natural Fertility, Forced

Reproduction') by Paola Tabet was first published in N. C. Mathieu (Ed.) *L'Arraisonnement des femmes: essais en anthropologie des sexes*, Paris: Editions de l'École des Hautes Études en Sciences Sociales (in the 'Cahiers de l'Homme' series), 1985, pp. 61–146. This is the first English translation, by Diana Leonard.

1989

'Identité sexuelle/sexuée/de sexe?' ('Sexual, Sexed and Sex-Class Identities') by Nicole-Claude Mathieu was included in Anne-Marie Daune-Richard, Marie-Claude Hurtig and Marie-France Pichevin (Eds) *Catégorisation de sexe et Constructions scientifiques* (Aix-en-Provence: Université de Provence), 1989, pp. 109–147 and in N.-C. Mathieu's collection *L'Anatomie politique: catégorisations et idéologies du sexe*, Paris, Côté-femmes, 1991. This is the first English publication (translated by Diana Leonard).

1991

An earlier version (of 'Rethinking Sex and Gender'), 'Penser le genre: Quels problemes?' by Christine Delphy appeared in Marie-Claude Hurtig, Michèle Kail and Hélène Rouch (Eds) *Sexe et genre: de la hiérarchie entre les sexes* (Paris: Éditions du Centre National de la Recherche Scientifique), 1991. The present version was translated (by Diana Leonard) and appeared first in *Women's Studies International Forum*, vol 16, no 1, 1993, pp. 1–9.

We are grateful to *Questions féministes, Feminist Issues, Women's Studies International Forum*, Éditions de l'École des Hautes Études en Sciences Sociales, Université de Provence, Éditions du Centre National de la Recherche Scientifique, and to Linda Murgatroyd for permission to reprint these works.

Chapter 1

Reconstructing French Feminism: Commodification, Materialism and Sex

Lisa Adkins and Diana Leonard

Sex in Question is a collection of articles by French feminists who were members of the group that established the journal *Questions féministes* with Simone de Beauvoir. These papers are, however, quite unlike the phenomenon that the English-speaking world has come to know as 'French feminism' because they are written from a shared materialist feminist perspective.[1]

We have chosen one article by each of five key members of the group and a sixth by an Italian feminist who is close to the group. This selection, from an obviously very substantial range of books and articles, relates particularly to issues that have received a great deal of attention recently in North America and Europe: the construction and inter-relationship of gender, sex and sexuality. We hope that this book will therefore give its readers an indication — albeit only an indication — of what the rigorous and powerful *Questions féministes* analysis has to contribute to English language theoretical debates. In particular, it shows that there are feminists who have been saying for 20 years what is often seen as a major insight of the last five years in anglophone circles: that not just gender but also sex is a social, not a Natural, division; and that both gender and sex can only be understood in relation to heterosexuality.

Of the original *Questions féministes* editorial group,[2] the work of some individuals is already known and has been key to a number of anglophone feminist debates. But several are, unfortunately, almost unknown in Britain, North America (except for Quebec) and Australasia. Simone de Beauvoir's *The Second Sex* (published in 1949 and translated into English in 1953), together with her novels and volumes of autobiography, and the example of her own life and political work, have been an important inspiration for feminists throughout the world, especially since the rebirth of the women's movement in the early 1970s.[3] Monique Wittig's novels, plays and political statements on heterosexuality and the category 'woman', and in particular her well-known and controversial statement that 'lesbians are not women',[4] have been of great significance in debates around women's creative writing, heterosexuality and gender, and the relationships of sexual identity, language, subjectivity and consciousness.[5] More recently her ideas have again been widely drawn upon in women's studies and in lesbian and gay studies for

1

arguments about the relationships between sex and gender, and performativity, gender and heterosexuality.[6] Christine Delphy's work on domestic labour and on materialist feminism found particular currency in Britain during the mid-1980s, when the infamous 'domestic labour debate', and, more importantly, the relationship between marxism and feminism, marked the heartland of feminist theory.[7] However, the works of Nicole-Claude Mathieu, Monique Plaza and Paola Tabet are much less well known, and Colette Guillaumin is known mainly for her work on racism and right-wing ideologies, rather than for her work on sex and difference.[8]

In addition, despite the fame of particular individuals, the writers in and around *Questions féministes* (*QF*) are rarely recognised in the anglophone feminist literature as constituting a feminist 'tendency'. On the contrary, their work is almost never discussed in conjunction, and each is treated as an atomised writer, dissociated from any particular feminist position. So the connections between their ideas are seldom — if ever — acknowledged, and they are usually not considered in textbooks that purport to introduce feminist ideas and to compare 'radical feminism' with 'liberal' and 'socialist' feminisms. These women have, however, for 20 years been contributing actively to a common project of developing a distinctive form of feminist analysis, despite a major split over lesbian separatism during the early 1980s, which was followed by a court case and two members of the original group establishing *Nouvelles questions féministes* (*NQF*).[9] This split did not, however, involve a disagreement around the central *QF* concern with the political/power relationship between men and women, the appropriation of women's labour and bodies, and how women's consciousness is grounded in their situation. The founder members continue in many respects 'to think alike' (something of fundamental importance in France) and most communicate interpersonally and cross-reference each other's work. However, the impact of their ideas, and the importance of the journal itself, was undoubtedly reduced.

The lack of recognition of French radical materialist feminism as a tendency, its rather uneven representation and its individualisation in anglophone feminist debates, is not, however, due to a simple lack of English translation. Most of the feminists associated with the group have had some of their key writings translated. Moreover, the (US based) journal *Feminist Issues* was established in 1981 precisely for the purpose of disseminating their ideas (though because of the split, Delphy's work has not appeared there since its first year). However, although *Feminist Issues* may have proved significant and important in introducing some of the work from *Questions féministes* into the North American context, as an outlet for publication it has been much less successful elsewhere.

One problem is, perhaps, an issue of translation. The articles have not always been made easy to read, and the words chosen do not always fit the ideas directly into anglophone debates. This has certainly led to some mis-understandings of the analyses and, as a consequence, to an underestimation of the relevance and significance of French radical materialist feminist work. The main problem, however, has simply been that the journal is difficult to get hold of in most countries. Even in Britain and Australia, it is held by only a few libraries, it is not widely known, and it is certainly not recognised as a key feminist journal. Thus, some writers from the group who are reasonably well established in feminist debates in the US — notably Guillaumin — have barely been heard of in Britain and are certainly not widely referenced or cited. Translations of other articles by various members of the group are scattered over a number of edited collections, pamphlets and journals. Only Monique Wittig and Christine Delphy's work and names are well known, largely because they have books available in English.[10]

Although the lack of availability and difficulties of translation have undoubtedly played their part in the rather limited engagement with French radical materialist feminism in English language debates, there are more important processes at work — processes that indeed gave rise to the problems of translation and access, etc. The first is the particular construction of 'French feminism' that has emerged, especially in American feminist writings; while the second relates to the meaning ascribed to 'materialism' in anglophone feminist theory. In the following sections we shall deal briefly with each of these in turn, and then finally turn to issues around the term 'gender', which the French have seldom used.

The Commodification of 'French Feminism'

Over the past 10 years or more, there has been enormous interest amongst feminists and others in analyses of sexual difference. Within this, particular attention has focused on psychoanalytic and deconstructive literary analyses, especially those by the French writers Luce Irigaray, Julia Kristeva and Hélène Cixous. Indeed, as many commentators have noted, there has been a veritable outpouring of publications around their work. What concerns us here is not so much the pros and cons of the actual work of these three writers; nor whether (as Delphy argues, 1995) it is the body of anglophone commentary on them that actually constitutes 'French feminism', since the three main authors disagree among themselves and two of them are actively opposed to feminism. Rather, what concerns us is the way in which their work has been represented as the sum total of 'feminist' theory being produced in France. We believe this construction has contributed to the exclusion of other French feminist writers — both the radical feminists represented here and also the socialist feminists.

This actually parallels struggles that occurred in France itself, where, from the start of second wave feminism after 1968, a well organised and financed group calling itself Psychanalyse et Politique (or Psych et Po) developed quite different analyses from those of the rest of the Women's Liberation Movement (the Mouvement de Libération des Femmes, the MLF).[11] The latter accepted Beauvoir's famous proposition that 'One is not born a woman, one becomes one', but Psych et Po

> drew heavily on psychoanalysis and on Lacan in particular to make the claim that 'woman has never existed'. They took the psychoanalytic specificity of women for granted, but argued that women have been repressed by patriarchy in such a way that we do not know what woman would be like if left to herself .... Organising themselves around the key figure of Antoinette Fouque ... the group declared itself against 'feminism' (Fallaize, 1993, pp. 8–9).

> The conflict between Psych et Po and the rest of the feminist movement has [been] unique to France and hounds us to this day. Psych et Po ... runs the publishing company 'des femmes' ... which in 1979 ... registered the feminist symbol (the clenched fist within a women's sign) and the name 'women's liberation movement' as its legal trademark and, in 1980, sued Editions Tierce, another feminist publishing company, for unfair commercial practices, when Tierce joined with the rest of the movement to protest this act of expropriation .... [T]he lack of formal structure [due to feminists' old distrust of institutions] left the door open for ... Psych et Po's leader ... to present herself to both government and media as the spokesman for the women's movement (Ezekiel, 1992, p. 78).

> The idea of female difference, so central to [the Psych et Po] strand ... developed rapidly in the mid-1970s. Three major theorists published important and influential texts ... which, though they differ in some important respects, all played a part in the project of bringing about what Psych et Po called 'the Revolution of the Symbolic', a revolution ... aimed at bringing the feminine into existence. Luce Irigaray's *Speculum. De l'autre femme* (*Speculum. Of the Other Woman*), published in 1974, attempts to locate and define the 'masculine feminine', which, she argues, needs exploration before we can think through the 'feminine feminine'. Julia Kristeva's ... *La Révolution du langage poétique* (*Revolution in Poetic Language*) also published in 1974 was regarded as a capital text locating the feminine in the pre-oedipal, and characterising it as a necessarily marginal, revolutionary force which disrupts language with what she calls the force of the semiotic .... The following year in 'Le Rire de la Medusa' ('The Laugh of the Medusa') and in another essay, 'Sorties' ('Exits'), Hélène Cixous began to theorise what the practice of an écriture féminine (a feminine writing) might be, a writing which would emerge from the feminine libidinal economy and its multiple nature. She called on women ... to write through their bodies' (Fallaize, 1993, pp. 8–9).

To follow the ways in which the conflation of French feminism with Irigaray,

Kristeva and Cixous has taken place outside France, we need to turn to the works that introduced feminist theory from France to English-speaking audiences. The first collection was Marks and Courtivron's *New French Feminisms* (1981), with two special issues of US journals (*Signs* and *Feminist Studies*) in the same year. In the mid-1980s, there followed Claire Duchen's *Feminism in France: from May '68 to Mitterrand* (1986) and *French Connections: voices from the women's movement in France* (1987), with Toril Moi's *French Feminist Thought* (1987). All present a range of views, and some even decry the actions of Psych et Po (see, for example, Marks and Courtivron, 1981, p. 31; and Duchen, 1986, p. 37). But nonetheless they all, and Moi in particular, suggest that the work of Cixous, Irigaray, Kristeva is particularly interesting — and overall their work is certainly given far more space and attention.

Subsequently, so much attention has been focused on these three particular writers (by such writers as Butler, 1990; and Grosz, 1989, who looks at Kristeva, Irigaray and the rather different work of Michèle Le Doeuff), that by the late 1980s and early '90s it was impossible to review the state of anglophone feminist thinking without considering the impact of their work. Indeed, the early 1990s has produced whole collections reflecting on the significance of shifts in anglophone feminism due to their ideas (see, for example, Fraser, 1992 and Delphy, 1995, pp. 198–9, fn 11).[12]

In the Introduction to one such collection (Fraser and Bartky's *Revaluing French Feminism*, 1992) — which reflects on the impact of 'French feminism' on US feminist politics — Fraser argues that 'French feminism' has contributed, and continues to contribute, to a major reconfiguration of US feminism through some of the problematics (for example, that of 'difference') set up within 'French feminism' being transplanted virtually wholesale into US feminist debates. Fraser is well aware that

> the reception of 'French feminism' has been partial and selective. It has focussed almost exclusively on one or two strands — the deconstructive and psychoanalytic — of a much larger, more variegated field. The result is a curious synecdochic reduction (Fraser, 1992, p. 1).

She traces this reduction to the publication of Marks and Courtivron's collection (1981), which first introduced French feminists to anglophone readers and started the construction of 'French feminism' as a distinctive cultural object (and, we would add, made it enticing and commodified it). Fraser notes that the 'curious . . . reduction' took place despite the fact that the collection itself did not present 'French feminism' in this way. It may have excluded any writings from French ' "syndicalist feminism" and feminist currents within leftwing parties', but it did present an otherwise wide-ranging (or 'relatively catholic') selection (Fraser, 1992, p. 19, fn 2). (In terms of our present concerns, Marks and Courtivron did indeed include the original editorial statement from the *Questions féministes* collective, together with short extracts from an early article by 'C. D.' (Delphy, 1975) and from one of Wittig's novels.)

However, despite her recognition of the restriction of 'French feminism' within anglophone debates, Fraser herself does not attempt to offer any explanation for it. On the contrary, she seems to find it inexplicable and almost impossible to trace, saying:

> We could doubtless learn much about the workings of our culture and its institutions if we could reconstruct the precise processes of this synecdochic reduction. It is all the more striking in that it occurred despite the strenuous protests of Monique Wittig, Simone de Beauvoir, and the editors of the journal *Feminist Questions* (Fraser, 1992: footnote p. 19).

The processes of this reduction are, however, less inexplicable than Fraser suggests. For if we consider the representation of 'French feminism' in Marks and Courtivron, we find the editors arguing in their introduction that 'Women concerned with the woman question in France use the words "feminism" and "feminist" less often than do their counterparts in the United States', and that this is because of a

> desire to break with a bourgeois past — with the inadequacies and fixed categories of humanistic thought, including feminism — [which] has led to a vigorous attack against the labels by one of the most influential and radical of women's groups (known originally as 'Psychanalyse et Politique'. . .) as well as by Hélène Cixous (Marks and Courtivron, 1981, p. x).

Marks and Courtivron thus, from the start, not only represent the whole of the French women's movement as distanced from 'feminism', but also situate Psych et Po as the 'most influential and radical' group in the country; as central to French feminist debates; and as *the* most exciting and innovative variety of feminism around: ' "Politique et psychanalyse" is the most original of the women's liberation groups in France and perhaps in the Western world' (Marks and Courtivron, 1981, p. 33).

However, as leading feminists in France have constantly argued, this variety of French feminism has *not* been as influential in France as the US feminist literature claims; and it was only this one group which distanced itself from the term 'feminism'. The majority protested loud and long, and argued for the importance of an autonomous, non-trademarked, activist women's movement.

> The French women's movement . . . is in constant danger, because of the existence of such groups as Psych et Po which pass themselves off

as *the* women's movement and exert considerable influence, thanks to the unfortunately all-too-warm reception the general public has given their ideology — a convenient neo-femininity developed by such women writers as Hélène Cixous, Annie Leclerc and Luce Irigaray... Unfortunately this is also the aspect of the French women's movement best known in the United States. Such books as... *New French Feminisms* give a totally distorted image of French feminism by presenting it, on the one hand, as if it existed only in theory and not in action and, on the other, as if the sum of that theory emanated from the school of neo-femininity — which celebrates women's cycles, rhythms, and bodily fluids, along with 'writing of the body' (*écriture du corps*) and women's 'circular thinking' (Beauvoir, 1984, pp. 234–5).

It is ironic that Psych et Po, which, while calling itself the movement, denounces feminism, has been embraced by feminists in foreign countries. For instance, it is to a large extent the work of this group and its sympathizers which has been dubbed 'French feminism' in the United States, despite numerous protests from the movement, a practice that shows no little arrogance on the part of American feminists (Ezekiel, 1992, p. 84).

Most French feminists thus see Marks and Courtivron's collection, not as introducing and representing French feminism in a relatively even fashion, as Fraser claims, but as a major contributor to the very process of reduction she finds so curious. What is also interesting about *New French Feminisms* is how its editors represent some of the feminists associated with *Questions féministes*. Specifically, as is quite common in anglophone feminist writing, they place Beauvoir and Wittig within and central to the exciting and innovative 'new French feminism' without noting their disagreements with Psych et Po and Cixous.[13] Also, while Marks and Courtivron certainly recognise the launch and existence of *Questions féministes* in their history of the women's movement in France, they see the journal as 'a significant political and literary event' (p. 35) because Beauvoir and Wittig were published together *in* it — rather than because they (and others) were jointly involved in establishing and editing the journal as a form of political activism. They underplay the fact that while Beauvoir's support for the Women's Liberation Movement (WLM) in France was well known and generous,

[Her] choice of contacts [in the 1970s] was by no means haphazard. Then and now, she sought out women who started with a materialist analysis of the situation of women (and the world), and strictly rejected any belief in 'the nature of women'. For example, Anne Zelensky, one of the people who has been active with her in the 'League for Women's Rights'; Christine Delphy, who edits the theoretical feminist publication (*Nouvelles*) *Questions Féministes*; and the group of women she worked with for many years on 'le sexisme ordinaire' (everyday sexism) for *Les Temps Modernes* (Schwarzer, 1984, p. 15).

The 'curious synecdochic reduction' of French feminism to the work of deconstructionist and psychoanalytic writers is also crucially connected to the disciplinary background of most English-speaking specialists on France (i.e. those most likely to read, write, comment, translate and produce histories and collections on 'French feminism'). Such specialists usually have disciplinary backgrounds in linguistics and literature, and so find far greater connection with French feminists writing fiction or literary theory than with those from sociology, psychology or anthropology. That is to say, the anglophone feminists most likely to be engaged in either promoting or critiquing French writing are much more interested in literary criticism and the construction of subjectivities and psyches through language and texts, than in French theorists who emphasise the significance of social relations and the economy in understanding the relations of the sexes and the construction of individual consciousness.[14] Thus, the representation of 'French feminism' in English-speaking debates (and the texts that actually get translated) has been profoundly influenced by the disciplinary location of French Studies specialists.

In the US, this tendency has been compounded by the specificities of its academic and political debates. Materialism has historically had little impact in the US. Marxism, for example, has never had the kind of impact on academic thinking in politics, economics and sociology, nor on political activism that it has in Europe. On the other hand, social psychological and particularly forms of psychoanalytic discourse have always been popular, powerful and central to North American theorists, and have held their ground in the arts and the social sciences in a way that has not been paralleled in Europe.[15] In addition, postmodernism, although often accorded an origin in European writers (Derrida, Barthes, Baudrillard, Lyotard), in feminist writing has been most developed in the US. Given this context, it is not surprising that it has been the psychoanalytic and deconstructive variety of 'French feminism' that has found most sympathy and popularity in the US — and is now held to constitute its totality.

To these reasons, Delphy (1995) adds the suggestion (echoing Ezekiel and Moses's[16] charges of imperialism) that Anglo-Americans have invented 'French Feminism' so as to put onto an Other the responsibility for ideas US feminists find dangerously attractive but which they do not dare to admit in themselves — but which they can then embrace. That is to say, the French, who carry exotic prestige in anglophone intellectual circles, are the means to (re)introduce 'an outdated [additive] epistemological framework' (Delphy, 1995, p. 194) and to 'rehabilitat[e] ... essentialism' (op. cit., p. 213) in(to) anglophone feminist debates, and to make it seem both serious and 'sexy'.

The 'curious reduction' of 'French feminism' to particular writers, and their subsequent erotisation and marketing is, therefore, not at all as inexplicable as Fraser suggests — and it does indeed shed light on 'the workings of our [American] culture and its institutions'. But, ironically, both her contribution and those of the majority of other writers in the collection she edited with Bartky, also have as their (albeit often critically evaluative) focus, this 'curiously reduced' version of feminist theory in France. So their book *itself* in turn is part of the very process she locates as strange and (to some extent at least) problematic. It subjects 'French feminism' to intense critical scrutiny, but accords next to no space to new readings and re-readings of other forms of French feminist theory.[17] The version that concerns us — radical materialist feminism — gets mentioned only so far as it contrasts with the psychoanalytic and deconstructive variety, and in order to be dismissed as outmoded.[18]

Similar critiques of materialist analyses — saying how they differ from other analyses and/or dismissing them as having little utility in terms of current debates — are common in feminism. In the next section, therefore, we turn to understandings of 'materialism' and in particular to the use of 'materialism' in British feminist debates, to see how these, in turn, contributed to a sidelining of French materialist feminism.

Materialism

To trace the reasons for the limited engagement with the *QF* group in Britain, we need to return to early representations of their ideas, and specifically to the accounts of Christine Delphy's work provided by British feminists in the early 1980s. These set in place a particular understanding of radical materialist feminism that, in Britain at any rate, has proved long-lived.

As we have already noted, Delphy's work, and in particular her work on domestic labour, is relatively well known in the UK. She attended some early 1970s British feminist conferences; she and Guillaumin, Mathieu and Plaza were involved in workshops with British feminists,[19] her work was translated and promoted by particular individuals and several of her papers were published in English in the mid-1970s (Delphy, 1976, 1977). Also, she was a visiting scholar at the University of Bradford in 1980. However, undoubtedly the most important moment in establishing her fame, or rather her notoriety, in the British context, was the publication of a review of her work in the first issue of the journal *Feminist Review*. This article, by Michèle Barrett and Mary McIntosh (1979), was important because its authors were prominent feminist sociologists and marxist/socialist feminists, and at that time marxist feminist sociology was the dominant mode of feminist theoretical analysis in Britain. Moreover, Barrett and McIntosh had themselves been key in establishing this mode of analysis — and indeed the journal *Feminist Review* itself. So their engagement with Delphy's work in the debut issue meant her name (at least) became widely known.

The review was published at a time when the search for a materialist analysis of gender was the order of the day. As Barrett herself has recently argued, it was a time when ' "things" — be they low pay, rape or female foeticide' (1992, p. 201) were thought about primarily in terms of marxist feminist categories — which meant in relation to the capitalist mode of production. Moreover, in such theorising, both capital and labour were viewed as ungendered categories.[20] In the book she published in 1980, *Women's Oppression Today*, Barrett herself dismissed any form of materialism that attempted to understand gender in terms of determinants which had not been specified by marxism, or any form of 'materialism that displaces the labour/capital contradiction from its centrality in the analysis of capitalist society' (ibid, p. 252). Her own discussion of the constitution of gender was largely in terms of ideology. For instance, she critiqued the then on-going debate about who benefited from domestic labour for its 'functionality for capitalism' approach, saying that family life should be understood in other terms — namely that capitalism was *historically* gendered because pre-existing family forms influenced its development; but that *now* the domestic sphere must be understood in terms of ideological processes and families' construction of gendered subjects (ibid, p. 173).

It is, therefore, not surprising that the ideas that were put forward by Delphy — that marriage constitutes a specific economic relation in which men and women are located in different relations of production; that women's labour is commodified and appropriated through *non-capitalist processes*; and that the *material* determinants of gender are constituted by the contradictions between the social categories 'men' and 'women' — were potentially extremely disruptive. They could not be tolerated by the dominant form of materialism articulated by Barrett and McIntosh (and other marxist feminists in Britain), and so, not surprisingly, their review of Delphy's work was very critical.

They taxed Delphy with, *inter alia*, misunderstanding marxism (especially in moving from an understanding of the material in terms of the capital/labour contradiction) and using marxist terminology incorrectly; with producing not a materialist understanding of gender but an economistic one (i.e. with seeing marriage and domestic life in purely economic terms, as a mode of production, and so not dealing with large areas of women's experience); with concentrating on marriage and ignoring motherhood; with ahistoricism in reducing 'women' to an unchanging economic class; and with ethnocentrism in generalising from French farm family data to other countries (i.e. with universalising the position of women).

We do not intend to rehearse Barrett and McIntosh's arguments in their entirety — nor indeed Delphy's equally robust reply in issue 4 (1980) of *Feminist Review*, where she responded that Barrett and McIntosh confused 'the materialist method, used . . . by Marx, and the analysis of capitalism which he made using it' (p. 83),[21] and asserted that their analyses were contradictory — and explicable only in terms of a 'desperate desire to continue to exempt men from responsibility for the oppression of women' (p. 79). What is important here is that because of the dominance of marxist feminism at the time, the whole of radical materialist feminism came to be seen as having been dismissed by Barrett and McIntosh's critique. Despite Delphy's demonstration that there were 'many distortions' of her work in Barrett and McIntosh's paper, and that 'their theoretical-political positions prevent[ed] them understanding [her ideas]', it was Barrett and McIntosh's views that were widely accepted and which have been repeated time after time, as *the* problems associated with (i.e. as *a complete refutation of*) (French) radical materialist feminism.[22] In other words, the power of marxist feminism to define materialism in the early 1980s in Britain meant that Delphy's analysis was, and continues to be, dismissed as a problematic mode of feminist analysis by a whole range of writers.[23]

Ironically, however, the version of materialism then defended by Barrett and others (i.e. understanding the material solely in terms of the capital/labour contradiction — in relation to what was held to be *the* economic mode of production) has itself now been declared bankrupt in terms of the analysis of gender by much the same group of feminists. Moreover, not only have they abandoned the search for a materialist analysis of gender, they have also articulated a full-scale critique of 'materialism' within feminism, and beyond.[24] This includes an assertion that materialism constitutes a reductive understanding of gender.

This critique assumes that in materialist accounts, economic relations (meaning those between capitalists and workers) are always held to be the dominant ones, and that such accounts therefore cannot attend to a whole range of elements recognised as constitutive of gender, such as sexuality, the body and subjectivity. In addition (and related) to this, materialism is widely held to have a number of other problems for feminist (and more generally for social) theory, including producing universalistic accounts and a mechanistic understanding of the constitution of social formation. That is to say, the kinds of critiques levelled at Delphy are now held to apply more or less wholesale to *all* materialist analyses. We would suggest, however, that this need to abandon 'materialism' in analyses of gender is a product, not of this type of analysis, but of the dominant (i.e. what was the marxist feminist) understanding of 'the material'.

Some understandings of gender do suffer from economism, that is to say, they understand gender solely in terms of economic relations and/or hold the economy to be the sole/dominant factor structuring relations, and that such explanations are unsatisfactory. But the inadequacies of such explanations are connected not only to their being attempts to show that the capitalist economy is solely/mainly responsible for women's oppression, but also to their limited understanding of what constitutes the economic domain, and how the economic domain is constituted.

If for years the marxist/socialist feminist project was to produce a materialist understanding of gender, this did not involve a re-analysis of the economic sector. *The* economy (what was meant by 'the economic sector' and 'the economic system') was taken for granted. Instead, understandings of gender were pursued through re-analyses of the ideological or cultural domains. These new analyses were therefore located within an already established model of social formation; where the economic domain was ungendered, and where the constituents of gender, such as sexuality, were not only declared non-economic, but also secondary to the economic. In other words, such attempts took place within a model of social formation in which there was an existing hierarchy as to what determined what.[25]

Those marxist feminists who recognised problems with using this model made various attempts (from the early-to-mid-80s) to rework materialism to give a fuller account of gender. Whilst these were extremely important and insightful, in retrospect they did not resolve the problem because some of the assumptions regarding the material, and in particular the construction of the economic domain, were retained.

For instance, in her work on 'The Material of Male Power' (in 1981), Cynthia Cockburn attempts to rework materialism to avoid the pitfalls of earlier marxist feminist analyses — particularly their economism. She argues for a fuller understanding of 'the material', to include not only the economic but also what she terms the physical, in which she includes issues of 'bodily physique and its extension in technology, of building and clothes, space and movement' (Cockburn, 1981, p. 43); and the socio-political, which includes 'male organization and solidarity, the part played by institutions such as church, societies, unions and clubs' (op. cit., p. 43). Cockburn claims this reworking of materialism would allow an understanding of gender which would go 'beyond men's greater earning power and property advantage' (op. cit., p 43), and thus allow the full significance of material relations for the constitution of gender to be explored.

This opening up of materialist analysis appears to go well beyond what had existed previously. For example, Cockburn's argument that the physical formed part of the material seems at first sight to allow the significance of previously marginalised factors — such as the body — to be addressed. However, while she does question the primacy of the economic in the analysis of gender, she does not interrogate this category itself. Instead, it continues to be assumed that the economic is gender neutral, and that it is entirely constituted by the capitalist mode of production. Gender, on the other hand — or what Cockburn terms the sex-gender system — is conceived as constituted through physical and socio-political processes. This is evident, for instance, when she explicitly allows ' "the economic" to retire into the background' in her account, so as to allow a focus on the physical and socio-political when seeking to understand gender. The separation of the (gender neutral) economic and sex-gender system is also evident in such assertions as:

> I set out to explore aspects of the process of mutual definition in which men and women are locked, *and* those (equally processes of mutual creation) in which the working class and the capitalist class are

historically engaged (Cockburn, 1981, p. 42, stress added)

and:

> The fact that a mode of production and a sex-gender system are two fundamental and parallel features of the organization of human societies should not lead us to expect to find any exact comparability between them, whether the duo is capitalism/'patriarchy' or any other (op cit., p. 56).

What also stands out from this account, ironically, is that the significance of factors previously unattended to in materialist analyses of the constitution of gender, could still not be addressed. For example, the significance of sexuality for gender in the labour market could not be considered within this framework (Adkins, 1995; Adkins and Lury, 1996).

Cockburn's more recent work (1991) still separates the economic from gender. She now, like others, distances herself from the production of a materialist understanding of gender, and has abandoned her earlier project of reworking materialism, using instead concepts of institutional and cultural power to understand gender. But although this shift again appears to break away from earlier analyses, in this case by paying attention to the pervasive operation of sexuality and emotions in the workplace, the full significance of the sexual and the affective for gender still cannot be addressed. For instance, Cockburn suggests that sexuality may enter into the labour process through employers' exploitation of sexuality for profit: 'the "sexy" uniform of a club waitress exploits for profit both her female sexuality and the male sexuality of the client' (Cockburn, 1991, p. 149). That is to say, sexuality may constitute a force of production. But the implications of the sexual constituting a force of production are not addressed in terms of gender. On the contrary, 'production' is *only* understood in terms of capitalism, so sexuality is seen as being appropriated in the workplace *only* for profit. Such questions as whether or not the appropriation of sexuality in the workplace may be a gendered phenomenon — for instance, why waitresses rather than waiters are required to wear 'sexy' uniforms — are not asked. The economic is still viewed as an ungendered category — as not constituting a potential source of gender — and, hence, gender is still separated from the economic.

So, despite some fairly major shifts in feminist analyses, there is still a prevalent ungendered understanding of the economic; and an understanding of gender as distinct from the economic. As the above discussion suggests, these assumptions preclude a full understanding of the processes at play in the constitution of gender. Understanding the economic only in terms of an ungendered capitalist mode of production, negates the ways in which the economic may itself be gendered. Indeed, countering this conception of the economic, stressing other divisions of labour, and recognising that what is 'labour' and what is 'material' can change, are some of the major contributions to feminism of the *QF* position. However, given the continued dominance within anglophone feminist debate of an understanding of 'materialism' that derives from early marxist feminist analyses, it is not surprising this alternative version of materialist feminism has been given little airtime.[26] Nor is it surprising that work which stresses the economic gets dismissed as narrow economism when the dominant reading of the phrase 'the economic' is so restricted.

Rather than suffering from economism, the work of French radical materialist feminists *recasts the meaning of the 'economic'* in a way that offers exciting possibilities, and a way out of a number of cul-de-sacs which have dogged feminist analysis. The authors represented here have never taken the definition of the economic to be restricted to the contradiction between capital and labour (to production for capitalism). On the contrary, they have always located the 'economic' far more broadly, and as a social and political product in a far wider sense. They see it as including — indeed they understand it as intrinsically organised in terms of — gender: that is, through the contradictions, the exploitative relations which exist, between the social groups 'men' and 'women'.

While it has proved very difficult for marxist materialist feminists to come to grips with the significance of, for instance, sexuality, sex, the body, and subjectivity for gender generally, and especially in areas such as the labour market where political economic frameworks were particularly strong, the *Questions féministes* position has not delimited 'production' to the organisation of, and the activities involved in, the production of goods and services for capital. Rather this tendency has viewed production as embedded in a range of social relations between men and women. This opens up the possibility of a much broader understanding of gender, and the papers here consider marriage and sexuality — housework, symbolic work, affective relations and bodily practices including sexual intercourse, childbearing and childrearing — as all, *simultaneously*, forms of gendered production. This version of 'materialism' also does not draw distinctions between, nor does it hierarchise, different modes of 'social' formation. For example, the 'sexual' and the 'economic' are not separated in ways that make it impossible to consider the relationship between the two. Rather, they are considered as co-constructed and constructing. Tabet, for instance, argues here that reproduction (including breast-feeding) should be seen as work, and as exploited work; while elsewhere she has analysed various sexual-economic exchanges — where sex is exchanged for something other than sex — and analysed the significance of these exchanges for the constitution of gender (Tabet, 1987).

This avoids the cul-de-sac in which marxist feminists found themselves. Because the latter separated gender and the economic, when they have turned their attention to sexuality, sex, the body, subjectivity, etc. — as they have increasingly recently — they lose sight of the 'material' (and vice versa). So, they shift instead to a reliance on the distinction between the 'material' and the 'cultural', with the result that gender has tended to be only partially conceived.[27] As Barrett recently commented when reflecting on the move away from issues of social structure to issues of political agency, or sexuality, etc. (and the associated disciplinary shift from the social sciences to the arts), the cultural may certainly have acted as a counterbalance to the material/socio-economic, but it is not

> adequate simply to shift attention in one direction or another . . . . The issues of what weight to attach to these various subject matters (the economic or the aesthetic, for example) will eventually have to be rethought (Barrett, 1992, p. 204).

The *Questions féministes* position, however, has never been restricted to either the traditionally 'material' *or* the 'cultural'.[28] Given this context, it is ironic that when radical materialist feminism is mentioned in anglophone feminist debate, it should continue to be dismissed on the grounds of its out-moded 'materialism' — accused, for instance, of hanging on to a distinction between the material and the ideal. For, on the contrary, the work from this perspective precisely constantly questions and challenges this problematic dichotomy: for instance, the idea that the sexual is distinct from the material, or that the aesthetic is separate from the economic. More importantly, it has been able to achieve an account of gender which is able to hold on to a range of structuring elements in a way surpassing many others.

Sex and Gender

This refusal to analyse gender in terms of the material/cultural or real/ideal distinction is particularly clear in relation to current debates on the use of the terms 'sex' and 'gender'. One of the most important developments in early 1990s' anglophone feminist theory is seen to be the destabilisation of the apparent orthodoxy regarding the relationship between sex and gender. It is no longer assumed that sex is a 'natural' or 'biological' category, with gender a social or cultural construction somehow imposed on top of it. 'Sex' is increasingly recognised as a socio-historical product, rather than a fixed, trans-historical, or taken-for-granted category.

The origins of this destabilisation have come from several sources (including Foucault, 1976b; Gatens, 1983; Laqueur, 1990), but the full force of the implications of the constructedness of 'sex' appears only recently to be being realised. Within North American feminism, Judith Butler's recent work (1990 and 1993) on deconstructing the sex/gender distinction through problematising the fixity of sex, has been particularly influential.

Butler questions the assumption that 'sex' is prior to gender, and argues instead that 'sex' is materialised through the regulatory apparatus of hetero-sexuality. She links the drawing of a radical distinction between sex and gender to such untenable dichotomies as real/ideal or nature/culture (which assumes in the sex/gender dichotomy that the socio-cultural 'acts' upon an asocial and fixed nature). This denies not only the historical construction of sex, but also of the body. Moreover, this destabilisation of sex/gender is seen to derive from the critiques of materialist models of social formation that we have mentioned. Butler herself says the problematic model of 'gender' has been 'crucial to the de Beauvoirian version of feminism' (Butler, 1993, p. 4).

However, although the sex/gender distinction has been relied upon in many 'materialist' feminist analyses of gender, this is categorically not the case for the *Questions féministes* group — which has the greatest claim to be the 'Beauvoirian version'. On the contrary, many in this tendency have long and explicitly refused to use the term gender at all *because* of the naturalisation of sex that this distinction entails. Instead of 'gender' they, like most feminists in France, have talked of 'rapports sociaux de sexe' (social relations of sex)[29] and 'différence',[30] while combating vigorously the neo-femininity school's *valorisation* of women's difference (see, Mathieu, 1977; Guillaumin, 1979; Delphy, 1976). They also exemplify the constructedness[31] of sex, reproduction, sexuality and the body and, far from locating sex as a fixed, 'biological' category, they 'seek to understand the relations which constitute and construct the social categories of sex' (Juteau-Lee, 1995, p. 20).

As stated at the beginning of this chapter, we have selected to present here writing from the *Questions féministes* group that is centred on the issue of the inter-relations of 'sex', 'gender' and 'sexuality'. It is, therefore, by no means, and does not purport to be, a full and exhaustive representation of all that French materialist feminism has to offer. It does, however, constitute an important, longstanding, developed perspective on an area currently of great concern to anglophone feminist debate.

'The Category of Sex' (first published in 1982)[32] provides an excellent brief introduction to the key ideas shared by the group. In it, Monique Wittig, a novelist and literary theorist, argues that the division of society into two sexes is the product, and not the cause, of oppression; that 'sex' is a political category and there would be no 'sex' without oppression; and that heterosexuality is of central importance in defining the sexes as natural, different and complementary. Thus, 'sex' is understood as a product of power relations between two opposed groups: 'men' and 'women'[33] — and constituted in a class relationship involving the appropriation of the work of one group by the other. There is here no separation of the body, 'biology' and other bodily processes from (what Anglos might call) other elements of 'gender'.

In 'Penser le genre: Quels problemes?' (1991) ('Rethinking Sex and Gender', 1993), Christine Delphy — a sociologist, who has long been involved in English language debates — traces the history of the anglophone concept of gender through the work of Margaret Mead, sex role theorists, and Ann Oakley. She shows how they progressively denaturalised the division of labour and psychological differences between men and women, and increasingly stressed cultural variation. But, she says, none of these authors questioned the assumption that gender is based on a natural, sexual dichotomy. She, like Butler, insists that the links between sex and gender — and sex, sexuality and procreation — must be questioned; and, moreover, that the relationship between the two is such that gender precedes sex. The social division of labour and associated hierarchical relations lead to physiological 'sex' being used to differentiate those who are assigned to be dominant, from those who will be part of the subordinate gender/class. She suggests that while the concept of 'gender' has helped our thinking develop, we should now dare to imagine 'non-gender': what a non-hierarchical society — a utopia (see, the fiction of Wittig) — might look like.

In 'Identité sexuelle/sexuée/de sexe?' (1989) ('Sexual, Sex and Sex-Class Identities', first translated in this volume) Nichole-Claude Mathieu — an anthropologist — uses ethnographies and structuralist analysis to produce a classification of three different ways of conceptualising the relationship between sex and gender:

- In the first, which is the most common way of seeing the relationship in western society, sex is experienced as an individual anatomical destiny which one follows through the identity of the gender that conforms to it. Here, 'gender translates sex'. They are homologous.
- In the second, which is commonly encountered in the social sciences and among socialist and cultural feminists, as well as in most 'traditional' societies studied by anthropologists, gender consciousness is seen as based on lived experience in a group (i.e. from 'socialisation' and living as a woman within the group of women). Here gender symbolises sex (and sex symbolises gender). They are analogous.
- In the third, found among radical feminists and political lesbians, a social/political logic is seen to exist between sex and gender, and identity is based on 'sex-class' consciousness: on recognising male domination. Here, gender is seen to construct sex (and heterosexuality is viewed as a social institution). Gender and sex are heterogeneous.

Delphy's ideas thus exemplify Mathieu's third way of conceptualising the relationship of sex and gender; but while Delphy suggests that the concept of gender has been useful in developing feminist ideas, Mathieu is less convinced. But both would probably agree (with Butler) that current use of 'gender' is often politically compromised and intellectually confusing.

A fuller exposition of the ideas outlined by Wittig is found in 'Pratique du pouvoir et idée de Nature' (1978) ('The Practice of Power and Belief in Nature', 1981a, b and abridged in this volume) by Colette Guillaumin. In the first part of her article she is concerned with the appropriation of women, but her understanding of the form of this appropriation differs from that of Delphy (1970, 1984), which is probably more familiar to anglophone readers. While Delphy concentrates on the appropriation of wives' (and other family members') work in family relationships, Guillaumin argues that 'gender' involves a bodily appropriation of all women. She thus looks at the ways in which, for women, both general relationships with men and the individual relationship of marriage are constituted by such appropriation. She shows how ownership of the body is gendered and, in so doing, she questions the utility of a disembodied understanding of labour, which she says is inadequate for the class of women. She proposes a concept of 'sexage': that the specific nature of women's oppression is their reduction to the status of natural objects, and the direct physical appropriation by men of their time, the products of their bodies, their sexual obligation, and their responsibility to care for other members of the group.

The second part of her article examines the different ways in which the complementarity of the sexes is produced, including biological categorisation and constructions of the body. Western societies have a long history of rationalising domination by attributing superiority or inferiority to supposedly stable, supposedly inherent, characteristics such as IQ, physiology, 'race' or sex. But ' "sex" is not a given, it is not *un fait de nature*; [and] her analysis makes visible the processes leading to [its] naturalization' (Juteau-Lee, 1995, p. 21). In so doing, Guillaumin interrogates the category of 'Nature', or what is 'natural': that is, the idea that things or persons have properties determined by internal characteristics of the things or persons themselves. She stresses in her analysis of sex relations, as also in her work on 'race', that it is because women (and non-whites) are subordinated that they are 'naturalised' — that is, attributed a particular nature, and *not* the other way about.

'Fertilité naturelle, reproduction forcée' (1985) ('Natural Fertility, Forced Reproduction', first translated in this volume) by Paola Tabet uses the currently less fashionable practice of comparative anthropology to good effect in questioning the assignment of reproduction to 'nature', and looks instead at variations in its organisation. She starts with a critique of the concept of 'natural fertility' used in demography and anthropology, showing no such thing exists, and that there are, on the contrary, worldwide 'constant interventions in sexuality which tend to produce a female organism which is specialised for reproduction. These interventions constitute a strong and complex transformation of the biological conditions of reproduction and, correlated with this, a very strong and complex sociological manipulation of the biological conditions of human sexuality'. She stresses that reproduction and sexuality are not given biological facts, but rather socially constituted and constitutive of female (and to a lesser extent male) individuals: that reproduction is a pivot of all relations between the sexes and of all sexual relations.

The final chapter — 'Nos dommages et leurs intérêts' (1978) ('Our Costs and their Benefits', a new translation for this volume) — is by Monique Plaza. Although better known for her critique of what she, as a social psychologist and practising psychiatrist, sees as the 'misuse' of psychoanalysis by Irigaray (Plaza, 1977, 1984), she is here concerned with aspects of Michel Foucault's work. Specifically, she critiques an attempt by Foucault to separate out violence from sexuality by saying that while violence in rape is unacceptable and should be punished, it is oppressive to penalise sexuality. Plaza argues rape is not like other violence, for example, a punch in the face, since whether an act is seen as 'rape' depends on the issue of consent, whereas a punch is never assessed in this way. This is because men rape those who are socially women/defined as sexual beings/whose bodies men have appropriated. Hence rape rests on the social difference between the sexes/social sexing/hetero-sexuality as sexual possession, and as such is essentially sexual. She argues that Foucault's work on sexuality is radical in seeing sexuality as not given and not a thing in itself, but rather as the product of social modalities of power over the body; but that it is reactionary in its 'refusal to know' the antagonism of men and women/the gendering of sexual practice. He does not see the consequences *for women* (the gender dimension) of contemporary society's 'constant arousal'/'deployment' of sexuality. In seeking to rewrite the law on rape in such a way as to punish violence but decriminalise sexuality, he is defending men's existing right to possess women's bodies.

These authors show the contribution that materialist analysis can make to a fuller understanding of the constitution of gender by their understanding of the significance of sex, sexuality and the body. They also show that feminist materialism is far from shackled to economic determinancy, and certainly does not imply a naive presumption of the determinacy of matter over conscious-ness or structure over agency.[34] The issues raised, and more importantly the way in which these issues are addressed within this form of feminist inquiry, are original and powerful ways of addressing current feminist problematics. By their unwavering commitment to an analysis of social categories as social instruments of repression, seeing 'the classification of human beings into two genders [as] as spurious as the classification of human beings into thirty-seven races; anatomical or physical differences between persons [being but] a pretext for [the] domination of one social group over another' (Pheterson, 1994, p. 262), French radical feminists have made extremely important contributions to understandings of gender that are of direct relevance to current anglophone debates. We hope this volume will enable their work to be read and recognised, instead of misunderstood and dismissed, and so encourage engagement with not only the articles presented here, but the whole body of their ideas.

Notes

We should like to thank Debbie Cameron, Claire Duchen, Judith Ezekiel and Paola Tabet who read and commented upon earlier drafts of this chapter.

1   While this collection itself provides a stronger demonstration of what materialist radical feminism is than any single definition, we can start by noting that the first editorial of *Questions féministes* says the journal is devoted to radical feminist analyses of the oppression of women, which are materialist in that they study

   the connections between sexist mentality, institutions, laws, and the socio-economic   structures   that   support   them...This   analysis

> ... define(s) men and women as two groups with opposed interests ....
> The economic inferiority of women in the workforce, their exclusion
> from power positions, including politics, and their restricted access to
> knowledge [is] linked with the division of labor between the sexes ... The
> overall power of men over women, the psychological devaluation of
> women (beyond their material exploitation), the sexual and physical
> violence against women, all result from this power and help to reinforce
> it (1977, translated in Marks and Courtivron, 1981, p. 217).

2   The founding collective in 1977 consisted of Simone de Beauvoir as Directrice de
    publication, and Colette Capitan Peter, Christine Delphy, Colette Guillaumin,
    Emmanuèle de Lesseps, Nicole-Claude Mathieu and Monique Plaza. Monique
    Wittig, who had been in the USA since 1976, joined from issue 4, November 1978.
    The journal was published until March 1981 by Éditions TIERCE.

3   For a select biography of work on Simone de Beauvoir by franco- and anglophone
    feminists, see, Patterson, 1994, pp. 30–4. Beauvoir has been important for the
    social sciences as well as for the humanities, and has survived shifts in disciplinary
    focus in women's/feminist studies. (See Barrett (1992) for a discussion of this
    shift.)

4   It is the final sentence in 'The Straight Mind' (1980a). This article deals with les-
    bianism as a political choice for feminists, a theme continued in 'One is Not Born
    a Woman' (1981). The preceding sentence gives some context:

    > it would be incorrect to say that lesbians associate, make love and live
    > with women, for 'woman' has meaning only in heterosexual systems of
    > thought and heterosexual economic systems. Lesbians are not women.
    > (Wittig, 1992, p. 52)

    In another article 'One is not Born a Woman' (1980b), which places lesbians
    outside the categories 'man' and 'woman', Wittig contends that what constitutes a
    woman is a 'particular social relation with a man, a relation that implies personal
    and physical obligations as well as economic obligations ... a relation that lesbians
    escape by refusing to become, or to stay, heterosexual' (pp. 83–4) (See Duchen,
    1986).

5   For a bibliography of work on Monique Wittig by franco- and anglophone
    feminists, see Crowder, 1994, pp. 533–4.

6   For example in Butler's (1990) analysis, where the performativity of gender is set
    in terms of the heterosexual matrix: 'that grid of cultural intelligibility through
    which bodies, genders, and desires are naturalized' (p. 151).

7   On the domestic labour debate, see Delphy and Leonard (1992, pp. 51–7 and p. 71,
    fn 8). The protagonists in the debate sought to establish whether capitalism or
    patriarchy benefited from women's unpaid work, and whether/how the
    oppression of women could be analytically and strategically incorporated within
    the accepted Left analysis of capitalism — or whether it was part of a different
    system and so required a different and separate political struggle.
        On Delphy's influence generally, see Jackson (1996).

8   A collection of Guillaumin's articles entitled *Racism, Sexism, Power and Ideology*
    was published in English by Routledge in 1995.

9   See Duchen, 1984 and 1987, pp. 78–110 and Garcia, 1994, pp. 853–5.
        NQF in 1981 involved Simone de Beauvoir as Directrice de publication,
    together with Christine Delphy, Claude Hennequin and Emmanuèle de Lesseps as
    the editorial collective.

10 Delphy, 1984; Wittig, 1992. Delphy's work has been translated and promoted by
    Diana Leonard, with whom she has also written a major book (Delphy and
    Leonard, 1992). Wittig writes in both English and French and translates her own
    work.

While Guillaumin's work should become more familiar to anglophone readers (see, note 8), we still unfortunately lack a translation of Mathieu's collected works (see Mathieu, 1991) and the very important collection of French feminist anthropology which she edited, *L'Arraisonnement des femmes* (Mathieu, 1985).

11 For commentaries on Psych et Po in English, see Huston, 1978; Douglas, 1980; Lewis, 1981; Duchen, 1986, 1987; Ward-Jouve, 1991, pp. 61–74; Kaplan, 1992, p. 165; and Beauvoir, 1984. For a bibliography of critiques in French, see Ezekiel, 1992 and especially *Chronique d'une imposture: du mouvement de libération des femmes á une marque commerciale* (Association pour les Luttes Féministes, 1981).

12 The fact that *Yale French Studies*, the premier journal for followers of 'French feminism', has now published a swingeing attack by Christine Delphy (1995) may presage a reassessment by US feminists. This is, however, by no means the first such protest, see, Gibbs *et al.*, 1980; Moses, 1987.

13 Wittig, though

> [s]ometimes erroneously grouped with Cixous and Irigaray under the rubric of 'l'écriture féminine' (female writing), . . . is adamantly opposed to exalting female difference. She advocates 'lesbian writing' in which the category of sex will be eliminated and language freed from its fetters of male domination (Crowder, 1994, p. 531).

14 See Barrett, 1992 for a discussion of current problems of disciplinarity and analyses of gender, especially between the arts and social sciences.

15 See Pheterson, 1994, for a discussion of the differences between US, Dutch and French feminist social sciences.

16 In a paper given at the Berkshire Conference on Women's History in June 1992, quoted in Delphy, 1995.

17 Apart from Simon's 'Two interviews with Simone de Beauvoir', there are only a few minor comments regarding any non-psychoanalytic French feminists. Thus, for example, Fuss discusses materialist feminist objections to Irigaray's analysis of pleasure (especially, Plaza, 1977) and the understanding of 'nature' and 'sex' as socially constituted, which she associates with 'materialists' Wittig, Delphy and Plaza — but her major concern is a critical engagement with Irigaray.

18 For instance, Fraser, again in her introduction, when discussing shifts in anglophone feminist thinking and debate, describes the ways in which (she says) there has been a move away from the assumption of early second wave feminism that 'the goal of women's liberation was to throw off the shackles of femininity, eliminate gender differences, and become universal human subjects' (1992, p. 5). This consensus — and in particular the assumption of a universal subject woman — was, she argues, discredited (sic) through a number of developments, including the analyses of 'French feminists' such as Cixous and Irigaray, who rejected universalism and endorsed differences. Fraser then goes on to mention (but not to describe) a current in French feminism — radical materialist feminism — which 'retains a humanist feminist commitment to universalism and a negative view of difference' (op. cit., p. 7). Although Fraser herself sees problems in the anti-universalist position (for instance in terms of the destabilisation of 'feminism'), she nonetheless, by describing French radical materialist feminism as *retaining* particular assumptions which most others have moved beyond, implicitly dismisses this (unexplored) mode of analysis.

19 The French participants also included Noelle Bisseret, Colette Capitan Peter and Emmanuèle de Lesseps. The workshops were originally funded by the Social Science Research Council and the Maison des Sciences de l'Homme.

20 See Mies, 1986; Acker, 1989; Cockburn, 1991; Delphy and Leonard, 1992; Adkins and Lury, 1996, for some critiques of this view.

21 Delphy's two foundations of materialism were

> that it is 'a theory of history . . . where this is written in terms of the domination of social groups by one another' (Delphy, 1976). Domination has as its ulterior motive exploitation. This postulate explains and is explained by the second foundation: the postulate that the way in which life is materially produced and reproduced is the base of the organization of all societies, hence is fundamental both at the individual and the collective level. (1980, pp. 87–8)

22 For example, twelve years later, in 1993, Landry and MacLean in their review of *Materialist Feminisms*, say

> Christine Delphy . . . whom we cite in the Preface [an article written in 1975 — the only piece of her work in their bibiography], has written manifestos for a materialist feminism. We find her description of this project . . . ultimately rather disappointing, and we would make some of the same criticisms of it that we make of Zillah Eisenstein's work . . . (see also, Barrett and McIntosh, 1979 for a fuller critique of Delphy). (Landry and MacLean, 1993, p. 15)

They then say that Eisenstein uses marxist terminology incorrectly, confuses status with class, assumes incorrectly that women constitute a class 'for itself' by means of their consciousness of themselves as women, and that seeing women as a class does not advance our theoretical grip on the relationship of capitalism and patriarchy but only loses the more radical insights of marxist (or socialist) feminism — and that she is ethnocentric (Landry and MacLean, 1993, pp. 33–34) — all of which are criticisms made of Delphy's analysis by Barrett and McIntosh.

23 Indeed, so powerful was the marxist feminist critique of Delphy's work that there was a general failure to recognise the parallels between her 'dual systems' approach and that proposed by Heidi Hartmann (1979, 1981), which was accorded great significance in feminist debates (cf., Nava, 1983).

Since that time the dual systems approach has of course itself been problematised (see, for example, Mies, 1986; Pateman, 1988; Acker, 1989; Cockburn, 1991; Adkins, 1995) and Delphy herself has moved on from this position (see Delphy and Leonard, 1992).

However, the 1980s dismissal was not total. Some British feminist sociologists did use Delphy's ideas in producing their own analyses. For example, Sylvia Walby's (1986) work on patriarchal relations in employment drew on Delphy's analysis of the domestic mode of production to consider the relationship between women's exclusion from, and segregation within, the labour market, and the exploitation of their domestic labour in the family; while Janet Finch (1983) drew on Delphy's work in her study of employers' use of wives' unpaid labour.

24 See Barrett (1992).

25 We should stress that this was *a* particular understanding of marxism.

26 Nor is it surprising that the major focus for attack should have been Delphy's work, since her earlier concentration on housework made her analysis the closest of the group to a classic marxist position. Her latest work with Leonard is broader, however, and also considers emotional, sexual and reproductive work within families.

27 See Adkins and Lury, 1996, for a discussion of such difficulties in relation to recent feminist analyses of the labour market.

28 So, for example, 'capital' is not understood in a taken-for-granted fashion, but rather its meaning is understood as a product of historical struggles between classes. Similarly, within French materialist feminism, it is recognised that 'domestic labour' may be organised by a range of processes including

aestheticisation, emotionalisation as well as changes in technologies — but it is the relations between men and women which constitute the relationship each gender has to that labour in terms of ownership, appropriation and exchange. In this sense parallels can be drawn between Bourdieu's (1984) revision of the notion of class and the understanding of the gender developed by French materialist feminists.

In his study of consumption and the significance of consumption for class formation, Bourdieu argues for the recognition of the significance of the accumulation and mobilisation of social and cultural capital in this process. He thus revised the notion of 'class' so as simultaneously to recognise the significance of circuits of both economic *and* social and cultural capital. His work has been critiqued by feminists for its lack of attention to gender — especially the ways in which the ownership and exchange of cultural capital is more limited for women than for men, and indeed may be linked to processes of oppression (see, for example, Delphy and Leonard, 1992; Skeggs 1996; Lury, 1996). For instance, Delphy and Leonard (1992) have shown how, in the family economy, women may be the agents in the creation of cultural capital, but they are not free to exchange this capital in the same way as men either on the market or in other circuits of exchange. Nevertheless (like French materialist feminists) Bourdieu does not separate off and hierarchises different modes of formation. The 'economic', the 'social' and the 'cultural' — whilst recognised as having different histories — are all located as 'material'.

29 This translation loses the oppositional flavour of the phrase in French.

30 Meaning here what in French is called '*la* différence': *the* one, between men and women. They do, of course, recognise that the modalities of this difference vary by class, historical period, race and nation, and that other systems of inequality put some women in power over other women, i.e. that there are also differences among and between women. But they do not see any of these differences between women as 'transcendental, foundational, fixed [or] trans-cultural' (Juteau-Lee, 1995, p. 21), as they are frequently articulated in forms of identity politics.

31 But their version of 'social constructionism' cannot be equated with 'social conditioning'; nor does it disembody sex/gender. Moreover it does not rest on a radical separation of 'nature' and the 'social'. It therefore challenges recent writings which attribute such characteristics to all constructionist analyses (see, for example, Butler, 1993, Moore, 1994).

See also Juteau-Lee (1995) for an analysis of the ways in which Guillaumin's work moves beyond strict constructionism.

32 The dates given throughout this book are those of the first publication of an article or book, and, where this first publication was in French, it is indicated when the piece was translated into English. The exception, of course, is where there is a direct quotation from an English version.

33   Believing that biological differences have no meaning outside a (hetero)sexist discourse, [Wittig] maintains that the very concepts of 'woman' and 'man' are political constructs whose function is to keep women subordinate to men. Rejecting the categorizing of people by sex is a necessary stage in eliminating the oppression of women; hence, her near-total suppression of the words 'woman' and 'man' in her fiction. (Crowder, 1994, p. 526).

34 The overturning of this assumption is usually attributed to Foucault (1969).

Chapter 2

The Category of Sex

Monique Wittig[1]

O. expresses a virile idea. Virile or at least masculine. At last a woman who admits it! Who admits what? Something that women have always till now refused to admit (*and today more than ever before*). Something that men have always reproached them with: that they never cease obeying their nature, the call of their blood, that everything in them, even their minds, is sex (Jean Paulhan).[2]

In the course of the year 1838, the peaceful island of Barbados was rocked by a strange and bloody revolt. About two hundred Negroes of both sexes, all of whom had recently been emancipated by the Proclamation of March, came one morning to beg their former master, a certain Glenelg, to take them back into bondage.... I suspect...that Glenelg's slaves were in love with their master, that they couldn't bear to be without him (ibid).

What should I be getting married for? I find life good enough as it is. What do I need a wife for?.... And what's so good about a woman? — A woman is a worker. A woman is a man's servant. — But what would I be needing a worker for? — That's just it. You like to have others pulling your chestnuts out of the fire... — Well, marry me off, if that's the case (Ivan Turgenev).[3]

The perenniality of the sexes and the perenniality of slaves and masters proceed from the same belief, and, as there are no slaves without masters, there are no women without men. The ideology of sexual difference functions as censorship in our culture by masking, on the ground of nature, the social opposition between men and women. Masculine/feminine, male/female are the categories that serve to conceal the fact that social differences always belong to an economic, political, ideological order. Every system of domination establishes divisions at the material and economic level. Furthermore, the divisions are abstracted and turned into concepts by the masters, and later on by the slaves when they rebel and start to struggle. The masters explain and justify the established divisions as a result of natural differences. The slaves, when they rebel and start to struggle, read social oppositions into the so-called natural differences.

For there is no sex. There is but sex that is oppressed and sex that oppresses. It is oppression that creates sex and not the contrary. The contrary would be to say that sex creates oppression, or to say that the cause (origin) of oppression is to be found in sex itself, in a natural division of the sexes pre-existing (or outside of) society.

The primacy of difference so constitutes our thought that it prevents turning inward on itself to question itself, no matter how necessary that may be to apprehend the basis of that which precisely constitutes it. To apprehend a difference in dialectical terms is to make apparent the contradictory terms to be resolved. To understand social reality in dialectical materialist terms is to apprehend the oppositions between classes, term to term, and make them meet under the same copula (a conflict in the social order), which is also a resolution (an abolition in the social order) of the apparent contradictions.

The class struggle is precisely that which resolves the contradictions between two opposed classes by abolishing them at the same time that it constitutes and reveals them as classes. The class struggle between women and men, which should be undertaken by all women, is that which resolves the contradictions between the sexes, abolishing them at the same time that it makes them understood. We must notice that the contradictions always belong to a material order. The important idea for me is that before the conflict (rebellion, struggle) there are no categories of opposition but only of difference. And it is not until the struggle breaks out that the violent reality of the oppositions and the political nature of the differences become manifest. For as long as oppositions (differences) appear as given, already there, before all thought, 'natural' — as long as there is no conflict and no struggle — there is no dialectic, there is no change, no movement. The dominant thought refuses to turn inward on itself to apprehend that which questions it.

And, indeed, as long as there is no women's struggle, there is no conflict between men and women. It is the fate of women to perform three-quarters of the work of society (in the public as well as in the private domain) plus the bodily work of reproduction according to a pre-established rate. Being murdered, mutilated, physically and mentally tortured and abused, being raped, being battered, and being forced to marry is the fate of women — and fate supposedly cannot be changed. Women do not know that they are totally dominated by men, and when they acknowledge the fact, they can 'hardly believe it'. And often, as a last recourse before the bare and crude reality, they refuse to 'believe' that men dominate them with full knowledge (for oppression is far more hideous for the oppressed than for the oppressors). Men, on the other hand, know perfectly well that they are dominating women ('We are are the masters of women', said André Breton) and are trained to do it. They do not need to express it all the time, for one can scarcely talk of domination over what one owns.

What is this thought that refuses to reverse itself, which never puts into question what primarily constitutes it? This thought is the dominant thought. It is a thought that affirms an 'already there' of the sexes, something which is supposed to have come before all thought, before all society. This thought is the thought of those who rule over women.

> The ideas of the ruling class are in every epoch the ruling ideas, i.e. the class which is the ruling *material* force of society, is at the same time its ruling *intellectual* force. The class which has the means of material production at its disposal, has control at the same time over the means of mental production, so that thereby, generally speaking, the ideas of those who lack the means of mental production are subject to it. The ruling ideas are nothing more than the ideal expression of the dominant material relationships, the dominant material relationships grasped as ideas: hence of the relationships which make the one class the ruling one, therefore, the ideas of its dominance. (Marx and Engels, 1845–6)

This thought based on the primacy of difference is the thought of domination.

Dominance provides women with a body of data, of givens, of a prioris, which, all the more for being questionable, form a huge political construct, a tight network that affects everything, our thoughts, our gestures, our acts, our work, our feelings, our relationships.

Dominance thus teaches us from all directions:

— that there are before all thinking, all society, 'sexes' (two categories of individuals born) with a constitutive difference, a difference that has ontological consequences (the metaphysical approach),

— that there are before all thinking, all social order, 'sexes' with a 'natural' or 'biological' or 'hormonal' or 'genetic' difference that has sociological consequences (the scientific approach),

— that there is before all thinking, all social order, a 'natural division of labour in the family', a 'division of labour [that] was originally nothing *but* the division of labour in the sexual act' (the marxist approach).

Whatever the approach, the idea remains basically the same. The sexes, in spite of their constitutive difference, must inevitably develop relationships from category to category. Belonging to the natural order, these relationships cannot be spoken of as social relationships. This thought, which impregnates all discourses, including common-sense ones (Adam's rib or Adam *is*, Eve is Adam's rib), is the thought of domination. Its body of discourses is constantly reinforced on all levels of social reality and conceals the political fact of the subjugation of one sex by the other, the compulsory character of the category itself (which constitutes the first definition of the social being in civil status). The category of sex does not exist a priori, before all society. And as a category of dominance it cannot be a product of natural dominance but of the social dominance of women by men, for there is but social dominance.

The category of sex is the political category that founds society as heterosexual. As such it does not concern being, but relationships (for women and men are the result of relationships), although the two aspects are always confused when they are discussed. The category of sex is the one that rules as 'natural' the relation that is at the base of (heterosexual) society and through which half of the population, women, are 'heterosexualised' (the making of women is like the making of eunuchs, the breeding of slaves, of animals) and submitted to a heterosexual economy. For the category of sex is the product of a heterosexual society that imposes on women the rigid obligation of the reproduction of the 'species', that is, the reproduction of heterosexual society. The compulsory reproduction of the 'species' by women is the system of exploitation on which heterosexuality is economically based. Reproduction is essentially that work, that production by women, through which the appropriation by men of all the work of women proceeds. One must include here the appropriation of work which is associated 'by nature' with reproduction, the raising of children and domestic chores. This appropriation of the work of women is effected in the same way as the appropriation of the work of the working class by the ruling class. It cannot be said that one of these two productions (reproduction) is 'natural' while the other one is social. This argument is only the theoretical, ideological justification of oppression, an argument to make women believe that before society and in all societies they are subject to this obligation to reproduce. However, as we know nothing about the work, about social production, outside of the context of exploitation, we know nothing about the reproduction of society outside of its context of exploitation.

The category of sex is the product of a heterosexual society in which men appropriate for themselves the reproduction and production of women, and also their physical persons by means of a contract called the marriage contract. Compare this contract with the contract that binds a worker to his employer. The contract binding the woman to the man is in principle a contract for life, which only law can break (divorce). It assigns the woman certain obligations, including unpaid work. The work (housework, raising children) and the obligations (surrender of her reproduction in the name of her husband, cohabitation by day and night, forced coitus, assignment of residence implied by the legal concept of 'surrender of the conjugal domicile') mean in their terms a surrender by the woman of her physical person to her husband. That the woman depends directly on her husband is implicit in the police's policy of not intervening when a husband beats his wife. The police intervene with the specific charge of assault and battery when one citizen beats another citizen. But a woman who has signed a marriage contract has thereby ceased to be an ordinary citizen (protected by law). The police openly express their aversion to getting involved in domestic affairs (as opposed to civil affairs), where the authority of the state does not have to intervene directly since it is relayed through that of the husband. One has to go to shelters for battered women to see how far this authority can be exercised.

The category of sex is the product of heterosexual society that turns half of the population into sexual beings, for sex is a category which women cannot be outside of. Wherever they are, whatever they do (including working in the public sector), they are seen (and made) sexually available to men, and they, breasts, buttocks, costume, must be visible. They must wear their yellow star, their constant smile, day and night. One might consider that every woman, married or not, has a period of forced sexual service, a sexual service that we may compare to the military one, and which can vary between a day, a year, or twenty-five years or more. Some lesbians and nuns escape, but they are very few, although the number is growing. Although women are very visible as sexual beings, as social beings they are totally invisible, and as such must appear as little as possible, and always with some kind of excuse if they do so. One only has to read interviews with outstanding women to hear them apologising. And the newspapers still today report that 'two students and a woman', 'two lawyers and a woman', 'three travellers and a woman' were seen doing this or that. For the category of sex is the category that sticks to women, for only they cannot be conceived of outside of it. Only *they* are sex, *the* sex, and [it is as] sex [that] they [are] made in their minds, bodies, acts, gestures; even their murders and beatings are sexual. Indeed, the category of sex tightly holds women.

For the category of sex is a totalitarian one, which to prove true has its inquisitions, its courts, its tribunals, its body of laws, its terrors, its tortures, its mutilations, its executions, its police. It shapes the mind as well as the body since it controls all mental production. It grips our minds in such a way that we cannot think outside of it. This is why we must destroy it and start thinking beyond it if we want to start thinking at all, as we must destroy the sexes as a sociological reality if we want to start to exist. The category of sex is the category that ordains slavery for women, and it works specifically, as it did for black slaves, through an operation of reduction, by taking the part for the whole, a part (colour, sex) through which the whole human group has to pass as through a screen. Notice that in civil matters colour, as well as sex, still must be 'declared'. However, because of the abolition of slavery, the 'declaration' of 'colour' is now considered discriminatory. But that does not hold true for the 'declaration' of 'sex', which not even women dream of abolishing. I say: it is about time to do so.[4]

Notes

1   'The Category of Sex' was first published in *Feminist Issues* in Fall 1982, pp. 63–8 (but dated as written in 1976), and later included in the collection of Monique Wittig's work: *The Straight Mind and Other Essays*, Boston: Beacon Press and Hemel Hempstead: Harvester Wheatsheaf, 1992, pp. 1–8.

2   Jean Paulhan, 'Happiness in Slavery', preface to *The Story of O*, by Pauline de Reage.
3   Ivan Turgenev, *The Hunting Sketches*.
4   Pleasure in sex is no more the subject of this paper than is happiness in slavery.

Chapter 3

Rethinking Sex and Gender

Christine Delphy[1]

Up till now, most work on gender, including most feminist work on gender, has been based on an unexamined presupposition: that sex precedes gender. However, although this presupposition is historically explicable, it is theoretically unjustifiable, and its continued existence is holding back our thinking on gender. It is preventing us from rethinking gender in an open and unbiased way. Further, this lack of intellectual clarity is inextricably bound up with, on the one hand, the political contradictions produced by our desire as women to escape domination, and, on the other, our fear that we might lose what seem to be fundamental social categories.

What is common to these intellectual impasses and political contradictions is an inability (or a refusal) to think rigorously about the relationship between *division* and *hierarchy*, since the question of the relationship between sex and gender not only parallels this question, but is, in fact, the self-same issue.

What I want to do here is argue that in order to understand reality, and hence eventually to have the power to change it, we must be prepared to abandon our certainties and to accept the (temporary) pain of an increased uncertainty about the world. Having the courage to confront the unknown is a pre-condition for imagination, and the capacity to imagine another world is an essential element in scientific progress. It is certainly indispensable to my analysis.

From Sex Roles to Gender

The notion of gender developed from that of sex roles, and, rightly or wrongly, the person who is credited with being the founding mother of this line of thought is Margaret Mead. Put very briefly, it is her thesis (Mead, 1935) that most societies divide the universe of human characteristics into two, and attribute one half to men and the other to women. For Mead, this division is quite arbitrary, but she does not condemn it unreservedly. She sees it as having many advantages for society, culture and civilisation.

Mead herself does not deal with either the sexual division of labour or differences in the status of men and women. As far as she is concerned, the division of labour is natural, and the few comments she does make about it show that she attributes it to the different reproductive roles of males and females, and to differences in physical strength between the sexes. These are, of course, the 'classic' reasons used within both anthropological and 'commonsense' (including feminist) thinking. Mead also does not question the hierarchy between the sexes. She either ignores it, or considers it legitimate. Nor does she discuss the prescribed differences between the sexes, except within the very limited domain of 'temperament' (under which heading she groups abilities, aptitudes, and emotional personality).

For a long time, Mead's analysis of prescribed differences was the major theme in the critique of sex roles — a critique that arose from a concern to defend the rights of individuals to express their individualities freely. In the process it was implied that 'masculine' and 'feminine' traits together constitute and exhaust the whole of human possibilities (see below).

Although the term is frequently accredited to her, Mead herself rarely uses the term 'sex roles' because she was not in fact concerned about these roles, still less with critiquing them. Her concern was rather the analysis and critique of feminine and masculine 'temperaments'. In fact, the idea of sex roles was critically developed from the 1940s to the 1960s, that is, in the decades commonly considered to be a period when feminism was 'latent' — through the work of Mirra Komarovsky (1950), Viola Klein and Alva Myrdal (Myrdal and Klein, 1956), and Andrée Michel (1959, 1960). All these authors worked within a Parsonian sociological perspective, and saw a *role* as the active aspect of a *status*. Broadly speaking, 'status' was the equivalent of the level of prestige within society, and each status had roles which the individuals who held that status had to fulfil. This perspective is clearly sociological in the true sense of the word: people's situations and activities are held to derive from the social structure, rather than from either nature or their particular capacities.

Thus, when these authors spoke of the 'roles' of women and men, they were already taking a large step towards denaturalising the respective occupations and situations of the sexes. Their approach was not actually opposed to Mead's anthropological approach, but rather developed it in two ways:

1 They confirmed the arbitary aspect of the division of qualities between the sexes, this time by an epistemological diktat: that is, by their postulate that everyone plays roles.
2 More importantly, they considered a social 'role' to be not simply the 'psychological' characteristics Mead had spoken about, but also (and principally) the work associated with a rung on the social ladder (a status), and hence a position in the division of labour.

The division of labour and the hierarchy between men and women therefore began to be accorded a cultural character, whereas Mead had considered them to be natural; and since they were cultural rather than natural, the authors stressed they were arbitrary. In addition, since the concept of sex roles also emerged within the framework of a feminist critique (even when the term feminist was not explicitly used), these authors all stressed that as the position of women was socially determined, it was changeable. Even though the concepts they used were Parsonian in origin, they questioned Parsons's theory and its premise of harmony between the sexes; and Andrée Michel, in particular, strongly criticised the containment of women within traditional roles, and also Parsons's idea that this was good for women and for society.

The term 'sex roles' then remained in use for a long time, until the concept of gender, which derived directly from it, appeared in the early 1970s. If we take one of the first works directly on 'gender', Ann Oakley's *Sex, Gender and Society*, published in 1972, we find the following definition:

> 'Sex' is a word that refers to the biological differences between male and female: the visible difference in genitalia, the related difference in procreative function. 'Gender', however, is a matter of culture: it refers to the social classification into 'masculine' and 'feminine'. (Oakley, 1985, p. 16)

Oakley's book is devoted partly to a critical account of recent research on the differential psychology of the sexes: to innate and acquired elements of aptitude ('talents' in Mead's terminology) and attitude ('temperamental') differences between women and men, and partly to an account of what anthropological research can teach us about the division of labour between the sexes. According to Oakley, psychological differences between the sexes are due to social conditioning, and there is no research that allows us to infer any biological determinism whatsoever. She also says that while a division of labour by sex is universal, the content of the tasks considered to be feminine or masculine varies considerably according to the society.

Oakley's use of the concept of gender thus covers all the established differences between men and women, whether they are individual differences (studied by psychologists), or social roles, or cultural representations (studied by sociologists and anthropologists). In addition, in her work the concept of gender covers everything that is variable and socially determined — variability being the proof that it is social in origin. She says: 'The constancy of sex must be admitted, but so too must the variability of gender' (op. cit., 1985, p. 16).

However, the facets that are missing from Oakley's definition, although they were already present in the work on sex roles, and which have become central to feminist positions and been developed subsequently, are the fundamental *asymmetry* (Hurtig and Pichevin, 1986) and *hierarchy* (Delphy, 1980; Varikas, 1987) between the two groups, or roles, or sexes, or genders.

Sex and Gender

With the arrival of the concept of gender, three things became possible (which does not mean they have happened):

1 All the differences between the sexes which appeared to be social and arbitrary, whether they actually varied from one society to another or were merely held to be susceptible to change, were gathered together in one concept.
2 The use of the singular ('gender' as opposed to 'genders') allowed the accent to be moved from the two divided parts to the principle of partition itself.
3 The idea of hierarchy was firmly anchored in the concept. This should, at least in theory, have allowed the relationship between the divided parts to be considered from another angle.

As studies have accumulated showing the arbitrariness of sex roles and the lack of foundation for stereotypes in one area after another, the idea that gender is independent of sex has progressed. Or rather, since it is a question of the content, the idea that both genders are independent of both sexes has progressed, and the aspects of 'sex roles' and sexual situations that are recognised to be socially constructed rather than biologically determined, have grown. Everyone working in the field has certainly not drawn the dividing line between what is social and cultural and what is natural in the same place — but then it would have been astonishing if they had. It is right that the question should remain open.

What is problematic, however, is that the on-going discussions around this question have presumed epistemological and methodological paradigms that should actually have been questioned. We have continued to think of gender in terms of sex: to see it as a social dichotomy determined by a natural dichotomy. We now see gender as the *content* with sex as the *container*. The content may vary, and some consider it *must* vary, but the container is considered to be invariable because it is part of nature, and nature 'does not change'. Moreover, part of the nature of sex itself is seen to be its *tendency to have a social content*/to vary culturally.

What should have happened, however, is that the recognition of the independence of the genders from the sexes should have led us to question whether gender is, in fact, independent of sex. But this question has not been asked. For most authors, the issue of the relationship between sex and gender is simply 'what sort of social classification does sex give rise to? Is it strong or weak, equal or unequal?' What they never ask is why sex should give rise to any sort of social classification. Even the neutral question 'we have here two variables, two distributions, which coincide totally. How can we explain this co-variance?' does not get considered. The response is always: sex comes first, chronologically and hence logically — although it is never explained why this should be so.

Actually, whether or not the precedence gets explained does not make much difference. The very fact of suggesting or admitting the precedence of sex, even implicitly, leads to one being located, objectively, in a theory where sex causes or explains gender. And the theory that sex causes gender, even if it does not determine the exact forms gender divisions take, can derive from only two logical lines of argument.

In the first line of argument, biological sex, and particularly the different functions in procreation of males and females that it provokes, necessarily gives rise to a minimal division of labour. I would include in this line of argument, with its naturalist premises, most contemporary anthropological accounts, feminist as well as patriarchal, from George Murdock (1949) to Martha Moia (1981) by way of Gayle Rubin (1975) [with just a few notable exceptions, such as Mathieu (1991) and Tabet (1982) — in this volume]. It fails to explain satisfactorily: first, the nature and the natural reason for this first division of labour; and second, the reasons it is extended into all fields of activity; that is, why it is not limited to the domain of procreation. It therefore fails to explain gender other than by suppositions that reintroduce upstream one or more of the elements it is supposed to explain downstream.

The second line of argument sees biological sex as a physical trait which is not only suitable, but destined by its intrinsic 'salience' (in psycho-cognitive terms) to be a receptacle for classifications. Here it is postulated that human beings have a universal need to establish classifications independently of, and prior to, any social practice.[2] But these two human needs are neither justified nor proven. They are simply asserted. We are not shown *why* sex is more prominent than other physical traits that are equally distinguishable, but which do not give birth to classifications that are (1) dichotomous and (2) imply social roles which are not just distinct but hierachical.

I call this latter line of argument 'cognitivist', not because it is particularly held by the 'Cognitivists', but because it presumes certain 'prerequisites' of human cognition. The best known academic version of such theories is that of Lévi-Strauss, who, while not a psychologist, bases all his analyses of kinship, and (by extension) human societies, on an irrepressible and pre-social (hence psychological) need of human beings to divide everything in two (and then into multiples of two). Lévi-Strauss (1969) was very much influenced by linguistics, in particular by Saussure's phonology (Saussure, 1959), and he devised by ana-logous construction what the social sciences call 'structuralism'.

A rather more recent version of this thesis has been presented by Derrida (1976) and his followers, who say that things can only be distinguished by opposition to other things. However, while Saussure is concerned purely with linguistic structures, Derrida and his clones want to draw philosophical conclusions about the importance of 'différance'. These conclusions themselves incorporate presuppositions about the conditions for the possibility of human knowledge, hence about the human spirit, which are very similar to those of Lévi-Strauss. Saussure's theory had no such ambitions, and its validity in its own field of reference — linguistics — should not be taken as a guarantee of its applicability elsewhere. We may agree things are only known by distinction and hence by differentiation, but these differentiations can be, and often are, multiple. Alongside cabbages and carrots, which are not 'opposites' of each other, there are courgettes, melons, and potatoes. Moreover, distinctions are not necessarily hierarchical: vegetables are not placed on a scale of value. Indeed, they are often used as a warning against any attempt at hierarchisation: we are told not to compare (or to try to add) cabbages and carrots. They are incommensurable. They do not have a common measure. Therefore, they cannot be evaluated in terms of being more or less, or better or worse than one another.

Those who adhere to Derrida's thesis thus fail to distinguish between the differences on which language is based, and differences in social structures. The characteristics of cognition, in so far as they can be reduced to the characteristics of language, cannot account for social hierarchy. This is external to them. They therefore cannot account for gender — or they can do so only at the expense of dropping hierarchy as a constitutive element of gender.

Hence, neither of the two lines of argument that might justify a causal link from sex to gender is satisfactory. The presupposition that there *is* such a causal link thus remains just that: a presupposition.

But if we are to think about gender, or to think about anything at all, we must leave the domain of presuppositions. To think about gender we must rethink the question of its relationship to sex, and to think about this we must first actually ask the question. We must abandon the notion that we already know the answer. We must not only admit, but also explore, two other hypotheses: first, that the statistical coincidence between sex and gender is just that, a coincidence. The correlation is due to chance. This hypothesis is, however, untenable, because the distribution is such that the co-incidence between so-called biological sex and gender *is* 'statistically significant'. It is stronger than any correlation could be which is due to chance.

Second, that *gender* precedes sex: that sex itself simply marks a social division; that it serves to allow social recognition and identification of those who are dominants and those who are dominated. That is, that sex is a sign, but that since it does not distinguish just any old thing from anything else, and does not distinguish equivalent things but rather important and unequal things, it has historically acquired a symbolic value.

The symbolic value of sex has certainly not escaped the theoreticians of psychoanalysis. But what has entirely escaped them is that this should be one of the final *conclusions* of a long progression: the point of arrival and not of departure. Unfortunately, this blind spot is one that many feminists share with psychoanalysts.

As society locates the sign that marks out the dominants from the dominated within the zone of physical traits, two further remarks need to be made.

First, the marker is not found in a pure state, all ready for use. As Hurtig and Pichevin (1986) have shown, biologists see sex as made up of several indicators which are more or less correlated one with another, and the majority are continuous variables (occurring in varying degrees). So in order for sex to be used as a dichotomous classification, the indicators have to be reduced to just one. And, as Hurtig and Pichevin (1985) also say, this reduction 'is a social act'.

Second, the presence or absence of a penis[3] is a strong predictor of gender (by definition one might say). However, having or not having a penis correlates only weakly with procreative functional differences between individuals. It does not distinguish tidily between people who can bear children and those who cannot. It distinguishes, in fact, just some of those who cannot. Lots of those who do not have penises also cannot bear children, either because of constitutional sterility or due to age.

It is worth pausing here, because the 'cognitivists' think sex is a 'prominent trait' because they think physical sex is strongly correlated with functional differences, and because they assume that the rest of humanity shares this 'knowledge'. But they only think biological sex is a 'spontaneous perception' of humanity because they themselves are convinced that it is a natural trait that no one could ignore. To them it is self-evident that there are two, and only two, sexes, and that this dichotomy exactly cross-checks with the division between potential bearers and non-bearers of children.

To try to question these 'facts' is indeed to crack one of the toughest nuts in our perception of the world. We must, therefore, add to the hypothesis that gender precedes sex, the following question: when we connect gender and sex, are we comparing something social with something which is *also* social (in this case, the way a given society represents 'biology' to itself)?

One would think that this would logically have been one of the first questions to be asked, and it is doubtless the reason why some feminists in France (for example, Guillaumin, 1982, 1985; Mathieu, 1980; and Wittig, 1992) have been opposed to using the term 'gender'. They believe it reinforces the idea that 'sex' itself is purely natural. However, not using the concept of gender does not mean one thereby directly questions the natural character of sex. So economising on the concept of gender does not seem to me the best way to progress.

'Sex' denotes and connotes something natural. It was, therefore, not possible to question 'sex' head on, all at once, since to do so involves a contradiction in terms. ('Naturalness' is an integral part of the definition of the term.) We had first to demonstrate that 'sex' is applied to divisions and distinctions which are social. Then we had not only to *separate* the social from the original term, which remains defined by naturalness, but to make the social *emerge*. This is what the notions of first 'sex roles' and then 'gender' did. Only when the 'social part' is clearly established as social, when it has a *name* of its own (whether it be 'sex roles' or 'gender'), then and only then could we come back to the idea we started with. We had first to design and lay claim to a territory for the social, having a different conceptual location from that of sex, but tied to the traditional sense of the word 'sex', in order to be able, from this strategic location, to challenge the traditional meaning of 'sex'.

To end this section, I would say that we can only make advances in our knowledge if we initially increase the unknown: if we extend the areas that are cloudy and indeterminate. To advance, we must first renounce some truths. These 'truths' make us feel comfortable, as do all certainties, but they stop us asking questions — and asking questions is the surest, if not the only way of getting answers.

Division, Differences and Classifications

The debate on gender and its relationship to sex covers much the same ground as the debate on the priority of the two elements — division and hierarchy — which constitute gender. These are empirically indissolubly united, but they need to be distinguished analytically. If it is accepted that there is a line of demarcation between 'natural' and socially constructed differences, and that at least some differences are socially constructed, then there is a framework for conceptualising gender. This means, or should mean, recognising that hierarchy forms the foundation for differences — for all differences, not just gender.

However, even when this is accepted as an explanation, it is not accepted as a politics, nor as a vision of the future, by feminists. It is not their Utopia. All feminists reject the sex/gender hierarchy, but very few are ready to admit that the logical consequence of this rejection is a refusal of sex roles, and the disappearance of gender. Feminists seem to want to abolish hierarchy and even sex roles, but not difference itself. They want to abolish the contents but not the container. They all want to keep some elements of gender. Some want to keep more, others less, but at the very least they want to maintain the classification. Very few indeed are happy to contemplate there being simply anatomical sexual differences which are not given any social significance or symbolic value. Suddenly, the categories they use for analysis, which elsewhere clearly distinguish those who think difference comes *first* and hierarchy *afterwards* from those who think the contents of the divided groups are the *product* of the hierarchical division, become muzzy, and the divergence between the two schools fades away.

This is especially clear in the debate on values. Feminist (and many other!) theorists generally accept that values are socially constructed and historically acquired, but they seem to think they must nonetheless be preserved. There are two typical variants on this position. One says we must distribute masculine and feminine values throughout the whole of humanity; the other says that masculine and feminine values must each be maintained in their original group. The latter view is currently especially common among women who do not want to share feminine values with men. I am not sure whether this is because they believe men are unworthy or incapable of sustaining these values, or because they know men do not want them anyway. But we might well ask how women who are 'nurturing' and proud of it are going to become the equals of unchanged men — who are going to continue to drain these women's time? This is not a minor contradiction. It shows, rather, that if intellectual confusion produces political confusion, it is also possible to wonder, in a mood of despair, if there is not, behind the intellectual haze, a deep and unacknowledged desire *not* to change.

In any case, both variants of the debate show an implicit interpretation of the present situation, which contradicts the problematic of gender. On the one hand, there is a desire to retain a system of classification, even though (it is said) it has outlived its function of *establishing* a hierarchy between individuals — which would seem to indicate that people do not *really* think that gender is a social classification. On the other hand, there is a vision of values which is very similar to Margaret Mead's, which can be summarised as: all human potentialities are already actually represented, but they are divided up between men and women. 'Masculine' plus 'feminine' subcultures, in fact culture itself, is not the product of a hierarchical society. It is independent of the social structure. The latter is simply superimposed upon it.

Hierarchy as Necessarily Prior to Division

This last view is contrary to everything we know about the relationship between social structure and culture. In the marxist tradition, and more generally in contemporary sociology whether marxist or not, it is held that the social structure is primary. This implies, as far as values are concerned, that they are, and cannot but be, appropriate to the structure of the society in question. Our society is hierarchical, and consequently its values are also hierarchically arranged. But this is not the only consequence, since Mead's model also allows for this.

Rather, if we accept that values are appropriate to social structures, then we must accept that values are *hierarchical* in general, and that those of the dominated are no less hierarchical than those of the dominants. According to this hypothesis, we must also accept that masculinity and femininity are not just, or rather not at all, what they were in Mead's model — a division of the traits which are (1) present in a potential form in both sexes, or (2) present in all forms of possible and imaginable societies. According to the 'appropriateness' paradigm (i.e. the social construction of values), masculinity and femininity are the cultural creations of a society based on a gender hierarchy (as well as, of course, on other hierarchies). This means not only that they are linked to one another in a relationship of complementarity and opposition, but also that this structure determines the *content of each of these categories* and not just their relationship. It may be that together they cover the totality of human traits *which exist today*, but we cannot presume that even together they cover the whole spectrum of human potentialities. If we follow the 'appropriateness' paradigm, changing the respective statuses of the groups would lead to neither an alignment of all individuals on a single model, nor a happy hybrid of the two models.

Both the other sorts of conjecture presuppose, however, that these 'models' (i.e. the 'feminine' and the 'masculine') exist *sui generis*, and both imply a projection into a changed future of traits and values that exist now, prior to the change in the social structure.

To entrust oneself to this sort of guesswork, which moreover is totally implicit, requires a quite untenable, static view of culture. Even if it was progressive when Margararet Mead was writing just to admit that cultures varied and that values were arbitrarily divided between groups, this view is no longer tenable. It assumes the invariability of a universal human subject, and this has been invalidated by historians' studies of 'mentalities', and by the social constructionist approaches inspired (even if generally unwittingly) by the marxist principles discussed above.

This vision of culture as static is, however, fundamental to all the variants of the notion of positive complementarity between men and women (even if those who hold such views do not recognise it).[4] They all presuppose that values precede their hierarchical organisation (as in Mead's model), and this stasis can only lead us back to 'nature': in this case, to human nature.

Such a point of view, and only such a point of view, can explain why Mead was afraid that everyone would become the same, which was counter to nature. The fear that a generalised sameness, or absence of differentiation, would be provoked by the disappearance of what is apparently the only kind of difference that we know (for this viewpoint ignores all other sorts of variance)[5] is, of course, not new; though currently the fear that the world will align on a single model often takes the more specific form that the single model will be the current masculine model. This (it is said) will be the price we shall have to pay for equality; and (it is said) it is (perhaps) too high a price. However, this fear is groundless, since it is based on a static, hence essentialist, vision of women and men, which is a corollary to the belief that hierarchy was in some way added on to an essential dichotomy.

Within a gender framework such fears are simply incomprehensible. If women were the equals of men, men would no longer equal themselves. Why then should women resemble what men would have ceased to be? If we define men within a gender framework, they are first and foremost dominants with characteristics that enable them to remain dominants. To be like them would also be to be dominants; but this is a contradiction in terms. If, in a collective couple constituted of dominants and dominated, either of the categories is suppressed, then the domination is *ipso facto* suppressed. Hence, the other category of the couple is also suppressed. Or to put it another way, to be dominant one must have someone to dominate. One can no more conceive of a society where everyone is 'dominant' than of one where everyone is 'richest'.

It is also not possible to imagine the values of a future egalitarian society as being the sum, or a combination, of existing masculine and feminine values, for these values were created in, and by, hierarchy. So how could they survive the end of hierarchy?

This vision of a society where values existed as 'entities', prior to their being organised into a hierarchy, is, as I have said, static and ultimately naturalist. But it is also not an isolated idea. It is part of a whole ensemble of ideas which includes: first, commonsense and academic theories of sexuality that involve a double confusion: a confusion of anatomical sex with sexuality, and of sexuality with procreation; and second, a deep cultural theme to which these theories themselves refer back: namely that each individual is essentially incomplete in so far as he or she is sexed. Emotional resistance and intellectual obstacles to thinking about gender both originate from this: from the individual and collective consciousness.

This is what I previously called 'a set of confused representations turning around a belief in the necessity of close and permanent relations between most males and most females' (Delphy, 1980). I wanted to call this set (of representations) 'heterosexuality', but it has been suggested that it would be better called 'complementarity'. Its emblem is the image of heterosexual intercourse, and this gives it a social meaning and an emotional charge which is explicable only by its symbolic value. It could, therefore, equally be called a *set* of representations of 'fitting together'.

It would be interesting to develop this reflection further in relation to two main sets of questions: first, how this whole set of ideas forms a view of the world as a whole which is more than the sum of its parts — which possesses a mystical and non-rational character (a cosmogony); and second, how this cosmogony informs and determines the explicit and implicit premises of much scientific research — including feminist research and lesbian research.

Imagination and Knowledge

We do not know what the values, individual personality traits, and culture of a non-hierarchical society would be like, and we have great difficulty in imagining it. But to imagine it we must think that it is possible. And it *is* possible. Practices produce values: other practices produce other values.

Perhaps it is our difficulty in getting beyond the present, tied to our fear of the unknown, which curbs us in our Utopian flights, as also in our progress at the level of knowledge — since the two are necessary to one another. To construct another future we obviously need an analysis of the present, but what is less recognised is that having a Utopian vision is one of the indispensable staging-posts in the scientific process — in *all* scientific work. We can only analyse what *does* exist by imagining what does *not* exist, because to understand what is, we must ask how it came about. And asking how it came to exist must involve two operations. The first I described earlier when I said that we must admit we do not know the answers when we think we do (Descartes's famous 'suspension of judgment'). The second operation is admitting, even if it is contrary to the evidence of our senses, that something which exists, need not exist.

In conclusion, I would say that perhaps we shall only really be able to think about gender on the day when we can imagine non-gender. But if Newton could do it for falling apples, we should be able to do it for ourselves as women.

Notes

1 An earlier version of this article, 'Penser le genre: Quels problemes?', appeared in Marie-Claude Hurtig *et al.* (Eds) *Sexe et genre: de la hiérarchie entre les sexes*, 1991, Paris, Éditions du Centre National de la Recherche Scientifique.

   The present version was translated (by Diana Leonard) and appeared first in 1993 in *Women's Studies International Forum*, **16**(1), pp. 1–9.

2 See, for example, Archer and Lloyd (1985), who say gender will continue because it is a 'practical way of classifying people'.

3 This is 'the final arbiter' of the dichotomous sex classification for the state, according to Money and Ehrhardt (1972, quoted by Hurtig and Pichevin, 1985).

4 There is, however, no single meaning to complementarity. The paradigm of hierarchy as the basis of division *also* implies complementarity, although in a negative sense.

5 This would mean that I would only talk to a male baker since I would no longer be able to distinguish a female baker from myself.

Chapter 4

Sexual, Sexed and Sex-Class Identities: Three Ways of Conceptualising the Relationship Between Sex and Gender

Nicole-Claude Mathieu[1]

This contribution began as a paper to the 10th World Congress of Sociology in 1982. The general theme was 'Sociological Theory and Social Practice'. In reaction to what appeared an implicit presupposition of the title (that social actors do not have a theory of their own practice — but that happily sociology is there to provide one), my paper was entitled 'The conceptualisation of sex in social science practice and women's movement theories'.[2]

At the time, only the women's movements and certain sections of the gay male movements had, in fact, furnished any sociological theorisation of the concept of sex — through their political questioning of relationships between the sexes, and hence of current notions of 'man' and 'woman'. Such ideas certainly did not exist, or at least were not explicit, in 1970s social sciences (see, Mathieu, 1971, 1973 and 1977).

The concept of sex involves the mental organisation of ideas (representations, myths, utopias, etc: 'thought' sex) and practices (social relations between the sexes: 'acted' sex), which are often contradictory. Whether the contradictions are emphasised or hidden, certain logics are set in place which this article will try to encompass.

The ambiguity of the idea of sex, as manifest in commonsense, social science and women's movements' analyses, comes mainly from a required overlying of biological and social sex, at least in western societies. This is as central to the political polemics of feminist analyses and strategies as to the omissions and distortions of 'scientific' analysis.

We therefore need to be aware of the *type of problematic* in which we are situated when we talk of relations between men and women, and especially when we use vague expressions like: 'as a woman/as women...'. This issue is particularly acute in political movements, which is why it was attempts by various feminist and lesbian tendencies to define the term 'women' that provided the basis on which I developed a provisional scheme of three main ways of conceptualising sex. I wanted to develop this grid so that it could also apply to social science analyses and to the social actors we 'study', including those in other societies — especially where there is an official acknowledgment of a divergence between biological sex and social sex.

Sex is often thought to arise from 'biology', unlike gender, which is seen as 'social'. Various non-western societies, and marginal phenomena within our own societies, are interesting, however, in that they show that neither the definitions of sex and gender, nor the boundaries between sexes and between genders, are so clear. The renewed interest in gender in the field of symbolic anthropology, which followed a feminist impetus to which I contributed (with the notion of social sex) during the 1970s, has become more and more concerned with the so-called 'third sex' or 'third gender'. Some authors (for example, Saladin d'Anglure, 1985) have tried to theorise such phenomena from the point of view of the ways in which they are alike (as counter-demonstrations to the binary thinking that contrasts men and women); but I have investigated the ways in which they *differ* as regards the *articulation* between sex and gender, and how they themselves often revert to systems of bi-categoral thinking.

My concern was thus:

— to study anthropological accounts of various striking examples of *conformity* and *transgression* between conceptions of sex and conceptions of gender, and to try to construct a classification;[3] and
— also to see if and how such a classification could broaden the scope of the scheme I had previously developed for western societies, based upon different meanings underlying the concept of 'woman'.

This involved considering (both representational and behavioural) phenomena at various levels:

— the (more or less diffuse) norms of whole societies, focusing on the ways in which what each considered inappropriate was defined and 'resolved';
— institutionalised forms of (permanent or occasional) 'deviance', to see if these were simply bendings, or on the contrary the quintessence, of the norm; and
— the self-definition of groups or individuals considered deviant or marginal, asking if this self-definition was a solution to a sense of being inappropriate which conformed to the norms or which subverted them.

The play of congruence and incongruence (between norm and marginality, and between sex and gender) was, thus, the focal point of the analysis — alongside the play of asymmetry and symmetry between the sexes in some of the phenomena studied.

This led me to distinguish three main ways of thinking about the relationship between sex and gender. In each we can distinguish simultaneously:

— a problematic of *personal identity* in relation to the sexed body and sexuality, but also in relation to the status of the person in the social organization of 'sex';

— a strategy of *relations between the sexes*;

— an understanding of the *relationship between biological sex and social sex* (or between sex and gender); and

— a definition of the *relationship between hetero- and homosexuality*, in other words, the relationship between sex, gender and sexuality.

Using a convenient, though simplifying, shorthand, and starting from the problematic of personal identity to which each of these ways of thinking refers, I have called them:

- Mode I: *'sexual' identity*, based on an individualistic consciousness of sex; where sex and gender are homologically connected: here gender translates sex.
- Mode II: *'sexed' identity*, based on a sex group consciousness; where sex and gender are analogically connected: here gender symbolises sex (and, conversely, sex symbolises gender).
- Mode III: *'sex-class' identity*, based on a sex class consciousness; where sex and gender are socio-logically connected: here gender constructs sex.

Note:

— Each of these three types of 'logic' can be an expression of either the norms of a society or a particular group, or it can derive from marginal or 'oppositional' individuals or groups.

— For any given society, group or individual, elements (for example, 'man' and 'woman') or phenomena (for example, 'homosexuality' and 'heterosexuality'), which might seem to be intrinsically linked, may not necessarily fall within the same way of thinking.

— Conversely, apparently contradictory 'opinions' or behaviours can belong to a single mode.

— The order in which these types are listed does not necessarily correspond to a linear historical evolution (particularly so far as the western women's movement is concerned).

Mode I: 'Sexual' Identity — Principle Referent: Sex

The first way of conceptualising sex is based in a problematic which I call *'sexual' identity* — based on *individualistic* consciousness of the psycho-socio-logical experience of biological sex. It is the perspective which is most common in western societies. Take, for instance, the following sentence from a 'lonely hearts' column: 'Why aren't things working out with my boy-friend? I still have everything necessary to be a woman ...' (in this context, periods, hence procreative capacity). Here 'a woman' is simply someone of the female sex.

In this problematic, personal psycho-social traits should fit with biological traits (and there are problems if they do not). Biological sex is seen as given, or to be determined.

The referent is thus an absolute sex bipartition, which is both natural and social simultaneously. Masculine corresponds (or should correspond) to maleness, and feminine to femaleness. The model is the western conception of heterosexuality as an expression of *Nature* (or in other societies, of an order of the world which has been *fixed*).

In the social relations which correspond to this perspective, a strategy of *femininity* is imposed on women, and that of masculinity taught to men.

Gender translates sex: a homologic connection is established between them. 'The' sex difference is seen as the basis of personal identity, the social order, and the symbolic order.

In the social sciences, most psychology and psychoanalysis is still located in this mode of thought.

Definitions and Resolutions of Incongruencies

In this 'naturalist' perspective, homosexuality is judged to be an anomaly or a perversion — a judgment shared by many homosexuals themselves (either prior to, or among those who remain outside recent political movements). In addition, one of the defensive arguments some homosexuals put forward to assume their 'deviance' — that homosexuality *also* exists in nature, i.e. among animals — shares the same logic.

The contradiction homosexuality represents within this first perspective is resolved at the level of *definition* in a way that might seem paradoxical:

1   On the one hand, each term in the partners' relationship continues to be defined by biology. Hence the simple definition: a homosexual couple = 1 woman + 1 woman, or 1 man + 1 man. Hence also, paradoxically, the self-definition given by some homosexuals: 'I sleep with (love, etc.) a woman, but it could equally be a man'.[4]

   (To present the choice of partner as a question of an individual whose sex is *contingent* (it could be one or the other) seems to me very different from the claim of bisexuality, where the formula is rather 'I love both men and women': one and the other. The latter thinking belongs to mode II.)

2   On the other hand, although the homosexual relationship is defined in biological terms, the bipartition of the basic heterosexual model must be recovered at the psycho-social level. Hence the current idea — sometimes acted out — that in a homosexual couple there will be *a*

'masculine' woman or *a* 'feminine' man. Only one of the pair is really considered homosexual and deviant: the one who does not (or is presumed not to) have the 'role', or the 'psychology', or the sexual behaviour (for example, in the 'active/passive' oppositional hierarchy), in other words, the *gender of their sex.*

Here we can see that sexual behaviour is an integral part, not of gender, but *of sex* differentiation, a differentiation which the gender assigned to one of the two homosexuals translates only after a fashion (*sic*).

However, this difficulty can be cancelled out. For instance, among the Swahili Muslims of Mombasa (Kenya), sex so strongly determines gender that *both* partners in a homosexual couple are considered feminine if they are women (and behave in a feminine way), and masculine if they are men (according to Shepherd, 1987). (Young male homosexuals have at most slightly feminine mannerisms, but only in private and mainly in the company of women; moreover, they are the only men outside the family admitted near women in this very sex-segregated society.) But if sex and gender are totally appropriate here — if, for instance, gender is not differentiated in a homosexual couple — it is because bipartition is taken back to another level, based on another value: the hierarchy of rank. Male and female homosexuality is relatively well tolerated — provided couples are based on an opposition of richer/poorer or older/younger. According to Shepherd, rank surpasses gender. Nonetheless, it should be noted that the procreative heterosexual model is still fundamental, and more pregnant (literally) for women, since, unlike young men, no woman can become homosexual *until after* she has been married.

In this logic where *gender bipartition fits sex bipartition, and primacy is given to sexual identity* — a logic which could be called 'sexualist' — gender is normally adapted to sex.

It is sometimes, paradoxically, necessary to do the opposite: to adapt sex to gender, to bend biology (or at least anatomy) to psychic experience, or to the cultural norm. This happens with *transsexuals* in modern societies. They mostly reject with horror being considered homosexual, and want to reach a 'true' heterosexuality by modifying their sex. The stress most of them put on becoming 'normal' is generally coupled with a traditional view of gender roles (the division of tasks, deportment, etc.) and 'phallogocentrism' (Runte, 1988). Like society as a whole, transsexuals reject what they consider to be the 'caricature' of the opposite sex presented by some homosexuals, and confuse homosexuals and transvestites[5] (*travestis*: cross-dressers) with equal contempt — as Annette Runte stresses in her analysis of three autobiographies by female-to-male transsexuals:

Those women in suits, those sad caricatures of men, those ... those travestites ... they are ridiculous, grotesque ... It's aberrant! In-sane! ... I am not a lesbian ... I am a man! (Daniel Van Oosterwyck, quoted in Runte, 1987 and 1988).

(We shall see that 'caricature', the exaggeration of gender traits, is specific to travestism, typical of mode II.)

'The difficult border-line between lesbianism and female transsexualism', as Runte puts it (1987) — the boundary to which female-to-male transsexuals lay claim — is, however, somehow denied by scientists (doctors and psychiatrists), as has been shown by Ines Orobio de Castro (1987) in her article on the asymmetric way in which transsexualism is perceived theoretically and treated in practice depending on whether the subject wants to become a man or a woman. Once a diagnosis of homosexuality has been eliminated, a male-to-female transsexual is considered to have the gender identity of a genuine 'woman'. But a female-to-male transsexual is considered primarily a 'masculine' homosexual woman rather than a man. It seems women cannot be conceived to be 'really' masculine. According to the author, the reason for this asymmetric attitude is not so much that it is more acceptable to see someone adopt the (inferior) status of a woman than the (superior) status of a man, as that there is a 'difference in evaluating the relation between sexual disposition and one's biological sex: a man's sexual practice [i.e. active/passive] being crucial to his maleness and a woman's *body* to her femaleness' (p. 213, stress in original). As noted above, in this mode, sexual behaviour is part of the definition of sex. At least men-to-women transsexuals and men psychiatrists agree on this point.

My interpretation, not inconsistent with that of Orobio de Castro, is that in the sexualist perspective of western societies, the sex of women is, above all, a 'no-sex male'. In fact, a woman does not have any sex, she is a 'not-male'. A man without a penis is thus necessarily a woman, *even though* the artificial sex constructed is not a female sex. However, a woman without a vulva or vagina cannot be a man, *because* the artificial penis is not a male sex.

Whatever modern transsexuals may think, certain forms of 'travestism' and transvestism are ways of dressing a *sex* modification (and not just a gender modification, as in mode II) — as can be seen from the *hijras* of India and the Inuit (Eskimos).

Hijras are eunuch-transvestites consecrated to a female deity. They certainly seem to belong in the 'sexualist' mode, because this is the very reason they are castrated. Perceived as neither men nor women, and above all as non-males, the cultural *ideal* (the religious norm) is that they should not only be asexed but *asexual* (this being tied also to a general, albeit ambiguous, valuation of asceticism and sexual abstinence in the culture). The individual homosexual *practice* of many of them is consequently seen as contradictory to their ritual role. (Moreover, the term 'hijra' is not the one used to describe a homosexual or effeminate man.) Being non-male (because they are castrated, because they are consecrated to a Mother goddess) and 'travestised' as women, they call themselves 'the wife' of their regular partner, their 'husband', and insist that the men with whom they have relations as prostitutes are not homosexuals, according to information given by Nanda (1986). (Note that Nanda presents the 'travestism' of the hijras as a 'caricature'. However, from the various photos in the book, they could be taken for women.)

One phenomenon of the 'third sex' that also seems to fit 'sexualist' ideology (unlike other forms of transvestism, such as that of the *berdaches* discussed in mode II), is that of the Inuit/Eskimos (according to accounts by Dufour, 1977; and Saladin d'Anglure, 1985, 1986).

Among the Inuit, as in most societies, biological sex determines gender, but biological sex is also *problematic* in a way close to that felt by modern transsexuals. For the Inuit, however, the problematic aspect is not something experienced by isolated individuals: it is tied to the very definition of social being. One or more people re-live *in each individual*, and she or he receives their name from them and their place in the kinship system. Now, whereas *names do not have a gender* (they can be applied equally to either sex), *they have a sex*: that of the eponym (the living or more often dead person, held to have given their name to the child).

Therefore, a contradiction often arises between the sex of the eponym and that of the baby. There are two solutions (which involved 2 per cent and 20 per cent respectively of the population studied by Saladin d'Anglure, 1986). There is either a sort of *transsexualism*: some children are said to have changed sex at the moment of birth. These are the *sipiniq*, whom Rose Dufour noted are mainly 'a boy foetus which changed into a girl at birth' (op. cit., 1977, p. 65). (This brings her informants, who say 'the opposite, a girl transformed into a boy, does not exist', into a singular harmony with western psychiatrists.) Or there are various degrees and diverse forms of *transvestism*, the varying degrees being explained by the fact that one can have several eponyms of different sex. Here a child is dressed and brought up in the gender that conforms to the sex of the eponym, or chosen by the eponym.

I think we have here a *transgression of gender* (of the 'normal' gender of the child, i.e. that which would conform to its sex) *by sex* (of the eponym).

However, at puberty, the transvestite Inuit children, who have been to varying degrees classified as belonging to the opposite sex/gender, take (and learn) the activities and behaviour of their biological sex/gender, with a view to marriage and procreation. Hence there is a reversion, which appears as *a second transgression of gender* (here of the eponym and hence the child) *by sex* (of the adolescent).

Here, the primacy of the hetero-*sexual* system in the sexualist logic of mode I is particularly manifest. This distinguishes it from the more 'hetero-*social*' logic of mode II.

Mode II: 'Sexed' Identity — Principle Referent: Gender

A second way of conceptualising sex is linked to a problematic which I call *sexed identity* — the past participle marking a recognition of an action, an elaboration, by the social on the biological: the idea of a division — a cutting, a section (sexion) — of the category *of* sex into two social sex categories.

Here, people do not situate themselves only individually in relation to their biological sex; personal identity is also strongly linked to a form of *group consciousness*. Sex is no longer experienced, as in mode I, only as an individual anatomical destiny to be carried out through the appropriate gender identity. Rather, gender is experienced as a collective way of life. There is here an awareness that social behaviours are imposed on people *on the basis of* their biological sex (as one of the 'group of men' or 'group of women').

Gender symbolises sex (and sometimes the other way around). An *analogy* is established between them.

True, the two social groups are still thought of as figured on a *biological* model, but there is more concern with how the biological difference between the sexes is socially expressed, i.e. with the cultural *elaboration* of difference. This problematic involves a social and cultural complementarity of the sexes, whether this is conceived as harmonic (as 'equality in difference') or dissonant (as implying more or less unavoidable 'sex antagonism'); and with variations from one society to another, and by class, historical period, etc.

This is the main problematic found in the social sciences: in social psychology, sociology and anthropology, in work on relations 'between' the sexes, on 'sex roles' (up-dated as 'gender' roles — to which we shall return) and in more recent work on the *construction of gender*.

As far as women's consciousness and strategies of relations between the sexes are concerned, what is at issue is *femininitude* and virility, which means that femininity and masculinity are seen as having to be *accomplished*, perfected, or revealed. These strategies are just as much imposed as femininity/masculinity in mode I, but here refer to a *group culture*, whether this one is valued or challenged.

This way of thinking is expressed by various tendencies in the women's movement, including 'cultural feminism' and 'cultural lesbianism'. They oppose, in a way, the social order elaborated on the biological order, *but* their referent remains biological bipartition. According to cultural feminists, the problem is women not being recognised and valued *enough*, but 'feminine culture' itself appears to derive from some sort of essence. Typical statements include: 'Woman has still to become' or 'The future is female' or 'Our culture is beyond the social'. Cultural lesbianism, which values lesbian culture as women's self-identification apart from male definitions, produces such statements as: 'The lesbian is the most woman of women.'

It is thus possible, within sexed identity, to be politically aware that the two sex groups are inequitably socialised, but to combine this with a tendency to (what I call) *anatomise the political* (as opposed to the 'politicising of anatomy' found in mode III).

Some English-speaking 'socialist feminists' or 'marxist feminists' (and the French so-called '[social] class struggle' tendency) can be situated in this way of thinking. They believe the injustice of the relative statuses of men and women needs to be corrected, sex roles equalised, their content eventually improved, and 'mentalities' changed, but without injuring the solidarity between men and women they deem necessary for 'global' (i.e. anti-capitalist, nationalist, etc.) struggles. Their terminology is revealing: they speak of *women's* struggle or issues, rather than of struggle or conflict between the sexes. The same logic also produces attempts (albeit by different tendencies) either to unveil the 'real' *powers* of women, which have been overlaid by male (or western) science, or to seek out mother-goddesses and a supposed original matriarchy: to re-discover and re-value women or Woman.

The concern is somehow to improve both men's and women's cultures or to make them equally visible, but it is assumed there will still be two sexes and two genders.

Mode II also applies to most of the so-called traditional societies studied by anthropologists, where there are rituals allowing individuals to think of themselves as 'a woman within the group of women' or 'a man within the group of men' (apart from their membership of other groups, such as age-classes, etc., which is also ritualised). In addition to rituals, many societies do have women's associations (for example, in West Africa), which administer women's lives, including their relations with men as a group. And in almost all societies there are meetings or places from which women are excluded and which are strictly reserved for men. In western societies, such a bipartition into sex groups exists in rural communities, and in the urban milieu has led to such institutions as the English men's clubs and women's associations.[6]

Strict segregation of the sexes may also give rise to non-institutional forms of solidarity among women, such as a protective solidarity against men among the Mundurucu of the Brazilian Amazon. In this matrilocal but patrilineal society, no woman can leave the village alone without risk of rape (see, Murphy and Murphy, 1974). More generally, solidarity among women for economic and emotional survival exists in many societies (see, Caplan and Bujra, 1978).

In Africa there have been 'women's' riots based on a strong tradition of women's associations (the most famous being that of thousands of Igbo and Ibibio women in Nigeria in 1929, where about 50 women were killed and as many wounded by British bullets). But these revolts pose a problem of definition. Some writers have described them as feminist, in the sense that the women were defending their interests, notably their economic interests. (They thought they were going to be taxed for their economic activity by the colonial administration that had previously only taxed men.) But for our present purpose, what is interesting is that, in their demonstrations against the authorities, women used obscene *sexual symbolism*, the very symbolism they *traditionally*, and collectively, used to punish any man who insulted a woman (and thereby all women).[7] We thus have a politico-economic demand based on a sexed group consciousness whose mode of expression refers to an identity 'as women': according to the women, they did not want to become 'as men' and feared that their children would die. Caroline Ifeka-Moller (1975) says that their putting forward their identity as reproducers (and not producers) shows the stability of an ideology that defines women by their procreative function in a male-dominated society. Women had gained some economic wealth in the area since the 1880s, but this had not eroded the political and economic control of men — which was reinforced by the colonisers and the world commercial crisis.

It seems clear that this kind of revolt, which moreover was supported by the men, ratifies the hierarchical complementarity of the sexes/genders. In this case, *sex is being used as a symbol of gender status*.

In this second perspective, the fit *between the biological and the social* (i.e. the model of hetero-social difference) is thought of, not as 'natural' or founded in some order of the world (as it is in perspective I), but rather as *necessary* if society is to function. It could be said to be a pragmatic perspective, in contrast to the idealist perspective of mode I.

The bipartition of gender is thus symbolic of Culture rather than an expression of Nature (see Lévi-Strauss on the artificial character of the family and the sexual division of labour[8]), and it can, therefore, admit greater *flexibility* of behaviour.

This is why I place here homosexuality self-defined by 'way of life' and sexual preference as a possible base for identity — as well as the assertion of a bisexual choice.

Definitions and Resolutions of Incongruencies

Instead of the management of *convergence* between sex and gender which seems characteristic of mode I ('transgressions of gender by sex' such as modern transsexualism, hijras's emasculation in India, transformist transvestism among the Inuit — or the denial of homosexuality as a 'gender' problem among the Swahili), in mode II we find the management of *divergence* between sex and gender, notably through what could be called *transgressions of sex by gender*.

1   At the *individual level*, *travestites* in modern western societies adopt more or less regularly the gender they desire (that of the opposite sex) without modifying their sexual identity (without contesting their anatomical sex). Unlike the majority of transsexuals, men dressed as women are often homosexual, and their sexed identity is defined in relation to the gay homosexual *community* — despite the contempt, if not rejection, they may suffer there, and the inferior status accorded them. See, for instance, the American female impersonators studied by Esther Newton (1979).

The importance of homosexuality as a group culture founding sexed identity, and the predominance of *gender* over sex in this way of thinking, are also paradoxically illustrated by the case of a man dressed as a woman and calling himself a '*lesbian*' man' who tried to get himself accepted by a group of lesbians and refused to join male homosexuals in gay demonstrations.[9]

If (non-transformist) travestism seems typical of mode II, and transsexualism of mode I, there are, nonetheless, (rare) instances of individuals who say they are transsexuals, but who, instead of seeking a convergence between sex and gender, play on divergence and also on 'homosexuality' (in their sense) to confirm a sex/gender status. For instance, a woman-to-man transsexual, Marie-Aude Murail, makes no allusion to any sort of surgery in her/his fictionalised autobiography *Passage*, but instead gives a self-description as 'an effeminate man', 'a chopped male' (see Runte, 1987 and 1988). As Runte says, 'In her imagination, she equals a "eunuch" and thus adopts the widespread vision of "woman" as a "deficient" man' (Runte, 1987, p. 221). (On women as non-males, see the views of psychiatrists on female-to-male transsexuals above; and on non-males as women, see the hijras.)

But — and it is this which classifies Murail's case in mode II — to confirm sex identity as a 'man', s/he tried (unsuccessfully) to integrate into the world of male homosexuals (notably by having sexual relations with them). S/he describes her/himself as 'a guy with breasts who sleeps with homos'. Because they love men, s/he is therefore a man. A *same-sex* relationship was needed to affirm sex and gender. (Whereas in mode I thinking, one must have contrasting sexes: a woman-to-man wants a woman as partner, and therefore should have surgery.)

For Murail, knowing that s/he is still physically a woman, but thinking of her/himself as a male homosexual, there is no longer any need to fear the label of lesbian as a caricature of a man. The incongruence of sex and gender was managed so well by the principle of sameness that s/he went so far as to assert: 'I am a lesbian, I love faggots.' Runte is right to say that Murail naturalises neither sex nor gender, and speaks of this statement as a paradox (Runte, 1987). For me, the paradox can be explained as follows: if we speak in terms of sex, which is the most important in transsexualism, Murail is a (homosexual) man; if we speak in terms of gender, Murail agrees to be a (woman) homosexual.

Finally, there is a parallel case of a man-to-woman transsexual (a hermaphrodite who was declared male as a child and subsequently, not very effectively, treated with male hormones) whose breasts were removed and who defined him/herself as 'a lesbian woman'. He/she sought identity as a woman in a lesbian group (dressed as a man, but addressed in the feminine), feeling (I quote) *'even more a woman* when in love with a woman'. (Here, we again find the idea expressed that 'the lesbian is the most woman of women'.)

2   Transgressions of sex by gender are also expressed through various *institutional* solutions to the incongruence between sex and gender.

Take, for example, the *marriages between men* that used officially to exist in the Azande kingdoms of southern Sudan prior to colonisation (see, Evans-Pritchard, 1970). In this hierarchical society, the court bachelor warriors could take boys as wives, provided, as in all marriages, they gave bride-wealth to, and performed services for, the parents of the young man. The boy was 'the wife' of 'the husband' and carried out the agricultural, domestic and sexual tasks of a wife for him. This institution was explained by the Azande as due to a 'lack of women' (many men married very late because of polygyny). Moreover, if the warrior proved a good son-in-law, the parents of the young male-wife might later propose one of their daughters in his place. The young man could, in his turn, take a boy as a spouse while awaiting a wife.

However, sexual relations between women (which were also attributed to large scale polygyny with seclusion of women and the violent repression of adultery) were strongly disapproved of by men, because

> once a woman has started homosexual intercourse she is likely to continue it because she is then her own master and may have gratification when she pleases and not just when a man cares to give it to her (Evans-Pritchard, 1970, p. 1432).

According to the ethnographer's informants, it seems women disguised such relations under the form of loving friendships (with a small ritual similar to the rites of blood-brotherhood between men), but for this they had to have their husbands' permission. It seems also that they adopted the behaviour of husband and wife (for example, the 'husband' could hit the 'wife') and used penis-shaped fruits and vegetables (*but*, it is also noted, they interchanged roles in the sex act).

Here, both forms of homosexual relations can be attributed to marked segregation between the sexes (with the men's group opposed to the women's group), but male homosexuality, which was encouraged, simply reproduced the system of male domination over women, while female homosexuality was perceived as a threat to men's control of women.

Marriage between men among the Azande thus shows perfectly that inversion of sex is not necessarily a subversion of gender. It corresponds to the primacy of heterosocial gender (i.e. a hierarchical differentiation and bipartition of tasks and functions in the division of labour, sexual labour included).

This is confirmed when we turn to *marriages between women*, an institution that has been reported in about 30 African societies, including some of the present day. Unlike marriages between men, those between women do not seem to imply homosexual relations, at least not in a recognised and official way. Rather what is at issue, with women, is procreation. It is generally a case of society's adapting to assure the continuity of an agnatic lineage in the absence of a (dead or non-existent) male. A woman will pay the bridewealth to become what the literature calls the 'female husband' of another woman. The latter produces children with a man who is only their genitor and who has no rights over them. The rights belong either to the lineage of the father of the female husband (i.e. to her lineage), or to the lineage of her own husband.

Within the great diversity of existing arrangements,[10] O'Brien (1977) has nonetheless distinguished two types of female husbands: the first involves a woman substituting for a man (for a father or brother, in which case the woman is generally acknowledged as the 'father' of the child; or for a husband or son, these being more likely to be declared the 'father'); and the second in which women act on their own account, are more 'autonomous', and then often closer to being social men. The latter type is linked to it being possible for women to manipulate wealth and/or attain important social and political positions in certain societies.

To become a 'husband' can thus be a means for a woman to express or acquire a better status (which was certainly not the case for the Azande boy-wives — but they were 'women' only temporarily). In the only study which has really been interested in the views of the women wives of the female husbands, recently carried out among the Nandi of western Kenya (Oboler, 1980), some women informants thought it less tiresome to be married to a woman than to a man, and they emphasised the greater sexual and social liberty this situation allowed them. Marriages between women, nevertheless, function on the model of gender opposition, with the 'female husbands' having men's prerogatives over their wives.

The principal attributes of gender — the differentiation of tasks and social functions — are therefore reproduced even within marriages between people of the same sex. This proves by mirror image that marriage is not principally defined by the reproductive function of opposite sexes (which can always be arranged), but rather is always about assuring a whole set of rights of the 'man' sex/gender over the 'woman' sex/gender.

Certain details show that female husbands are not socially completely men, nor boy wives completely women, but even so one cannot talk of a 'third sex' here.

This expression is used more and more in relation to certain forms of institutionalised transvestism, such as that of the Inuit which we placed in mode I, and also the '*berdaches*' — a phenomenon which still existed in nineteenth-century North America among the Plains and Western Indians — which seems closer to perspective II.

Unlike Inuit transvestism, which is 'sexualist' and where there is 'reconversion' at puberty (probably because in this society *any* individual is liable to live out a divergence between their biological and social sex), the transvestism and adoption of tasks and behaviour of the opposite gender by the North American berdaches involved only *some* individuals, and became institutionalised only at adolescence or during adult life. Berdache boys who became social women, and girls who became social men, have been classed (according to the various native cultures and according to authors' interpretations) as 'third sex', 'gender mixing status', or 'gender crossing' phenomena.[11] Without getting into the debate, we can draw from it, for our present purpose, that berdaches mainly married, or had sexual relations with, people of the same sex but opposite gender — and it must be said, *because* of the opposite gender. As Whitehead says (1981, p. 93), berdaches 'conformed for the most part to a social, rather than anatomic, heterosexuality'.

Cases of bisexuality and even heterosexuality of the berdaches have been reported in some Indian societies (cf. Callender and Kochems, 1983, for examples); but what remains striking is that berdaches did not have sexual relations *with each other*. (Real homosexuality for them would consist in having relations with someone of the same sex-gender.) Hence the absence of same-with-same maintained the difference — principally of the genders, and occasionally of the sexes. Moreover, whether Indian tribes accepted homosexuality for 'ordinary' people or not, this was not confused with, and did not automatically entail, the status of berdache — nor, notably, the powers as shamans, which institutional crossing of gender boundaries often confers (as with the changes of sex/gender among the Inuit, see, Saladin d'Anglure, 1988).

As far as representations of *relations of biological and social sex* are concerned, some individual berdaches seem to have tried, at the level of *personal* identity, to recover a fit between sex and gender (between sexual identity and sexed identity) characteristic of mode I. Among the Mohave (Devereux, 1937) for instance, berdaches denied their 'real' physical sex. They resented anyone referring to it, called it by the anatomical terms for the other sex, and even imitated the physical sex of their gender. *Alyha* (men in the role of women) imitated menstruation and pregnancy, and *hwame* (women in the role of men) denied their menstruation and claimed the paternity of their spouse's children.

This could be interpreted as a sort of will to transsexuality analogous to that of mode I. But modern transsexuals are in opposition to their society as long as they have individual changes of gender; they only begin to be *institutionally accepted* (i.e. legally: through a change in their identity papers) when they can 'prove' their sex and gender are congruent, due to anatomical alteration. On the contrary, the interesting thing about the Mohave berdaches is that on the one hand, their change of gender is accepted by society, because it is institutionalised; but on the other hand, their pretence of a change of sex is joked about and sometimes ridiculed. (Allusions and questions with a sexual content are addressed to their partner or spouse — rather than to them themselves, since their individual decision is respected, but also as their capacity to exercise vengeful witchcraft is feared, or more simply their physically violent reaction, especially when it is a born male berdache.) It seems that because Mohave society ratifies the change of gender, it doesn't 'need' to fabricate stories about a change of sex, though it tolerates them.[12] The bipartition of gender is enough to guarantee the heterosexual norm.

Despite the variations from one culture to another, it does seem that berdachism should be classified in mode II (where gender predominates over sex, and hence where bisexuality can be integrated), because:

— it shows transgression of sex by gender, unlike mode I (where there is transgression of gender by sex in modern transsexualism and Inuit transvestism);
— and it maintains the difference between partners, whether this be social or physical, unlike mode III (which is unifying in its refusal of gender roles, see below).

This rapid overview of examples shows this second perspective can integrate all forms of 'sexual choice' (hetero-, bi-, or homosexual) without departing from the norm of 'hetero-gender' (grounded in the idea of a hierarchical bipartition of sex). Indeed, some forms of male homosexuality, whether ratified *or condemned* by the wider society, can reveal the hierarchy of gender just as well as collective rituals of travestism from one sex to the other (gender reversal). For instance, homosexuality can be the maximal expression of the *sexed group consciousness* of the dominant group (the one determining gender), as in the ideology of supervirility of such enclosed groups as contemporary American 'leather' bars (cf. the novel by John Rechy, 1979), and the SA Nazis.

The only 'pragmatic' problem for society as a whole is precisely how to circumscribe male homosexuality, i.e. how simultaneously to gain its advantages (virile fraternity against women) while avoiding its inconveniences (lasting homosexuality and a loss of control of women and the birthrate). As Himmler said in his speech to the SS generals on the 18th February, 1937:

> We are a State of men, and despite all the faults such a system presents, we absolutely must hold on to it. For it is the best institution... [But] we must prevent... the advantages of men's fellowship degenerating into defects... I know many comrades in the Party think they have to... present themselves as particularly virile and behave coarsely and brutally towards women... I consider there is too strong a masculinization of the Movement as a whole, and that this masculinization contains the germ of homosexuality. I want you to make sure that your soldiers dance with girls — as I have shown you — at the midsummer fête (cited in Boisson, 1987, pp. 217–31).[13]

Different societies have different ways of managing male homosociality and homosexuality. The 'best' solution is obviously a relationship which, while provisionally feminising (in gender) one of the partners (by inferior status, age, or knowledge), does not *effeminise* him (either in gender or sex), but leads to full heterosexual virility. This seems to have been the case in the relationship between master and pupil in classical Greece, where there was no contradiction — for men — between homosexuality and marriage.

Male homosexuality in mode II does not necessarily mean an incongruence between sex and gender (as in mode I), nor is it a subversion of gender and sex (as in mode III). It can even *serve* the virility/feminitude model — under some conditions and within certain limits — to the point of being *prescribed*: for example, the pederastic relationship intended to individually initiate a future young warrior was legally imposed in ancient Sparta. (Unlike pedagogic pederasty among noble Athenians, which, though valued, was not obligatory; see Gisella Bleibtreu-Ehrenberg, 1987, quoting the works of Patzer.)

This also applies to many well-known cases of collective male initiation rituals in Melanesia (cf. for example, Herdt, 1984). Here, homosexual practices, including ingestion of sperm, are peculiar in not only giving boys access to virility (in separating them from the world of women, which is common to all initiations), but in also completing their *physiological* masculinity. Not only the sexed component of masculine identity, but also the *sexual* component, has to be reinforced,[14] hence *elaborated*.

In these societies, which are violently male dominated, individuals' gender membership is, to everyday appearances, strictly determined by their sex membership. Although there are some occasional ceremonies of *travestism* (these are rituals of reversal that only confirm the radical difference between the sexes/genders), no case of institutional and long-term *transvestism* analogous to that of the berdaches has been reported from Melanesia (according to Herdt, 1984, p. 74, note 6). What we do find, however, are attempts *to annul the difference between the sexes* — or rather to annul women — at the symbolic level, which are very different from those possible with mode I thinking.

In the latter, according to the Inuit for instance, the 'first woman' was a man impregnated by another man who had split the penis of the former so that he could give birth (cf. Saladin d'Anglure, 1977). It was then only at the birth of humanity, or at the birth of an individual (a *sipiniq*, boy transformed into girl), that a woman could be a transformed man. (In the other examples we have seen, although non-man, a woman is nevertheless fixed as woman.)

In the Melanesian examples, the annulling of difference is situated not 'at the origin' but in the continuing reactualisation of a sort of male pansexualism. The male sex is conceived as the unique source and ultimate principle of *all* sexual identity: it absorbs, or eliminates, the characteristics of the female sex. Among the Gimi of New Guinea, for instance, the ideal state of total masculinity is attained through rituals (male rites with sacred flutes and also cannibal mortuary rites performed by women for men's survival; see Gillison, 1983) and, synonymous with masculine identity, 'the power to create is derived from the union of sexual opposites *in a male form*' (Gillison, 1980, p. 170). Moreover, men's appropriation of female biological powers also affects female substances themselves. Thus, for the Gimi, menstrual blood, which resulted from the first mythical copulation, is polluting and debilitating for women as well as men: it *is* 'killed' and transformed sperm (Gillison, 1986); while for the Baruya of New Guinea, 'women's milk is born of men's sperm' (their husbands' sperm, which they ingest, just as young initiated men ingest the sperm of their non-married and unrelated elders) (Godelier, 1982).

In these societies, hetero*sexuality* could be said to be viewed as eminently dangerous, male sex as problematic, and masculine gender (the superiority of men) as under threat. But there is still an idea of an (asymmetric) complementarity of the sexes among the Baruya, at least in the public version of the origins shared by men and women, where Sun and Moon represent male and female principles. (There is another, but esoteric version of this myth, reserved for the most initiated men, where Moon is the younger brother of Sun. 'As a result of the process, female powers end up masculine, clad in the livery of their masters'; Godelier, 1982, p. 115.) However, among the Gimi the principle of gender asymmetry is pushed to its logical extreme, because here only one single *sex* remains (incarnate in men and women):

> ... for the Gimi, kin relations derive from only one substance, sperm, and only one source, the penis. This single entity can be either alive and moving upwards, like seminal fluid, or 'killed' and falling downwards, like menstrual blood, but it is indivisible ... the sexual symbolism of the Gimi does not admit any complementarity (Gillison, 1986, p. 66).

Baruya men practice ritual initiatory homosexuality; but Gimi men practice secret ritual bleeding ceremonies symbolising menstruation (Gillison, 1989) — somehow casting out femininity. Could one put forth the hypothesis that the Gimi 'no longer need' to complete their masculinity and virility by means of men, because not only are women here the instrument of masculinity,[15] but also here *women are men*?

If only the male sex remains, but there are two perfectly hierarchised genders, there is a maximal divergence between sex and gender. *Transgression of sex by gender* is complete. Gender no longer translates sex (as in mode I), for here the unicity of sex translates the univocality of gender: the logical and utmost end of asymmetry.

Do the Gimi then come close to a third way of conceptualising the relationship between sex and gender, where gender *constructs sex*? Seemingly not, because their acceptance of the primacy of (masculine) gender leads to a negation of (female) sex, whereas in mode III, refusal of gender hierarchy leads to an attempt to elaborate a new definition of sex.

Mode III: 'Sex' Identity (or Sex-Class Identity) — Principle Referent: Heterogeneity of Sex and Gender

The principle referent of the 'sexed' identity of mode II, the concept of gender, does not question the bipartition of societies into two sex groups. It is simply concerned with developing more or less symbolic 'variations' on this theme.

In the third way of conceptualising the relationship between sex and gender, by contrast, gender bipartition is seen as separate from/foreign to the biological 'reality' of sex (the latter being anyway harder and harder to pin down) — but not separate from the efficiency of the ideological *definition* of sex, as we shall see. The idea that sex and gender are heterogeneous (different in kind) means that sex differences are no longer thought to be 'translated' (mode I) or 'expressed'/'symbolised' (mode II) through gender. Rather, *gender is thought to construct sex*. A *socio-logical*, and political, connection is held to exist between them, involving an anti-naturalist logic and a materialist analysis of the social relations of sex.

Instead of the static ideas of 'inequality' and 'hierarchy' between the sexes and of male 'dominance' present in modes I and II, mode III puts forward dynamic ideas of domination, oppression and exploitation of women by men. And it precisely *questions* who (or rather what) are these 'women' and 'men' who seemed so obvious in mode I and so fluctuating in mode II.

Given there are no human beings in a state of nature (which is an old idea, but one which gets curiously forgotten when people start to talk about the 'sexes', and above all about 'women'); and given that there is nearly always *an* asymmetry in gender (including in the 'transgressions' gender imposes upon sex — to which we shall return in the conclusion), we move from an idea of difference to one of social *differentiation* of the sexes, and thence to social construction of the difference. Attention turns, therefore, in the social sciences, from the cultural construction of gender to the cultural construction of sex, and particularly of sexuality.[16]

Two aspects of the relationship between the biological and the social can then be studied:

1 how societies *use the ideology of the biological definition* of sex to construct a 'hierarchy' of gender, which in turn is based on the oppression of one sex by the other;
2 how societies *manipulate the biological reality* of sex to serve this social differentiation.

Claude Lévi-Strauss (1956) speaks of the artificial establishment, through the division of labour, of a social and economic mutual dependence *between the sexes*, leading to marriage and the family. The family, he stresses, is a (cultural) 'remodeling' of the (natural) biological conditions of procreation (see note 8).

However as regards social interventions in this field, people have up to now scarcely considered anything except the limitations (abortion, infanticide, temporary prohibitions on sexual relations, etc.) that can be imposed on the fecundity of women, in the use of their 'natural' capacities. This is stressed by Paola Tabet in 'Natural Fertility, Forced Reproduction' (1985, included in this volume), and she, by contrast, draws upon the (usually violent) means employed to *maximise* the biological possibilities in very diverse societies (ranging from hunter-gatherers through agrarian to industrial societies). Her demonstration of the social *manipulation* of the reproductive conditions of the human species (which is rather infertile compared with other mammals) allows her to show how 'difference' between the sexes is socially constructed by means of constraints on, principally women's, sexuality. Given the dissociation of sexual desire (and orientation) from reproductive hormonal mechanisms in human females, these constraints operate in most societies via the regular imposition of coitus (principally in marriage) and through the *transformation of the psycho-physical constitution* of women, channelling their polymorphous desire towards heterosexuality — and specialising them for reproductive ends.

Anthropology has long demonstrated men's appropriation of women's reproductive capacities through the interplay of kinship, marriage and control of women. Tabet's research shows how these (potential) reproductive capacities are, moreover, made to yield a return in the form of (forced) actual reproducing.

Faced with (what Tabet calls) the 'domestication' of women's sexuality, it is difficult to consider sex a simple, 'natural', biological given. Rubin too considered that: 'At the most general level, the social organization of sex rests upon gender, obligatory heterosexuality, and the constraint of sexuality female' (Rubin, 1975, p. 179).

Many feminist writers (notably, Edholm, Harris and Young, 1977; and Mies, 1983) have criticised Marx and the marxist tradition for leaving the division of labour between the sexes with a natural status, and called for analyses of the *relations of production* between the sexes. Tabet, for her part, shows that we should consider reproduction as work. It is socially organised, like all work, and we can analyse the relations of *reproduction* between the sexes in the same way as marxists analyse work. In many cases it is exploited work, where the worker (here the woman) is expropriated from the control and management of the instrument of reproduction (her body), of the conditions and rhythms of the work (for example, her succession of pregnancies), and of the quantity and quality (the sex) of the product (the child).

In her analysis of sex relations in western society, Colette Guillaumin suggested using the term '*sexage*' to designate *the class relationship* whereby the bodies, work and time of women as a whole are appropriated for the personal and social benefit of men as a whole (Guillaumin, 1978a, b, abridged in this volume). This involves both private appropriation (legalised in marriage) and collective appropriation (real though 'less visible' in our society than in others), together with the contradictions that arise between the two. She also showed that these relations of material appropriation, where women (like men and women in certain types of slavery) are treated like things, present an 'ideological discursive face', a discourse of Nature, where the notion of 'thing' merges with that of Nature. (This aspect, she says, is specific to *modern* naturalism.) 'Having an existence as a material, manipulable thing, the appropriated group is *ideologically materialised*' (this volume p. 103). Dominants and dominated are then considered as two species, with one, women, derived directly, without mediation, from Nature (cf. also Mathieu, 1973 and 1977).

In mode III, gender (i.e. the imposition of heteromorphic social behaviours) is thus no longer conceived as the symbolic marker of a natural difference, but as the operator of one sex's power over the other. Since women as a class are ideologically (and materially) defined in society by their anatomical *sex*, so objectively are men as a class by theirs. Here we find again an adjustment between biological and social sex, but (unlike mode I) this is seen now as a social, historical fact due to the material exploitation of women and the oppressive ideology of gender, and (unlike mode II) as not strictly 'necessary' to the reproduction of societies.

This is the reason I call 'sex' identity the class consciousness corresponding to mode III in women's movements (among political lesbians and 1970s radical feminists), and, to a small extent, in the men's movements created in response to feminism. It is an identity of resistance to gender. In the women's movements this sex-class consciousness entails a 'politicisation of the anatomy' (as opposed to the 'anatomisation of the political' of mode II). 'Woman' is no longer conceived as femaleness translated into femininity (mode I); nor as femaleness elaborated (well or badly depending on the point of view) into femininitude[17] (mode II). Instead, women are seen as constructed femaleness: objectively appropriated and ideologically naturalised females.

Pushing the logic of Lévi-Strauss's analysis of the division of labour to the limits (and calling it, like Freud's theory of the construction of femininity, a 'feminist theory manquée'), Rubin saw in this division

> a taboo against the sameness of men and women, a taboo dividing the sexes into two mutually exclusive categories, a taboo which exacerbates the biological differences between the sexes and thereby *creates* gender. The division of labour can also be seen as a taboo against sexual arrangements other than those containing at least one man and one woman, thereby enjoining heterosexual marriage. (Rubin, 1975, p. 178)

After all, says Rubin, 'Lévi-Strauss comes dangerously close to saying that heterosexuality is an instituted process' (p. 180).

If we consider how homosexuals define themselves in this mode, homosexuality is no longer envisaged as an individual accident (mode I), nor as a fringe which is as much a foundation to identity as the norm and hence to be reclaimed with a right to exist and to have a group culture (mode II). Rather, it is seen as a political attitude (conscious or unconscious) of struggle against the heterosexual and heterosocial gender underlying the definition of women and their oppression. A typical slogan is the 1970 definition of the New York 'Radicalesbians': 'A lesbian is the rage of all women condensed to the point of explosion.' Simone de Beauvoir wrote that 'One is not born a woman, one becomes one.' The most radical trends of political lesbian movements challenged both the word 'woman' and the word 'homosexual', because both referred to the bi-categorisation of gender and sex which they rejected: 'Lesbian is the only concept I know of which is beyond the categories of sex

Table 4.1

	I. 'Sexual' Identity	II. 'Sexed' Identity	III. 'Sex' (Sex-Class) Identity
Personal identity in relation to the sexed body and to the place of the person in the social organisation of sex	• Individualistic consciousness Individual anatomic destiny	• Group consciousness idea of a section/sexion into two social categories based on sex. Men's/women's culture	• Class consciousness
Logic/ideology	• Naturalist perspective, 'sexualist', idealist Principal reference: Sex	• Pragmatic perspective (flexibility) Principal reference: Gender	• Materialist perspective, antinaturalist (and/or Utopian)
Basic opposition	• Fixed opposition male = masculine female = feminine (laisser-faire Nature)	• Flexible opposition femininitude/virility (to reveal or elaborate Nature)	• Dialectical opposition men as a class/women as a class
Relation established between sex and gender (biological sex/social sex)	• Homological connection between S. and G. = Gender translates Sex	• Analogical connection between S. and G. = Gender symbolizes Sex and vice versa	• Socio-logical and political connection between S. and G. = Gender constructs Sex
Problematic	• Problematic of the fit between S. and G.	• Problematic of social complementary of sexes and genders	
Main concepts	• Sex difference	• Difference. Differentiation of genders Dominance of men/power of women	• Differentiation of the sexes. Domination Oppression-exploitation of the class of the sex 'women' by the class of the sex 'men'
Resolution of problems	• Managing the convergence of S. and G., with priority to Sex, to the bi-partition of sex	• Managing the divergence between S. and G. with priority to Gender, to the bi-partition of gender	• Disassociation/heterogeneity of S. and G. with refusal of Gender
Model (Pattern)	• Heterosexuality as expression of Nature	• Hetero-sociality. Hierarchical bi-partition of gender	
Relation hetero/homosexuality	• Homosexuality, contradictory with heterosexuality	• Masculine homosexuality, not contradictory with heterosexuality Bi-sexuality is possible	

	Examples	*Examples*	*Examples*
Resolution of incongruencies between Sex and Gender	• Transgressions of Gender by Sex (managing the convergence of S. and G.) — modern transsexuals — Inuit-eskimo transvestism ('third sex'?) — castrated transvestites in India (Hijras)	• Transgressions of Sex by Gender (managing the divergence between S. and G.) — modern 'travestites' — North American Berdaches ('third sex'?) — marriages between men and marriages between women (Africa)	• Homosexuality as resistance to Gender
Conceptions of homosexuality	• Homosexuality conceived as antinatural, natural or random	• Homosexuality as group culture Homosexuality of men as the quintessence of gender hierarchy Institutionalised homosexual rituals	• Certain homosexual and feminist political trends as attempt to abolish Gender
Politics	• Politics = respect for anatomy (pro-life, anti-abortion movements, etc.) • Individual resistance	• Gender reversal rituals • Group resistance, defence of minority rights as such (gays, lesbians, and women) • Anatomisation of politics (cultural feminism and cultural lesbianism) • Women's struggle — Igbo women's war	• Politicisation of anatomy (radical feminism and political lesbianism) • Struggle of (the) sex(es) — feminist revolt in Africa (Kono) — anti-marriage movement in China
Human Sciences	• Psychoanalysis and psychology (most part of) Studies on biological determinism of Gender Sociobiology	• Psychosociology, sociology, ethnology (most part of) Studies on the cultural elaboration of differences/Social construction of gender	• Studies on the social construction of sex and sexuality/modification of sex

(woman and man), because the designated subject (lesbian) is *not* a woman, either economically, or politically, or ideologically', wrote Monique Wittig (1980a, pp. 83–4, reprinted 1992, p. 20) — defining lesbians as 'escapees from [the] class' of women, like runaway slaves.

The self-conception of homosexuality in mode III is thus a strategy of resistance. The rejection of sexual relations between men and women is seen, according to the political current, either as logical and 'preferable', or — viewing these relations as class collaboration — as logical and imperative. (The 'politicising of anatomy' that this implies is the opposite of naturalism.) In addition, subversion of gender is manifest here by same-sex couples very commonly rejecting the bipartition of 'masculine' and 'feminine' attitudes and roles characteristic of modes I and II.

Sex-class consciousness does not seem to be restricted to western countries. Certainly, it is more often sexed group consciousness that presides in the (usually individual) rebellion of women against their condition in most 'traditional' societies (and also in our own). And anthropologists have all too often carelessly neglected women's painful consciousness because 'it doesn't have any effects' — or, as we would say, because it overcomes neither alienated consciousness and fatalism, nor ... repression. (See, Mathieu, 1985a, for an analysis of the dominated consciousness of women and how anthropologists have interpreted it. Also Tabet, 1987, for examples of forms of prostitution, or rather of 'sex for compensation', as attempts by women to affirm themselves as subjects.)

Also, group consciousness certainly does not necessarily question the bipartition of gender and sex. Indeed, it may actually prevent class conscious-ness. In western countries it was probably the conjunction of women's group consciousness (especially in the English-speaking countries, see note 6) *plus* individualistic values (applicable in theory to all subjects, whatever their sex) that made class consciousness among women emerge, passing from the old notion of 'the battle of the sexes' to that of sex-class struggle and women's liberation.

Non-western examples of forms of sex-class consciousness can be found. For instance, in China a marriage resistance movement existed between 1865 and 1935 (when the Japanese invaded) in three districts of the Pearl River Delta around Canton (cf. Topley, 1975 and Sankar, 1986). This spontaneous and unorganised movement involved up to 100000 women at the beginning of the twentieth century. Most of those involved were illiterate or semi-literate women, working in silk production, who chose not to marry and who lived in small communities called 'seven sisters associations', in reference to the Pleiades constellation.

Another instance is the revolt of Kono peasant women in eastern Sierra Leone in 1971. David M. Rosen (1983) justifiably distinguishes this protest from the Igbo 'women's war' (presented in mode II), because it was directed not only against the authorities, as in the Igbo case, but also against the men themselves. Kono women expressed a consciousness of unequal economic competition between the sexes, in which men always kept the best part for themselves through all the fluctuations in the economy.

The Kono protest took place after the annual ceremony to initiate girls into the women's secret association (*Sande*). This was, as usual, preceded by parades and dances by women and their daughters exhibiting *wild* plants, the ritual symbol of the association's feminine qualities. The (abnormal) event of women recommencing parades *immediately after* the initiation shows clearly that the demonstration turned to account the sexed group consciousness of the women (very strong in this society as in many others in West Africa); but the symbolism used in the economic demand was (unlike the Igbo) not the one traditionally attached to women as a group (wild forest plants), but rather *cultivated* plants (the ones women cultivate). These were the very object of their demands as a class of producers and of their anger against the men. (Among the Igbo, the symbolism used was that customary to women and to relations between the sexes.)

There was, therefore, a double transgression of the group consciousness usually expressed in the ceremonies tied to the initiation ritual: the women both restarted the parades and dances, which were usually only preparatory; and they abandoned ritual symbolism. This transgressed both ritual rules and the 'normal' representation of the *relationship* between female sex and gender. The degree of subversion of the system can be measured by some women threatening to leave the Kono District because 'there was *no room left for women*'. (This is very different from the Igbo, where women expressed a fear of *no longer being* women.)

Conclusion: Gender or Social Sex?

So far we have treated 'transgressions of sex by gender' and 'transgressions of gender by sex' in a general way. But whatever the mode of conceptual articulation between sex and gender, we can nearly always uncover an asymmetric functioning of gender in terms of sex, even in apparent transgressions.

Some of these have already been noted in passing. We can now review them briefly, and add a few new ones from among the many possibilities:

- Although homosexuality may be relatively tolerated among the Swahili of Mombasa, and it poses no gender problem, there is a difference by sex. Girls must have been married (have had reproductive sexuality) before living in a homosexual couple, but boys need not (can have early non-reproductive sexuality).
- Although female couples in this society may be as equally characterised by a relationship of economic dependency as male couples, the 'dominant' lesbian would not be admitted to men's meetings, while the 'passive' homosexual man is allowed into the company of women (Shepherd, 1978).

- Although transvestism exists for both sexes among the Inuit, it is the first menstruations (i.e. reproduction) which brings about a return to the sex/gender of origin for a girl, and the killing of the first game (i.e. production) for a boy.
- Although transsexualism exists in Inuit thinking, it is primarily the sex of boys which is transformed at birth. The sex of girls is hence more of a 'given'.
- Although transsexuals may be deeply convinced they are of the other sex, psychiatrists ratify non-males as 'women' and treat non-females as . . . females (homosexual women).
- Although the Azande themselves consider homosexuality in both sexes to be a result of their organisation of marriage, it is institutionalised for men and repressed among women (who are all in heterosexual marriages).
- Although marriages between women can be imagined to sometimes include sexual relations, they are officially made for the purposes of reproduction, whereas marriages between men are officially made for the exercise of sexuality.
- Although gender-crossing exists for both sexes among North American Indian berdaches, the technical skills of the male-to-woman are often judged superior to those of ordinary women, while those of the female-to-man rarely judged superior to those of ordinary men.
- Although gender-crossing qualifies both sexes for shamanism and confers talents for healing in the case of the berdaches as among the Inuit, the extent and quality of performance seem superior in males-who-became-women than in females-who-became-men. (To which it can be added that, even where there is no gender-crossing, when men and women shamans coexist in the same society, the former generally have higher status and qualifications; see, for example, Godelier, 1982.)
- Although among the Mohave, the female-become-man may have as many recognised privileges as a husband as the male-become-woman has duties as a wife, the condition of the (born female) berdache is more difficult. She finds it much harder to get a wife than the (born male) berdache to get a husband. People mock her more readily than him (since they fear his violence, even though he is supposed to be a woman); and above all she 'is not safe from being raped' — which is what happened in the case analysed by Devereux, where a (born female) berdache vied with a man to retrieve her/his unfaithful wife, as any man would have done. (In the rapist's own words, he showed her/him 'what a real penis can do'. After the rape s/he became an alcoholic and turned to men; Devereux, 1937, p. 215.)
- Although in some occasional collective ceremonies of travestism (co-called rituals of inversion), each sex is supposed to caricature the opposite, the caricature of women by men is much stronger and more

deliberate than that of men by women. (See, for example, Bateson, 1936 for the Iatmul of New Guinea, and Counihan, 1985 for contemporary Sardinia. The same applies in Greece today, according to personal communications from M.-E. Handman and M. Xanthakou.)

- Although both sexes are obliged to enter marriage, sexuality *as such*, that is to say without a reproductive goal, is prohibited for women but not for men in many societies. There are, for instance, prohibitions on sexual relations after the menopause, or once one of a woman's children has produced a child. Pre- or extra-marital relations are more often, or more extensively, authorised for men than for women, and the latter are married younger. Finally, polyandry (which is rare anyway) is usually diachronic, while polygyny is synchronic.

- Although in theory the division of labour between the sexes could be considered, as Lévi-Strauss says, a prohibition on each sex doing the other's tasks, there are in fact no strictly feminine activities. Rather, as Paola Tabet demonstrates (1979), in every society women are forbidden to do certain tasks; this is a function of the degree of technical complexity of the tools, men reserving for themselves possibilities for *control* of the key means of production and defence (hence mastery of the symbolic and political organisation).

While recognising the usefulness of my first suggestion as to the need for a sociological definition of sex (Mathieu, 1971), Bernard Saladin d'Anglure reproached me for seeing only two sex categories in our society: '...in so doing, she "restrains" (*arraisonne*) sex categories in the same way as she reproaches men for restraining women (cf. N.-C. Mathieu, 1985)'[18] (Saladin d'Anglure, 1985, pp. 155-6). More generally, he reproached both the new anthropology of the sexes and branches of 'feminism' (but which ones?) for continuing to think dualistically. This results, he says, in their concealing — in their 'overlooking' — the 'third sex' (*tiers-sexe*), whose existence and structural importance he himself sets out to explore.

Saladin's concern is to find a reconciling third sex. Mine is to reveal the avatars (transformations) of sex oppression beneath what appear to be 'third' sexes. In applying myself to the ways in which the relationship between sex and gender is conceptualised, I hope to have shown:

1 some diverse ways in which societies (and not I) restrain the third sexes/genders so that they do not subvert, and may even strengthen the social effectiveness of bi-categorisation (as for instance do theories of androgyny); and

2 that this bi-categorisation generally functions to the detriment of the social sex 'women'.

By '*social sex*' I mean both the ideological definition given to sex, particularly that of women (which can be covered by the term 'gender'), *and* the material aspects of social organisation which utilise (and transform) anatomical and physiological bipartition.

I prefer this term to 'gender' because, up to now, *sex* (the definition given to it in both its *material* and its ideal aspects — *aspects idéels* to use Godelier's expression) has functioned effectively as a parameter in concrete social relations and symbolic elaborations, despite their variability.

This has tended to get masked by the current use of 'gender', particularly in Anglo-Saxon women's studies. 'Gender' is now used exclusively and for all purposes, and this has made the concept lose part of the heuristic value we had wanted to give it. People now talk, for instance, of 'gender relations of production'. But despite crossings of gender, and even of sex, these 'gender' relations of production consist of the exploitation of women. Without doubt there are 'third', 'man-woman' genders, but at the base and at the bottom of the gender hierarchy, there are certainly females, whose social sex is 'women'.

Notes

1   'Identité sexuelle/sexuée/de sexe?' was first published in Anne-Marie Daune-Richard, Marie-Claude Hurtig and Marie-France Pichevin (Eds) *Catégorisation de sexe et Constructions scientifiques*, Aix-en-Provence, Université de Provence, 1989, pp. 109–47, and reprinted in the collection of Nicole-Claude Mathieu's work: *L'Anatomie politique: catégorisations et idéologies du sexe*, Paris, Côté-femmes, 1991.

This is the first publication in English, translation by Diana Leonard.

2   The 10th World Congress of Sociology, Mexico, August 1982, Symposium 33 (Strategies for Women's Equality), first session ('Theoretical Considerations on the Creation, Maintenance and Conceptualization of Sex Inequalities'). The scheme I proposed there for western societies was subsequently developed. In parallel with this I was working on women's consciousness and the relationship between sex and gender in societies studied by anthropology. The present article is an attempt at a classification integrating western and non-western material. It was first published in Daune-Richard *et al.* (1989) and then in Mathieu (1991).

3   I use the term *transgression* here not only in its restricted and behavioural sense of 'contravening a norm or law', but also in its full, etymological meaning: *transgredi*, from *trans* 'beyond' and *gradi* 'to progress': to pass beyond a limit or frontier.

The notion of frontier inevitably implies a conceptual definition of the 'nature' of the two objects between which the phenomenon of transgression takes place, and of the criteria on which their difference is thought, hence their systemic relationship. In geology, for instance, one does not speak of the daily tides as 'transgression by the sea', but only of the lasting encroachment of the earth by the sea, where what was land is land *no longer*. And a 'transgressive stratification' is a seam (sedimentary or volcanic) which is superimposed on strata of a different nature (meaning here of 'different origin'). This is why I talk of phenomena of (respective) transgression between conceptualisations of sex and of gender.

Some (conceptual and behavioural) incongruencies between sex and gender membership may be transgressions of *one* norm *without* their resolution transgressing the systemic definition of the relationship between sex and gender. Moreover, some conceptual and behavioural transgressions of this definition may be 'normed' by the society as a whole, or by a group within it.

As we shall see, the transgression of a norm is not necessarily the subversion of a system of thought. But if the transgression of conceptual limits is not necessarily 'abnormal', it can in other contexts constitute a veritable heresy.

4   The delicious subtleties of the *Petit Robert* dictionary (1973 edition) contradict this aspect of the definition:

Heterosexual. *Adj.* Feeling a normal sexual longing for individuals of the opposite sex.	Homosexual. *Noun.* Person who feels sexual longing more or less exclusively for individuals of their own sex. *Adj.* Relative to homosexuality.
Antonym Homosexual.	*Ant.* Heterosexual.
Heterosexuality. Normal sexuality of the heterosexual.	Homosexuality. Tendency, conduct of homosexuals.
Ant. Homosexual [*sic*].	[*sic:* no antonym]

Thus, heterosexual (given here only as an adjective, although used substantively in the entry heterosexuality) is a *quality of normality* and not a specific *category* of persons like homosexual (given as noun). But if heterosexual can only qualify, it can only qualify *people* ('feeling . . .'), while the adjective homosexual ('relative to homosexuality') qualifies a *phenomenon*, a thing which happens (heterosexual is not given as relative to heterosexuality).

And this heterosexuality is a . . . sexuality, underlined again as normal, and hence *the* sexuality. In contrast, homosexuality is a 'tendency', a 'conduct', which, moreover, one tries to draw back to heterosexuality by designating this longing as 'more or less exclusive'. One doesn't expect the definition: 'Heterosexual. Person who feels sexual longing more or less exclusively for individuals of the opposite sex' — though it would be perfectly correct.

There is so thorough a refusal to consider heterosexuality as a conduct, as one 'phenomenon' among several possible, that at the moment of its nominal categorisation, it finds itself opposed to . . . 'homosexual'. As much as to say that homosexuals are a strange phenomenon, to the point, moreover, where homosexuality itself *has no* antonym: *it is not the opposite* of heterosexual 'normality'. It is *an incongruence*: something to be resolved.

(By a sad twist, we can see that AIDS — said at the start to be a homosexual problem, and due to (bad) 'conduct' — has recently led the media to substantivise the term 'heterosexual': *the* heterosexuals also, it is now recognised, transmit AIDS.)

5   In French, the author distinguishes *travestissement* and *transvestisme*. She says that the former, with its connotations of disguise, parody, exaggeration, caricature, falsification, mask and dupery, more suitably designates the *occasional* collective or individual behaviour where no one is duped, though they are fervently involved, as in a '*coup de théâtre*'. Transvestism, however, supposes a 'real' crossing of boundaries, at least in the consciousness of the actors involved, and some *permanence* of performance, without necessarily going to an extreme.

In English, the term 'transvestism' usually covers both meanings, but in this article the French distinction has been maintained where necessary through the neologisms 'travestism' and 'travestites'. The literal translation of *travestissement*, 'travesty', has not been used since it carries other connotations [translator's adapted note].

6   This tradition may well have played a part in the advance and strength of Anglo-Saxon feminist movements at the end of the nineteenth century, in contrast to the 'latin' countries, where women were simply excluded from men's meetings and did not form women's associations.

7   A practice found in other African societies, see Ardener, 1973.

8   In order to make clear the artificiality, the non-naturalness, of the sexual, so-called 'division' of labour, Claude Lévi-Strauss noted (1956) that we could equally well start from its negative characteristics and call it a *'prohibition of tasks'*, just as we speak of the prohibition of incest. (The latter could conversely be called 'the principle of division of marriageable rights between families'.)

> ... when it is stated that one sex must perform certain tasks, this also means that the other sex is forbidden to do them. In that light, the sexual division of labor is nothing else than a device to institute a reciprocal state of dependency between the sexes (Lévi-Strauss, 1956, pp. 275–6).

> Now, exactly in the same way that the principle of sexual division of labor establishes a mutual dependency between the sexes, compelling them thereby to perpetuate themselves and to found a family, the prohibition of incest establishes a mutual dependency between families, compelling them, in order to perpetuate themselves, to give rise to new families (ibid, p. 277).

> ... if social organization had a beginning, this could only have consisted in the incest prohibition since, as we have just shown, the incest prohibition is, in fact, a kind of remodeling of the biological conditions of mating and procreation... compelling them to become perpetuated only in an artificial framework of taboos and obligations. It is there, and only there, that we find a passage from nature to culture, from animal to human life... (ibid, p. 278).

9   Personal communication from C. Menteau.
10 Marriages between women certainly present a great variety of concrete forms and meanings, according to the kinship structure, economic and political organisation and relations between the sexes of the societies concerned, and a debate exists as to how to interpret it (cf. particularly Amadiume, 1987; Huber, 1968/69; Krige, 1974; Obbo, 1976; Oboler, 1980; and O'Brien, 1972 and 1977, where one will also find other references).

The list of the populations recorded in the literature by O'Brien (1977, p. 110) is as follows:

1   Yoruba, Ekiti, Bunu, Akoko, Yagba, Nupe, Ibo, Ijaw, Fon in West Africa;
2   Venda, Lovedu, Pedi, Hurutshe, Zulu, Sotho, Phalaborwa, Narene, Koni, Tawana in Southern Africa;
3   Kuria, Iregi, Kenye, Suba, Simbiti, Ngoreme, Gusii, Kipsigis, Nandi, Kikuyu, Luo in East Africa;
4   Nuer, Dinka, Shilluk in Sudan.

11 For recent debates on the question of the berdaches, see, particularly: Désy, 1978; Whitehead, 1981; Callender and Kochems, 1983, 1986; Blackwood, 1984; Blackwood (Ed.), 1986. Callender and Kochems (1983, p. 445) give a list of 113 North American cultures that recognised individuals as having berdache status, including 30 recognising it for women.

Evelyn Blackwood (1984, p. 29, note 7) gives a list of 33 societies in North America where the institutionalised existence of a 'cross-gender role' for women was attested: in the Subarctic region — Ingalik, Kaska; in the Northwest — Bella Coola, Haisla, Lillooet, Nootka, Okanagon, Queets, Quinault; in California/Oregon — Achomawi, Atsugewi, Klamath, Shasta, Wintu, Wiyot, Yokuts, Yuki; in the Southwest — Apache, Cocopa, Maricopa, Mohave, Navajo, Papago, Pima, Yuma; in the Great Basin — Ute, Southern Ute, Shoshoni, Southern Paiute, Northern Paiute; and on the Plains — Blackfoot, Crow, Kutenai.

12 Whitehead (1981, pp. 89 and 92–3) connects the presence of 'mystifications of anatomy' — of possible redefinitions of physiology allowing a 'cross-sex identity'

in addition to a 'cross-gender identity' — among the Indians of the South West to the fact that it is principally in these tribes that women berdaches are to be found.

    Blackwood (1984), however, prefers to consider it essentially a question of 'cross-gender role'. She attributes the existence of women berdaches in the tribes of the West, in comparison to their relative absence among the Plains Indians, to the former having had a more egalitarian mode of production.

13   Himmler encompassed with equal disapproval: the masculinisation *of women* in Party organisations ('such that in the long run sexual difference, polarity, will disappear. From there it is a short step to homosexuality'); the weight of the Christian Church (which he described as 'an erotic association of men which terrorises humanity', which undervalues 'the woman', and which, moreover, had 'burnt five or six thousand (German) women' — one daren't ask if Himmler had a sense of the irony of History); and the 'slavery' in which women keep men in America (so much so that homosexuality there 'has become a measure of absolute protection for men').

    He preached 'a chivalrous attitude' to women, not only to favour (obviously reproductive) contacts between the sexes, as in the time of 'the healthy and natural regulation' in villages, but because 'the movement, the conception of a national socialist world, can only exist if it is carried by women: because men seize things with their understanding, while a woman grasps with her heart'. (On the way in which the movement was 'carried' by women, with their exclusion from all leading or intellectual positions, see Rita Thalmann (1982), especially chapter II 'The Masculine Order (*Der Männerbund*)'.)

14   Smearing the body with sperm is also sometimes a way of reinforcing a person, man or woman, who is in a state of physical or ritual weakness.

15   In relation to the Gimi rites, one can only recall Lévi-Strauss's comparison of cannibalism and ritual travestism, even though it refers to other contexts:

Represented in the ritual, cannibalism translates the way in which men think of women, or rather in which men *think masculinity through women*. Conversely, ritual clowning translates the way in which men think of themselves as women, i.e. try to assimilate femininity into their own humanity.' (Lévi-Strauss, 1975, p. 353, stress added)

16   As witnessed by at least the *titles* of such works as Ortner and Whitehead, 1981, Tabet, 1985 or Caplan, 1987, even if the authors do not share the same theoretical orientation.

17   Femaleness, femininity, 'femininitude' (*féminitude*)...these and other terms have been used and proposed, with sometimes different meanings and applications, by other authors (cf. notably, 'femineity' in Ardener, 1973 and Hastrup, 1978; and '*fémelléité*' in Descarries-Bélanger and Roy, 1988).

18   Besides being amusing (since neither I nor others were unaware of the existence in western societies of theories about the homosexual 'third sex' or about androgyny — any more than we ignored the work of Roland Barthes on 'Sarrasine' by Balzac, which anyway I cited), the charge is historically misplaced. *At the time* when I wrote (1971 and not 1977 as stated in Saladin's article), it was a question of letting women enter *into the analysis*, next to men, as a social and not a biological category; of giving women access to the sociological definition which was accorded only to the category of men. (And, if the idea is 'passée' to the point of appearing banal, the epistemological question of women being rendered invisible in everyday and 'scientific' discourse is far from resolved, see Michard-Marchal and Ribéry, 1982 and Mathieu, 1985b.) In other words, it was, paradoxically, a question of first introducing the bi-categorisation from a methodological point of view: of making the reciprocal determination of the two social categories understood. This was (and often still is) hidden in analyses, despite its evidence in the facts.

Chapter 5

The Practice of Power and Belief in Nature

Colette Guillaumin[1]

Apologue

This morning, in the Avenue General Leclerc in Paris, I saw what popular opinion calls a madman, behaving in a way that psychiatrists call psychotic. He was making sweeping gestures with his arms and leaping from one side of the pavement to the other. He talked and talked and scared the passers-by with great gyrations, apparently enjoying this immensely, since he burst out laughing each time he managed to induce a fearful response.

So he frightened the passers-by. Well, yes, if you like; though in fact this man in his 60s only grabbed at women with his enveloping gestures — at old and young women, but not at men. He even tried to grab hold of the genitals of one young woman — and laughed even more at this.

Now people only take publicly what belongs to them. Even the most unrestrained kleptomaniacs are covert when trying to take something that does not belong to them. However, as far as women are concerned, there is no need to be covert. They are common property, and, if we hear truth through wine and from the mouths of babes and madmen, this truth is told us plainly often enough.

The very publicness of the seizing; the very fact that in many people's view — and anyway in that of men in general — it assumes such a 'natural' character and seems almost a 'matter of course', is one of the daily, violent expressions of the materiality of the appropriation of the class of women by the class of men. Theft, swindling, and embezzlement are done covertly; and to appropriate male people requires a war; but not so the appropriation of female people, that is, women, for they are already property. And when people speak of the exchange of women, wherever it may occur, this truth is made clear. For what can be 'exchanged' is *already* possessed. Women are the property of whoever exchanges them, before the exchange takes place. When a male baby is born, he is a future subject, who will have to sell his own labour power, but not his own materiality, not his own individuality. What is more, as proprietor of himself, he will also be able to acquire the material individuality of a female; and, on top of that, he will dispose of the labour power of that same female, using it in whatever way suits him, including demonstrating that he is not using it. (. . .)

Habits of speech tell the same story. The appropriation of women is explicit in the very banal semantic habit of referring to female social actors by their sex as a matter of priority (as 'women'). This irritates us very much and obviously has many meanings, but its real import in fact passes unnoticed. In any context, whether it be professional, political, etc., all appellations in the domain are omitted or refused to actors of the female sex, while the same appellations designate, of course, only the other (male) actors. The following phrases, for example, were collected within one 48-hour period:

> A *pupil* has been punished with compulsory detention for a month; a *girl* has been reprimanded
> (report of disciplinary action at the École Polytechnique);
> A company director, a lathe-operator, a croupier and a woman . . .
> (about a group meeting to give their opinion on some matter);
> They killed tens of thousands of workers, students and women
> (Castro on the subject of the Batista regime).

These phrases, whose imprecision (as we believe) about job, status, and situation as soon as it is a question of women, so exasperates us, cannot be faulted for omitting information. On the contrary, they are factually correct. They are photographs of social relationships. What is said, and said only about female human beings, is their effective position in class relations: that of being primarily and fundamentally women. This is their social existence; the rest is additional and — we are made to understand — does not count. Corresponding to an employer, there is a 'woman'; corresponding to a polytechnic student, there is a 'woman'; corresponding to a worker, there is a 'woman'. 'Women' we are, and this is not one descriptive term among others for us: it is our social definition. (. . .)

From popular wisdom to the vulgarities of the local pub, from sophisticated anthropological theory to legal systems, we are ceaselessly told that we are appropriated. At best we rage against it, but mostly we are apathetic. However, we would doubtless be politically at fault if we rejected without examination such a set purpose, since, coming from the antagonistic class, it ought on the contrary to arouse our keenest interest and most careful analysis. After all, in order to know, it is enough to listen, without shrinking, to the daily banal discourse that reveals *the specific nature of the oppression of women*: appropriation. (. . .)

Introduction

Two facts dominate the account which follows — a material fact and an ideological fact. The first is a *power relation* (yes, a 'power relation' and not just 'power'): the power play that is the appropriation of the class of women by the class of men. The other is an *ideological effect*: the idea of 'nature'; of a 'nature' that is supposed to account for what women are supposed to be.

The ideological effect is not at all an autonomous empirical category. It is the mental form taken by certain determined social relationships. The fact and the ideological effect are two sides of the same phenomenon. The first is a social relationship in which actors are reduced to the state of appropriated material units (and not simply to bearers of labour power). The other, the ideological-discursive side, is the mental construction that turns these same actors into elements of nature — into 'things' even in the realm of thought.

In Part I of this article, 'The Appropriation of Women', we shall see the concrete appropriation: the reduction of women to the state of material objects. In Part II, 'The Naturalist Discourse', we shall see the ideological form that this social relationship takes: that is, the predication that women are 'more natural' than men.

Everyone — or almost everyone — acknowledges that women are exploited: that when they sell their labour power in the labour market its price is much lower that that of men, since on average the wages of women are only two-thirds of those earned by men. Everyone — or almost everyone — agrees that the housework performed by all women, whether or not they are otherwise employed, is unpaid work. This exploitation of women is the basis of all thinking about the relations between the sex classes, whatever its theoretical orientation. So when the exploitation of women is analysed and described, the idea of 'labour power' occupies a central position. But, strangely enough, it is used in the perspective of a social relationship from which women as a class are precisely absent. In this perspective, labour power is presented as 'the only thing the worker has to sell, his ability to work'.[2] But while this is correct for the man worker today, it is not true of women workers, nor of any other women today. This meaning of labour power, as the ultimate thing that can be used to earn a living, is inadequate for the whole class of women. (. . .)

A whole class, which makes up about half the population, (. . .) does not suffer just the monopoly of its labour power, but also a relationship of direct, physical appropriation. To be sure, this type of relationship is not unique to the relationship between the sexes. It was also characteristic of plantation slavery, which disappeared from the industrial world scarcely a century ago (United States in 1865, Brazil in 1890) — although this does not mean that slavery disappeared completely. Another form of physical appropriation was present in serfdom, which characterised the feudal landed estates and disappeared only at the end of the eighteenth century in France (the last serfs were emancipated around 1770, and serfdom was abolished in 1789), but which persisted for more than a century longer in certain European countries. (. . .)

The direct physical appropriation in relations based on sex, which I shall try to describe in this article, includes the pre-emption of labour power; and it is through the form this pre-emption takes that we can detect it is a material appropriation of the body. However, it has a certain number of distinct characteristics, of which the essential one (as in slavery) is the fact that *in this relationship there is no form of measurement of the pre-emption of labour power.* (. . .)

If relations of appropriation do indeed generally imply a monopoly of labour power, they are logically and also historically prior to it. The possibility of selling ONLY one's labour power, without being appropriated oneself, is the result of a long and difficult process. Physical appropriation appeared in most known forms of slavery: for example, in that of Rome (where, moreover, the totality of slaves of a master was called his *familia*), and in that of the eighteenth and nineteenth centuries in North America and the West Indies. On the other hand, certain forms of slavery where the duration was limited (to a certain number of years of service, as in Hebrew society; in the Athenian city-state, with certain reservations; and in seventeenth-century America), and certain forms of serfdom which fixed limits on the usage of the serf (for example, the number of days per week), are transitional forms between physical appropriation and the monopoly of labour power. What concerns us here is *physical appropriation itself: the relation in which it is the material unit which produces labour power which is appropriated, and not just labour power.* Called *slavery* and *serfdom* (in the feudal economy), this type of relation can be designated by the term *sexage*[3] in the modern domestic economy, where it concerns the relations between sex classes.

PART I: The Appropriation of Women

The Concrete Expression of Appropriation

(. . .) The particular expressions of this relation of appropriation (of the whole group of women, and of the individual material body of each woman) are:

1 the appropriation of time;
2 the appropriation of products of the body;
3 the sexual obligation; and
4 the physical charge of disabled members of the group (disabled by age — babies, children, old people — or illness and infirmity), as well as of *healthy members of the male sex group.*

Appropriation of Time

Time is *explicitly* appropriated in the marriage 'contract', insofar as there is no measurement of it and no limit placed on its use. Time is expressed neither in an hourly form, as is the case in standard work contracts, whether for wages or not (contracts for hire or in exchange for maintenance always specify work and free times — holidays, days off, etc.); nor in the form of a money measure (no monetary evaluation of the wife's work is envisaged).

What is more, this appropriation of time *does not just involve the wife, but also members of the group of women in general*, since, in fact, mothers, sisters, grandmothers, daughters, aunts, etc., who have made no individual contract with the husband, the 'head of the family', also contribute to the maintenance and upkeep of his property (living or inanimate). Doing the laundry, caring for children, and the preparation of meals, etc., are sometimes taken charge of by one of the mothers or sisters of the spouses, or by their daughter or daughters, etc. This is not by virtue of a direct contract of appropriation, as in the case of the wife (whose naked appropriation is demonstrated — first and foremost — in the legal obligation of sexual service), but as a function of the general appropriation of the class of women. This implies that *their time* (their work) may be disposed of without contractual compensation, and may be generally and indiscriminately disposed of. *It is as if the wife is actually owned by the husband, and each man has use of the class of women, and particularly each man who has acquired the private use of one of them.* (. . .)

Appropriation of Products of the Body

'It was not the hair of *our* Burgundian women which we sold, but their milk.' These words, straight from the mouth of an old male writer (on television on 16 December, 1977), say clearly enough that, contrary to what many of us believe, neither our hair nor our milk belong to us, for if they are sold, it is by their lawful owners. (. . .)

But still present proof of the appropriation of products of the body is that in marriage *the number of children is not the subject of contract*: it is neither fixed nor subjected to the wife's approval. (. . .) The wife must and will bear all the children her husband wants to impose on her. And if the husband exceeds what is convenient for him, he puts all the responsibility on the wife. She must give him everything he wants, but only what he wants. The status of abortion, which was clandestine for such a long time, existing without existing, confirmed this relationship. Abortion was *the recourse of women whose husbands did not want the child*, as much as the recourse of women who themselves did not want the child.[4]

We know that children belong to the father, and, in France, until a short time ago, for a mother to be able to take her child out of the country, she had to get the father's authorisation. The converse was not the case. Today, in rich countries, the ownership of children is not economically advantageous.[5] Children, however, remain a very important instrument of blackmail in case of marital disagreement. Men demand ownership of them, but not the material burden — which they hasten to confer to another woman (mother, servant, wife, or companion), according to the rule which requires that the possessions of the dominant group be materially taken care of by one (or some) of the possessions of the same. The ownership of children, a 'production' of women, is, in the last resort, juridically in the hands of men. Children continue to belong to the father even when, in the case of separation, their mother has material charge of them.[6] (. . .)

The individual material body of a woman belongs, in what it produces (children), as in its divisible parts (hair, milk), to someone other than herself — as was the case in plantation slavery.[7]

Sexual Obligation

(. . .) When you are a woman and after a certain time you meet an ex-lover, his main preoccupation seems to be to sleep with you again. Just like that, it seems. For, after all, physical passion does not seem to have much to do with this attempt. Obviously not. It is a clear way of showing that the essential thing in the relationship between a man and a woman is *physical usage*. Physical usage expressed here in its most reduced, most succinct form — sexual usage. It is the only physical usage possible when the encounter happens by chance and there are no stable social ties. It is not sexuality that is in question here, not 'sex'; it is simply usage. It is not 'desire'; it is simply control, as in rape. If the relationship is re-established, even in an ephemeral way, it must be once again through the usage of the woman's body.

There are two main forms that this *physical sexual usage* takes: that in which there is a non-monetary contract — marriage; and that which is directly paid for in cash — prostitution. Superficially they are opposed to each other, but it actually seems, on the contrary, that they confirm each other in their expression of the appropriation of the class of women. The apparent opposition is based on the intervention or non-intervention of payment: that is, of a *measure* of this physical usage. Prostitution consists in the fact, on the one hand, that the practice of sex is remunerated by payment of a specified sum; and, on the other, that this remuneration corresponds to a determined length of time (which can vary from a few minutes to a few days) and to codified acts. The main characteristic of prostitution is that the physical usage purchased is sexual, and sexual only (even if it sometimes takes forms that seem remote from what is strictly sexual relations, and shows common characteristics with prestige-giving behaviour, maternal conduct, etc.). *Sale* limits the physical usage to sexual usage.

Marriage, on the contrary, extends physical usage to all possible forms of this usage, with the sexual relationship in the central position, but encompassing other forms. (. . .)

The Physical Charge of Members of the Group

The relations of sex classes and the 'ordinary' relations of classes bring into the state of a thing, of a tool whose instrumentality is applied (or applicable) to other things (agriculture, machinery, animals); sexage, like house-slavery, concerns reduction to the state of a tool whose instrumentality is applied in addition and fundamentally to other human beings. In addition and fundamentally, because women, like all dominated people, of course, carry out some tasks which do not imply a direct and personalised relationship with other human beings; but *always* they (and only they nowadays in Western countries) are dedicated to assuring, outside of the wage system, the bodily, material, and eventually the emotional, maintenance of the totality of social actors. It is a matter of services which are (1) required (unpaid, as we know), *and* (2) given in the framework of a lasting personalised relationship. (. . .)

To be sure, these tasks of physical maintenance *also* exist in the monetary work sphere and are *sometimes* carried out professionally for a wage (but it is not by chance that, even under those conditions, here and now, it is almost exclusively women who do these jobs). But if we compare the number of paid and unpaid hours dedicated to these tasks, the overwhelming majority of them are carried out outside of the sphere of paid work.

Socially, these tasks are carried out in the context of a direct physical appropriation. For example, religious institutions absorb women whom they assign 'free of charge' to this work in hospices, orphanages, and various asylums and homes. As in the context of marriage (besides, they are married to God), it is in exchange for their upkeep and not in exchange for a wage that the women called *sisters* or *nuns* do this work. And certainly it is not a question of religious 'charity', since when it is men who are grouped together in these sacred institutions, they undertake none of the tasks of maintenance of humans at all. It is a matter of a fraction of *the class of women* who, having been brought together, carry out socially, without pay, the tasks of the physical care of the sick, the young, and the unattached elderly. (. . .)

Effects of appropriation on individuality
To speak of the physical maintenance of bodies is to say little. There are misleading appearances here that we think we know about. In fact, what does *physical material maintenance* mean? First of all, it means a constant presence. No clocking-in here, but a life whose entire time is absorbed, devoured, by face-to-face interaction with babies, children, a husband, and also elderly or sick people.[8] Face-to-face, because their gestures, their actions, hold the mother–wife–daughter–daughter-in-law directly within their domain. Each gesture of these individuals is full of meaning for her and modifies her own life at every moment: a need for something, a fall, a request, some acrobatics, a departure, a pain obliges her to change what she is doing, to intervene, to worry about what has to be done immediately, about what will have to be done in a few minutes, at such and such a time, this evening, before such and such a time, before leaving, before X arrives, etc. Each second of her time — and without hope of seeing this absorption end at a fixed hour, even at night — she is *absorbed into other individualities*,

diverted from the activity which is going on, to other activities.[9] (. . .)

Furthermore, the material attachment to physical individualities is also a *mental* reality. There is no abstraction: every concrete gesture has an aspect that is full of meaning, a 'psychological' reality. Although they relentlessly try to coerce us into not thinking, this attachment cannot be lived mechanically and indifferently. Individuality rightly is a precarious conquest, often denied to a whole class, whose individuality is forced to become diluted, materially and actually, into other individualities. A central constraint in the relations of sex classes, this deprivation of individuality is the sequel or the hidden face of the material appropriation of individuality. For it is not obvious that human beings so easily distinguish themselves one from another, and constant proximity/physical burden is a powerful hindrance to independence and autonomy. (. . .)

Surely it is no accident that the members of the dominant sex class are 'disgusted' by their children's shit and, as a result, 'cannot' change them. No one would even dream of thinking that a man could change the clothes of old or sick people, could wash them or do their laundry. But women do it, and 'must' do it. They are the social tool assigned to those tasks. And it is not only hard and obligatory work (there is other hard work that does not depend on the social-sexual division of labour); it is also work which, in the social relations in which it is done, destroys individuality and autonomy. Performed outside the wage system, in the context of the appropriation of her own person, attaching the woman to determined physical individuals, 'familiars' (in the literal sense of the word), with whom the ties are strong (whatever the love–hate nature of them), it dislocates the fragile emergence of the subject. (. . .)

Material Appropriation of Bodily Individuality

Appropriation of Physical Individuality and Labour Power in Sexage

Like any dominated group, we embody labour power. However, the fact of embodying labour power is not in itself material appropriation. The coming into being of a proletariat, along with industrial development, broke the syncretic link between appropriation and labour power that used to exist in slave or feudal societies (let us say, in an agricultural landed society).

Today, this non-equivalence, this distinction, is expressed in the *selling* of labour power. This introduces a *measuring* of labour power which is more clear-cut than had been the time limitation put on the utilization of labour power under serfdom. The selling of labour power is a particular form of its usage: it is an evaluation, both monetary and temporal, even if there is a tendency to confuse this evaluation with its maximum usage. The person who sells is selling so many hours, and he or she will be paid for these hours in either a monetary or some other form. In any case there is always evaluation. However the labour power is employed, whatever the tasks done, the sale involves two elements of measure — time and wages. Even if the price is fixed by the buyer (as is the case in the industrial system and in all the relations of domination where monetary exchange takes place), and even if the sale of labour is revealed to be difficult (as in the case of times of unemployment), the seller, *as a material individual*, disposes of *his or her own* labour power (it is not a question here of concluding whether it gets him or her very far or not), and thus distinguishes his or her individuality from the usage of that individuality.

Unlike other dominated groups with labour power, we women are, in the relations between the sexes, non-sellers of our labour power; and our appropriation evinces itself precisely in this fact. We are distinct from those oppressed people who can bargain *beginning with* the disposition of their labour power — that is, to exchange it or sell it.

There is a great suggestive power, for practical and tactical reasons, in evaluating in terms of money the amount of work performed within marriage; and this has been done. But we can ask ourselves if this does not contribute to hiding the fact that this work has, as one of its specific characteristics, the fact of not being paid. It would, moreover, be more correct to say that its intrinsic character is the fact of being *non-paid*.[10]

If it is non-paid, it is because it is not 'payable'. If it cannot be measured or converted into money (measurement and money being doublets), this means that it is acquired in another way. And this other way implies that it is acquired in aggregate, once and for all, and that it no longer has to be evaluated in terms of money or timetables or by the job — evaluations which generally accompany the ceding of labour power. And it is precisely these evaluations that do not take place in this case.

When evaluations take place in a relationship, they establish a contractual-style relationship: so much X in exchange for so much Y; so many hours for so much money; etc. Not all social relationships are translatable into contractual terms, and a contract is the expression of a specific relationship. Its presence or absence (which is highly relevant to the collective relationship of sexage) is the mark of a particular relationship. (...) For example, the paid labour force is *within* the contractual universe, slavery is *outside* of it. The generalised sexed relationship is not translated, and *is not translatable*, into contractual terms (which is ideologically interpreted as being a guaranteed relationship outside the contractual universe and founded in Nature). This is habitually obscured by the fact that the *individualised* form of this relationship is itself considered to be a contract: marriage.

This individualised form, through its banal appearance of being contractual, contributes to hiding the real relationship which exists between sex classes as much as it reveals it. The reason for this is that the contractual universe confirms AND assumes, *before all other things*, the quality of proprietorship in the parties to the contract. Minors, the insane, those under guardianship, i.e. those who are still the property of their father and who do not have possession of their subjectivity (which means in fact that they cannot have property of their own, as it is expressed in the Civil Code), do not have the power to make a contract. In order to make a contract, the ownership of material goods (land and funds put into play in the contract) and possibly the ownership of living things (animals, slaves, women, children) seems superficially to be the determining factor. But what in fact is the determining factor is *self-proprietorship*, which, in default of any 'property of one's own', is expressed in the possibility of selling one's own labour power. This is the minimum condition for any contract. But the fact for the individual of being the material property of someone else, excludes that person from the universe of contracts. It is not possible for anyone to be at one and the same time self-owned and the material property of someone else. The nature of such social relationships as sexage or slavery is, in a certain way, invisible, because those who are involved in them as the dominated ones, do not have a degree of reality very different from that of an animal or an object — however precious these animals or objects may be.

The sale or exchange of goods, and *especially of that which emanates from one's own body, which is what labour power is*, constitutes the proof of self-proprietorship: I can only sell what belongs to me. (. . .)

It was not due to some incomprehensible aberration that during the nineteenth century the earnings of women and children went to the husband/father and belonged to him. Only since 1907 (in France) have women had the right to draw their own wages (but still without having the personal right to work; the husband had the right to decide this, and he thus kept the ownership of his wife's labour power until 1965). This legal fact is made even more interesting by the fact that, in practice, women themselves did draw their own wages, since their husbands were for most of the time notable by their absence in the class where women worked for wages (there was little marital stability). But this wage that they drew did not belong to them legally; it belonged to the owner of the woman-work-tool.[11]

Sexage

The reduction to the state of a thing, more or less admitted or known about in relations of *slavery* or *serfdom*, exists today in industrialised urban centres, under our very eyes, dissimulated/exposed in marriage — an institutionalised social relationship if ever there was one. But the idea that a class is *used* (literally: manipulated like a tool) — that is, treated like a cow or a reaper — is, in the very progressive minds of our contemporaries, supposed to be ascribable to past ages or to despotisms as oriental as they are primitive; or at best to be the expression of a provocative cynicism. We do not see what we have before our eyes — even when we belong to the enslaved class.

For all that, marriage is only the institutional (contractual) surface of a generalised relationship: the appropriation of one sex class by the other. It is a relationship which concerns the entirety of the two classes and not a part of each of them, as a consideration of the marriage contract alone might lead one to believe. The marriage contract is only the individualised expression — in that it establishes an everyday and specific relationship between *two* particular individuals[12] — of a general class relationship, where the whole of one class is at the disposition of the other. And if, in fact, the individualisation of this relationship almost always happens (around 90 per cent of women and men are married at one time or another in their lives), marriage is nonetheless only the restrictive expression of a relationship — it is not in itself this relationship. It legalises and confirms a relationship that exists *before* it and *outside* of it: the material appropriation of the class of women by the class of men — sexage.

However, marriage also contradicts this relationship. If it expresses and limits sexage by restricting the collective use of a woman and by giving this usage to a single individual, it also deprives other individuals of his class of the usage of this particular woman. She would, without this act, remain common property. This is only ideally speaking, however, because in practice the *enjoyment* of the common right belongs either to God (nuns), to fathers (daughters, in which state one remains until one becomes a wife, according to the Civil Code), or to pimps (for women who are officially 'common property').

This contradiction at the centre of social appropriation itself operates between collective appropriation and private appropriation. A second contradiction takes place between the appropriation of women, whether it be collective or private, and their *reappropriation* by themselves, their objective existence as social subjects — in other words, the possibility of their selling, *on their own authority*, their labour power on the classical open market. This contradiction is also revealed by marriage. In France, it is only since 1965 (Article 233 of the Civil Code) that a wife herself has been able to make the decision to work; in other words, that she has been able to do this without her husband's authorisation. However, the abolition of this authorisation by the husband was not accompanied by any modification of Article 214, which codifies the relations between spouses and ratifies the type of appropriation characteristic of marriage. In the stating of the respective contributions of the husband and the wife to the responsibilities of the marriage, this article brings out that the contribution of the wife is different in essence from that of the husband. The husband is supposed to bring in the cash: that is, in most cases, to sell his labour power. The contribution of the wife, on the other hand, is based either on her dowry and inheritance ('pre-existing' money), or — and it is this which is the main thing — on 'her activity in the home or her collaboration in her husband's occupation'. This is to say, the wife is not supposed to *sell* her labour power in order to support the conjugal commonality, nor even to furnish a *specific quantity* of this labour power to the commonality, but 'to pay with her own person', as the popular saying so correctly puts it, and *to give her individuality directly to her husband without the mediation of either monetary or quantitative considerations.* (...)

Social appropriation (the fact, for individuals of one class, of not being material properties) is a specific form of social relations. It exists *here and now and only between sex classes*, and it runs up against the solid incredulity that usually greets facts so 'obvious' as to be *invisible* (as housework was before feminism). This type of social relation can only find acceptance if it is 'in the past' (slavery or serfdom) or 'elsewhere' (so-called primitives of various kinds).

On the Invisibility of Appropriation

The appropriation of women, the fact that it is their materiality *en bloc* that is acquired, is accepted at so deep a level that it is not seen. From the ideological point of view — that is from the point of view of the mental consequences (or the mental aspect) of a material fact — the attachment of serfs to the land and the attachment of women to men are in part comparable. The dependence of serfs on the land appeared at the time to be just as 'inevitable', just as 'natural', and must have been just as little called into question, as the present-day dependence of women on men. And the popular movement which, at the time of the birth of the communes, detached certain individuals from the feudal land-owning chain (or which used those who had already 'dropped out' of this chain by fleeing),[13] is perhaps comparable to that which today lets a small but increasing number of women escape from patriarchal and sexist institutions (from marriage, from the father, from religion, which are the obligations of their sex class).[14] But there is this difference: the serfs were the movable goods of the land, and it was land (*and not directly they themselves*) that was appropriated by the feudal land-holders, while women are directly — as was the land itself — appropriated by men. The plantation slaves of the eighteenth and nineteenth centuries were, like women, objects of direct appropriation; they were independent of the land and belonged to the master.

The Means of Appropriation

What are the means by which the appropriation of the class of women is carried out?

1 the labour market;
2 spatial confinement;
3 show of force;
4 sexual constraint; and
5 the arsenal of the law and customary rights.

The Labour Market

The labour market does not allow women to sell their labour power in exchange for the minimum necessary for existence — their own existence and that of the children they will inevitably have. They are thus *constrained* by this market, which grants them, in France, on average only two-thirds of a man's wage. (Until the beginning of the twentieth century women's wages in France were only half those of men[15]). Above all, this labour market imposes on them an unemployment rate considerably higher than that of men. (. . .) In this way women are forced to find employment as a wife, that is, to sell THEMSELVES and not to sell just their labour power, in order to live and let their children live.

Spatial Confinement

The place of residence for a married couple is still today fixed by the husband ('mutual agreement' only means acceptance by the wife, since in case of disagreement it is the husband who decides, unless the wife takes him to court). The general principle is thus fixed: the wife must not be anywhere except in her husband's home. For property which can move but not speak (pigs, cows, etc.), there were invented enclosures made of stakes, metal, rope, or electric fencing (consult manufacturers' catalogues). For property which moves *and speaks* (thinks, is conscious, what more can I say?), a comparable thing has been tried — female property belongs in the gynaeceum, the harem, or the house (in both its meanings[16]). But, in addition, because of their character as speaking property, their confinement has been embellished with internalisation — the perfect example of an internal fence, whose efficiency can hardly be improved upon.

The internalisation of this enclosure is effected by positive training and also by negative training. The first kind goes thus: 'Your place is here, you are the queen of the house, the magician of the bed, the irreplaceable mother. Your[17] children will become autistic, psychotic, idiots, homosexual, failures, if you don't stay at home, if you are not there when they come home, if you don't breast-feed them until they are three months, six months, three years old, etc., etc.' In brief, you are the only one who can do all this; you are irreplaceable (most of all, by a male). The second kind of training goes something like this: 'If you go out, other guys like me will pursue you until you give in, will threaten you, will make your life impossible and exhausting in a thousand ways. You have permission (it is an order) to go to the grocery, the school, the market, the city hall, and down the main street where the shops are. And you may go there between seven o'clock in the morning and seven o'clock in the evening. That's all. If you do anything else, you'll be punished in one way or another, and in any case I forbid it for *your* safety and *my* peace of mind.' This sort of thinking has even entered labour laws: 'If you are of the female sex, you will only have the right to work at night in those places where you are "irreplaceable" (we are definitely not in fact replaced) — in hospitals, for example.' The bitter inventory of the times and places which are closed to us, the spaces which are forbidden, and the emotional training through gratifications and threats, is a list which is beginning to be drawn up today.

Show of Force (Physical Violence)

Physical violence exercised against women, which was also in a sense *invisible* in that it was considered as an individual, psychological, or circumstantial 'failing' (like the 'mistakes' of the police), is now more and more being revealed for what it is. First, it is quantitatively not exceptional; and above all, it is socially significant of a relationship.[18] It is a socialised sanction of the right which men abrogate to themselves over women — this man over that woman, and also over all other women who 'do not walk the straight and narrow.' This is related to spacial confinement and sexual constraint.

Sexual Constraint

Nowadays we are largely in agreement about the fact that sexual constraint, in the form of rape, provocation, cruising, harassment, etc., is first and foremost a means of coercion used by the class of men to subdue and frighten the class of women, at the same time as it is the expression of their property rights over this same class.[19]

Every woman who has not been officially appropriated by a contract which restricts use of her to a single man — in other words, every woman who is not married or who acts alone (travelling about alone, eating alone, etc.) — is the object of a competition that reveals the collective nature of the appropriation of women. This is the meaning of brawls over women, and I have always been distressed to see that most women accept this monstrosity and do not even perceive that they are being treated like a seat at a rugby match or a piece of cheese; that in fact they accept the 'value' that is immanent in them — that of *an object* which can be disposed of. To gain the maximum benefit from their common property right, men will bring into play among themselves their prerogatives of class and prestige, as well as their physical strength. This does not necessarily take an apocalyptic form, with bruises and black eyes, but the competition between individuals of the dominant sex class to take (or recover, or benefit from) every 'available' woman — that is, *automatically* every woman whose material individuality is not officially or officiously fenced in — expresses the fact that the *totality of men* have the use of *each woman*, since it is a matter of negotiation or struggle between them to decide who *gets off with the bit*, as it is so exactly put. (. . .)

So-called 'sexual' aggression is as little sexual as it is possible to be. Moreover, it is not by chance that literary symbolisation of masculine sexuality is derived from the police (confessions, torture, jailers, etc.), sadism, and the military (strongholds, brutality, laying siege, conquest, etc.); nor by chance that, reciprocally, relationships of force have a sexual vocabulary (to screw, to fuck over, etc.).

It is difficult to distinguish between constraint by pure physical force and sexual constraint, and in fact they do not seem to be very clearly distinguished in the minds and actions of those who use them. If the legislator distinguishes them, it is only in terms of the *ownership of children*, who can always arrive unexpectedly. This is why, in the legal sense, rape only occurs through penile-vaginal coitus, and only outside of marriage. Sexual violence towards a woman is only considered to be rape if she is liable to produce children for *a man without his consent*. (. . .)

The Arsenal of the Law and Customary Rights

The arsenal of the law determines the modalities of the private appropriation of women, if not the collective appropriation itself, unspoken and uncontractualised as we have seen it to be. In one sense, it determines the limits insofar as it only intervenes in marriage — the restrictive form of the collective appropriation of women. But if the appropriation of women is evident through the diverse arrangements that marriage includes (labour power, parent–child relationships, and rights over children, place of domicile, etc.), women's non-existence as subjects extends far wider than the network of laws relating to it. If laws which refer to the possession of property and its disposition to children, and to decisions of all kinds, are explicitly male (and where this is not made explicit it is still the case in practice),[20] a more 'general' notion, such as citizenship, is just as sexed. The law in the French Code which treats the question of a *name* is particularly meaningful in this regard and expresses the non-proprietorship of oneself for women. One of the very first laws of the Code forbids every citizen on pain of punishment to adopt another name than that which appears on the birth certificate, which is visibly not applied to women since in marriage customary law imposes the name of their husband upon them.[21] (. . .) I do not think that the fact of taking another name than that given at birth (which does not conform to the law, at least for *a citizen, a subject*) has ever led to the prosecution of any woman when it was a question of her *married name*. Better still, the law itself confirms the customary law, since it specifies that at the time of divorce (the ending of appropriation) 'each spouse' is obliged to take back his or her name. What appears from the Code as a whole, and what is particularly marked in this example, is that women are not fundamentally legal subjects; they are not subjects before the law.

Summary of Part I

1   *The material appropriation of the bodies of women,* of their physical individuality, has a legalised expression: the contractual relationship of marriage. This appropriation is concrete and material; it is not a

question of some metaphoric or symbolic 'form'; nor is it a question of an appropriation which only occurs in ancient or exotic societies.

It is manifested by the object of the contract: (1) the *unpaid* character of the wife's *work*, and (2) *reproduction*: the children belong to the husband, and their number is not specified.

It is manifested by the *material, physical taking of possession*, by physical usage, which is sanctioned in the case of 'disagreement' by physical constraint and violence.

Unlimited physical usage, the utilisation of the body, and the non-payment for work — that is, the fact that there is no measure of the labour that comes from the body — express the fact that the individual material body of a woman belongs to her husband, who has the contractual right to make unlimited use of it, with the exception of murder (since rape does not exist in marriage, violence must be 'severe and repeated' to give her the right of escape).

Some tens of years ago, the appropriation was also manifested by the possibility the husband had of selling, for wages, the labour power of his wife, since in fact her wage belonged to him and came as a matter of right to the owner of the wife.

2   This ownership is also expressed by the *nature of certain of the tasks performed*. We know that certain tasks are empirically *associated with the relationship of bodily appropriation*, with the fact that those dominated are material property. This can be historically established for the pariah castes in India and for household slaves in the United States of America (in the eighteenth and nineteenth centuries). These tasks of material maintenance of bodies (the bodies of the dominant group, of each of the owners in slavery and marriage, but also, *and at the same time*, the bodies of other properties of these same owners) including feeding, care, cleaning, rearing, sexual maintenance, physical-emotional maintenance, etc.

When the sale for money of the labour power of those appropriated is possible, this labour power, for a still undetermined time and now for wages, remains practically the only one assigned to these tasks. Those appropriated do, indeed, perform all possible tasks, but they are the only ones to perform the tasks of physical material maintenance. Over 80 per cent of service personnel in France are women; in the United States service personnel are Afro-American men and women; in India they are men and women of the pariah castes. Here, today, in France, practically all daily household helpers are women, almost all nurses are women, as well as social workers and prostitutes, three-quarters of all school-teachers are women, etc.

If labour becomes subject to contract, saleable, this does not mean *ipso facto* that physical appropriation, the ceding of bodily individuality, does not persist — elsewhere, in another relationship.

3   Contradictions: (1) The class of men in its entirety appropriates the

class of women in its entirety and in the individuality of each woman; AND, on the other hand, each woman is the subject of private appropriation by an individual of the class of men. The form of this private appropriation is marriage, which introduces a certain type of contracting into the relations between the sexes.

The social appropriation of women thus includes, *at the same time*, a collective appropriation and a private appropriation, and there is a contradiction between the two.

(2) A second contradiction exists between physical appropriation and the sale of labour power. The class of women is materially appropriated in its concrete individuality (the concrete individuality of each of its members), therefore it is not free to dispose of its labour power; and, at the same time, it sells this labour power on the wage market. In France, changes in the law have marked the stages in the presence of women as sellers of labour power on the labour market. (This class has been on the labour market for a long time, but as appropriated persons and not as sellers; its members were hired out by their owners to a boss.) The first stage was the right to one's own wage (ownership of her wage by a woman in 1907); and the second was the right *to work without the husband's permission* (1965).

This second contradiction thus bears on the simultaneity of the relationship of sexage (concrete material appropriation of her bodily individuality) AND the classic work relationship, where she is simply the seller of her labour power.

These two contradictions govern all analyses of the relations of sex classes, or, if you prefer, of the relations of sexage. Collective appropriation of women (the one that is the most 'invisible' today) is manifested by and through private appropriation (marriage), which contradicts it. Social appropriation (collective and private) is manifested through the free sale (only recently) of labour power, which contradicts it.

4   Physical appropriation is *a relation between owner and object* (not to be confused with a relation between two 'subjects'). It is not symbolic; it is concrete — as the material rights of the one over the other remind us. The *appropriated* individuals *being things*, IN THIS RELATIONSHIP, the ideological-discursive face of the appropriation will be a discourse which asserts that the appropriated dominated individuals are natural objects. This *discourse of Nature* makes plain that the relationship is set in motion by natural mechanical laws, or possibly by mystical-natural laws, but in no case by social, historical, dialectical, or intellectual laws, and even less by political ones.

PART II: The Naturalist Discourse

(...)

From Appropriation to 'Natural Difference'

Things Within Thought Itself

In the social relationship of appropriation, *the physical material individuality which is the object of the relationship* is at the centre of the preoccupations which accompany it. This relationship of power, perhaps the most absolute which can exist (physical ownership — direct in the same way that products are appropriated), entails the belief that a corporeal substratum motivates, and in some way 'causes' this relationship, which is itself a material-corporeal relationship. The material taking possession of the human individual leads to a *reification* of the appropriated object. The material appropriation of the body causes a 'material' interpretation of conduct.[22] (1) The ideological-discursive face of the relationship turns appropriated material units into *things within the realm of thought itself*; the object is expelled 'out' of social relationships and inscribed in a pure materiality.[23] (2) As a corollary, the *physical* characteristics of those who are *physically appropriated* are assumed to be the *causes* of the domination which they undergo.

The owner class builds a statement about *natural constraints* and *somatic evidence* onto the practices imposed on the appropriated class, onto the place this class occupies in the relationship of appropriation, and onto the appropriated class itself. 'A woman is a woman because she is a female' is a statement whose corollary, without which it would have no social meaning, is that 'a man is a man because he is a human being'. As Aristotle said,

> It is then part of nature's intention to make the bodies of free men different from those of slaves, the latter being strong enough for the necessary menial tasks, the former erect and of no use for that kind of work (*Politics*, 1, 5, 25).

In the relations of sex classes, the fact that those who are dominated are things in the realm of thought, is explicit in a certain number of traits which are supposed to connote their specificity. We find this in the discourse on women's *sexuality*, in that on their *intelligence* (its absence or the particular form that it is supposed to take among women), and in that on what is called their *intuition*. In these three domains it is especially clear that we are considered as things: that we are seen in exactly the same way as we are actually treated — everyday, in all spheres of existence and at all times.

Take sexuality, for example. Either the dominant group assigns a fraction of the class of women to sexual use — supposedly to be the only ones to embody 'sexuality' (and sexuality alone): for instance, prostitutes in urban societies, 'widows' in some rural societies, 'coloured mistresses' in societies based on colonisation, etc. The women imprisoned in this fraction of the class are *objectified as sex*. Or the dominant group is ignorant of women's sexuality, and they boast about this ignorance — as do both orthodox and heterodox psychoanalysts. Or, in a third mode, women's sexuality is quite simply thought not to exist: women have no desire, no carnal impulses — as the classic virtuous versions of sexuality explain to us, from the Victorian middle class, which called it 'modesty' (i.e. absence of interest in it),[24] to the working class, who believe that women submit to men's sexuality without having any themselves (unless they are 'fast' — a characteristic that is not highly thought of and not found very frequently). This is also, when all is said and done, what is implicit in the diverse Christian ecclesiastical versions, where woman is more temptress than tempted. We may well ask ourselves how she can be a temptress without having any reason to be so. It is true that, a woman with no more brains or resolution than sexuality must undoubtedly be the work of the devil.

The absence (of desire, of initiative, etc.) reverts to the fact that ideologically women ARE sex — wholly sex, and used as such. And they have, of course, no personal appreciation, nor any impulses of their own toward sex: a chair is never anything but a chair; a sexual organ is never anything but a sexual organ. Sex is woman, but she does not possess a sexual organ; a sexual organ does not possess itself. Men *are not* sex, but they possess a sexual organ. Indeed, they possess it so well that they regard it as a weapon and effectively give it the social attribution of a weapon in situations of male bravado, as well as in rape. Ideologically, men have the free use of their sexual organ, and practically, women do not have the use of themselves. (. . .) The class relationship which makes the latter objects includes even their anatomical-physiological sex, without their being able to make any decisions about, or even have any simple autonomous actions in, this matter.

The version that makes women into 'devouring sexual organs' is only the obverse ideological face of the same social relationship. If the least autonomy appears in sexual functioning itself (in the most reduced and most genital meaning of the term), this autonomy is seen as a devouring machine, a threat, a ball-crusher. Nor are women human beings who have, among other characteristics, a sexual organ; they *are* always and directly *a sexual organ*. The universe of object relationships, the grim denial that women could be anything but a sexual organ, is a denial that they could have a sexual organ: that they could be sexed.

Sexuality is the domain in which the objectification of women is the most visible, even to those not predisposed to notice it. (. . .)

The same applies in the realm of intelligence. Women's 'specific' intelligence is the intelligence of a thing. Supposed to be naturally alien to intellectual speculation, they do not create with their brains; nor are they supposed to have deductive ability: logic. Considered to be even the incarnation of illogicality, women can get by, if the worse comes to the worst. But to achieve this, they stick to practical reality. Their mind does-not-have-

the-impetus-or-power-necessary-to-tear-itself-away-from-the-concrete-world
— from the world of material things, to which they are attached by an affinity
of thing to thing. (. . .)

And *intuition* (so specifically 'feminine') classes women as the expression
of fluctuations of pure matter. According to this notion, women know what
they know *without reasons*. Women do not have to understand, because they
know. And what they know comes to them without their understanding it and
without their using reason. In them, this knowledge is a direct property of the
matter of which they are made.

That which is called 'intuition' is very indicative of the objective position
of oppressed people. They are, in fact, reduced to making very close analyses
(contrary to what is claimed), using the tiniest and most tenuous elements of
the data that can reach them from the outside world, for *access* to this world,
as well as *action* in it, is *prohibited* to them. This mental exercise of putting
fragmented details into place is glorified and called deductive intelligence when
done by members of the dominant group (and it is developed at great length in
detective fiction); but it loses all of its intellectual character as soon as it is
manifested in woman, where it is systematically deprived of comprehensible
meaning and takes on a metaphysical character. The operation of denial
(*dénégation*) is truly stupefying in the face of particularly brilliant intellectual
exercises, which use heterogeneous elements to construct a coherent whole and
propositions applicable to reality. (. . .)

Being in a dominant position leads one to see those who are appropriated
as matter, and as a kind of matter that has diverse *spontaneous* characteristics.
Only those dominated can know that they *do* what they do, and that what they
do does not spontaneously spring from their bodies. (. . .)

The ideological aspect of the practical conflict between dominators and
those they dominate, and between appropriators and those they appropriate,
precisely concerns *consciousness*. The dominators generally deny the consciousness of those they appropriate, and they deny a consciousness to them
precisely because they take them to be things. Furthermore, they try
incessantly to make them swallow their own consciousness, because it is a
threat to the *status quo*; while the dominated individuals eagerly defend and
develop it by all means possible. (. . .)

*'Natural' Things. Or How the Idea of Nature and the Notion of
Thing are Fused*

The current idea of nature and those of former times are not exactly the same.
The one we know today took form around the eighteenth century.

The old idea of nature, which we can call Aristotelian for the purposes of
simplification, expressed a finalistic conception of social phenomena: a slave
was made in order to do what she or he did; a woman was made in order to
obey and be submissive; etc. The idea of the nature of a thing meant scarcely

anything other than the place in actual fact that a thing had in the world. It was almost completely identical with the idea of *function*. (...)

In the naturalist ideology developed today about dominated groups, three elements can be distinguished. The first is the *status of thing*, which expresses the actual social relationship. The appropriated individuals, being material possessions, are *materialised* elements *within thought itself*. The second element corresponds to what can be called a *design of order*: a finalistic and teleological system, which can be summarised as follows. Things being what they are (that is, the appropriation by certain groups, or by one group, of others, or of one other) is what makes the world function properly. Therefore, it is fitting that this situation should remain as it is, and this will avoid disorder and the over-turning of true values and eternal priorities. (In the fragile minds of the dominators, the slightest sigh of impatience by a dominated person triggers visions of the most apocalyptic turmoil — from castration to the ending of the earth's rotation.)

The third element specific to modern thought since the eighteenth century, 'naturalism', proclaims that the status of a human group, like the order of the world that has made it the way it is, *is programmed from within the living matter*. The idea of endogenous determinism came to be superimposed on that of finality — to be associated with it, but not to abolish it, as is sometimes too quickly believed. The end of theocentrism did not mean the disappearance of metaphysical finality. There is, thus, still a discourse of finality, but it is about an internally programmed 'nature': instinct, blood, chemistry, the body, etc.; not of a single individual, but of a class in its totality, each member of which is only a fragment of the whole. This is the strange idea that the actions of a human group, of a class, are 'natural'; that they are *independent of social relationships, that they pre-exist all history and all determined concrete conditions*.

From the 'natural' to the 'genetic'

The idea that a human being is internally programmed to be enslaved, to be dominated, and to work for the profit of other human beings, seems to be strictly dependent on the *interchangeability of individuals* of the appropriated class. The 'internal programming' of domination in the dominated individuals, happens to the individuals belonging to a class which has been appropriated as a class. That is, it takes place when collective appropriation precedes private appropriation. For sex classes, for example, the appropriation of the class of women is not reducible solely to marriage — which certainly expresses it, but not completely, as we saw in Part I of this article. In other words, *the genetic idea is associated with and dependent on the relationship of class appropriation*. It is a non-random appropriation, which is not the result of chance for the appropriated individual, but of a social relationship which is the foundation of the society. And thus it implies the existence of classes born of this relationship: classes that would not exist without it.

This ideological fact comes into play when all women belong to a group which is *appropriated as a group* (sexage) and when the private appropriation of women (marriage) stems from it. If this were not the case, we would find ourselves confronted with a random power relationship — acquisition by simple coercion, such as enslavement by war-time capture or military raids, and (if it exists, which is dubious) by marriage by capture.[25]

The appropriation of *an individual* who does not already belong to a statutorily appropriated class (within which the private appropriation of each particular individual can freely be carried out) takes place through open conflict and recognised relationships of power and constraint. To take a slave from a neighbouring people or from a free class, war or abduction are necessary. This was how slaves were recruited in the ancient city-states; and this is how the first white and black servants and slaves were recruited for the European colonies in America in the seventeenth century. To acquire a slave 'normally' *within an already existing slave class*, it is enough just *to buy her/him*. To acquire a woman in a society where there is *an existing class of women*, it is enough to '*ask for*' her or to *buy* her.

In the first case, the appropriation is the result of a power relationship — power which comes into play as the *means* of acquiring *material individualities which were not previously explicitly and institutionally destined for appropriation*. It does not seem that in this case the appropriation is accompanied by a developed and precise idea of 'nature'; it remains embryonic. By contrast, when an appropriated class is set up and logically ordered — and then characterised by a constant symbolic sign[26] — the idea of nature is developed and made precise, accompanying the class as a whole and each of its individuals from birth to death. Power is then not involved except as a *means of controlling those who are already appropriated*. The idea of nature does not seem to have been present in the ancient Roman and Hebrew societies, which practised slavery as the result of war or debt; but in modern industrial society, with plantation slavery, the proletarianisation of peasants in the nineteenth century, and sexage, there has developed a complex and scientised belief in a specific 'nature' of dominated and appropriated individuals.

Furthermore, the idea of nature has become progressively more refined. This is because the ideological interpretations of the forms of material appropriation are nourished by scientific developments — as they also affect the meaning and choice of these developments. If the idea of a specific nature of those who are dominated or appropriated ('racised', 'sexised') has 'benefited' from the development of the natural sciences, so for the last 50 years the attainments of genetics and then of molecular biology are coming to be swallowed up by that bottomless well which is the ideological universe of appropriation — the real instigator of this research.

The idea of a *genetic* determination of appropriation, and belief in its 'programmed' character (Darwin had begun to speak of the 'marvellous instinct of slavery'), are thus the product of both a particular type of appropriation (where one entire class is institutionally appropriated on a stable basis and considered as the reservoir of *exchangeable material individualities*) AND the development of modern science. This juncture is scarcely ever found except in the relationships of sexage[27] and those of eighteenth and nineteenth century slavery in the first industrial states. (. . .)

> ### All Human Beings are Natural but Some are More Natural than Others

The simultaneous occurrence of subjection, material servitude and oppression, on the one hand, and of the highly intellectual discourse of Nature, that great organiser and regulator of human relationships, on the other, is today principally 'embodied' in the class of women. They are seen as the favoured location of natural impulses and constraints. If, in the past, this burden has weighed on other social groups (for example, the group of Afro-American slaves, the first industrial proletariat, and the peoples colonised by the industrial metropolises), today, in these same metropolises, the imputation of naturalism is focused on the group of women. It is with respect to them that the belief in a 'natural group' is most constraining — most unquestioned. If the accusation of having a specific nature still today affects formerly colonised people, like former slaves, the social relationship that succeeded colonisation or slavery is no longer a relationship of direct material appropriation. Sexage, however, is still a relationship of the appropriation of the bodily material individuality of the entire class. As a result, there is a *controversy* about the question of the supposed 'nature' of former colonised people and former slaves; but about that of women there is no controversy. Women are considered by everybody to have a particular nature; they are supposed to be 'naturally', and not *socially*, specific. (. . .)

In all cases, the imputation of a natural character is made about *appropriated* and dominated individuals. Only those who are in the dominated group in a relationship of domination are natural. (. . .) Nature is absent from the spontaneous definitions of dominant social groups. Strangely absent from the natural world, the latter have disappeared from the universe of definitions. Thus, a bizarre world takes shape — where only those who are appropriated float in a universe of eternal essences. This completely encircles them, they do not know how to escape from it, and within it, enclosed in their 'being', they fulfill duties that only nature assigns to them — since nothing, absolutely nothing, in sight could make one think that another group is also involved.

Appropriation is a Relationship

'Difference' is the result of . . .

This burden which weighs on us, the imputation of being 'natural', the imputation that everything — our life, our death, our acts — is imposed on us by Mother Nature in person (and for good measure, she also is a woman), is expressed in a discourse of noble simplicity. If women are dominated, it is because they are 'not the same'. They are different, delicate, pretty, intuitive, unreasonable, maternal, non-muscular, lacking an organising character, a little futile, and unable to see beyond the end of their noses. And all this happens because they obviously have a smaller brain; slower nervous reactions; different hormones which behave irregularly; because they weigh less; have less uric acid and more fat; run more slowly and sleep more. It is because, stupid creatures, they have two X chromosomes instead of an X and a Y — which is the satisfactory way to have chromosomes. (...) In short, because they are different.

How are they different? In what way? In what way are they different? Being different all by oneself, if one thinks of it grammatically or logically, is an impossibility, just as is a 40-foot ant with a hat on. Being different is not like being curly-haired; it is being different FROM — different from something else. But, of course, you will say, women are different from men. We know perfectly well from whom women are different. Yet if women are different from men, men themselves are not different. If women are different from men, men themselves are men. We say, for instance, that men in this region have an average height of five feet four inches and (throughout the world) are carnivorous, walk at a rate of two and a half miles per hour, and can carry 66 pounds for such and such a distance, etc. But what is certain is that women, who are different from men, do not have an average height of five feet four inches, and do not always eat meat (because it is reserved for men in most cultures and in the poorer classes). And yet, though different from men and delicate and lacking strong muscles, they still carry heavy loads. However, when it comes to the work done here and now by women, everyone averts their eyes. I am not talking about road-building in Eastern Europe, but about the 20–30 pound bags of groceries women carry every day, plus a child in their arms — groceries and child being carried in a horizontal direction for several hundred yards and in a vertical direction up one to six flights of stairs. And I am not talking about terrace-builders in India, but about the loads handled in France in the isolation of farms or behind the walls of factories, such as the child picked up and put down and picked up again to waist and face level an incalculable number of times, in a movement little resembling weight-lifting, because that allows (apart from the satisfaction of its uselessness) regularity, calm, the use of both arms, and the docile immobility of the weight being lifted — advantages that the strong personality of a human being a few months or years old does not offer.

Well, sure enough, women are different from men, who themselves are not different. Men do not differ from anything. (...) We are different — it is a fundamental characteristic. We are different, as one can 'be retarded' or 'have blue eyes'. We succeed in the grammatical and logical feat of being different all by ourselves. Our nature is difference.

We are always 'more' or 'less'. We are never the term of reference. The height of men is never measured relative to ours, whereas our height is measured relative to that of men (we are 'smaller'), which is only measured relative to itself. It is said that our wages are a third less than those of men, but it is not said that men's wages are half as much again as ours. They just are men's wages. (Yet we should say it nonetheless, for to say only that women earn a third less than men hides the fact that *in practice* men earn half as much again as women. For example: a woman's wage of 1000 francs against a man's wage of 1500 francs.) We say of blacks that they are black relative to whites; but whites are just white. Moreover, it is not even certain that whites have a colour. It is no more certain that men are sexed beings. They *have* a sexual organ, which is different. It is we who *are* sex, wholly sex.

Moreover, there isn't really such a thing as masculine (there is no grammatical *male gender*). One says 'masculine' because men have kept the general for themselves. In fact, there is a general and a feminine; a human and a female. I look for the masculine, and I don't find it. And I don't find it because there is no such thing — the general takes care of men. They are not very insistent on identifying themselves as a gender (males) while they are a dominant class. They are not eager to find themselves denoted by an anatomical characteristic — they who are *men*. 'Man' does not mean 'male'; it means the human species. We say 'men' the way we say 'sparrows' and 'bees', etc. Why in the world would they want, like women, to be only a portion of the species? They prefer to be the whole, which is easy to understand. Are there perhaps languages where there is a grammatical masculine gender?

As for us women, what I am saying is that we are not even a portion of the species; for if 'woman' designates the female gender, this in no way means 'human being', that is, the species. We are not a portion of the species, but a species — the female. We are not an element of a whole, one of two elements of a sexed species, for example. No, all by ourselves we are a species (a natural division of the living), and all by themselves men are men. Thus there is the human species, composed of human beings, which can be divided into males. And then also there are women. And they are not in the human species, and therefore do not divide it up.

The dominant group, as the great Standard, could not ask for anything better than that we should be different. What the dominant group cannot stand, on the contrary, is similarity: *our* similarity. They cannot stand that we have — that we want — the same right to food, to independence, to autonomy, to life; and that we take these rights or try to take them. (. . .) It is our similarity to them that they repress in the most decisive way. All they ask is that we be different. They even do all that they can to see to it that we are paid no wage, or a lesser wage; that we have no food, or less food;[28] that we have no right to decision-making, but only to be consulted; and that we love our very chains.[29] They want this 'difference' — they love it. They never stop telling us how much it pleases them. They impose it with their actions and their threats, and then with their beatings.

But this difference — in rights, food, wages, independence — is never spoken of in this form: its real form. No. It is a 'difference', an exquisite internal characteristic with no relation to all those sordid material questions. (...)

... is the result of appropriation.

(...) The term 'appropriation' has been very frequently used in the last two or three years. The reappropriation of the body is much talked about, and doubtless not by chance. But in using this term one expresses a truth so crude and violent, so difficult to accept, that at the same time its meaning is distorted — which happens when the literal meaning has been ignored. 'Appropriation', turned into an image or a 'symbolic reality', both expresses and dresses up a brutal and concrete reality. So this term is used in a timid way, which claims that, in order to take back the ownership of our physical materiality, all we have to do is dance. This is a way of speaking the truth in order not to have to face it. So appropriation is admitted, but *as if it were abstract*, in thin air, coming from nowhere, some sort of quality, like difference. We are appropriated. Full stop. By nothing, we are expected to believe. One word or ten makes it seem as though what is said is not really true. A characteristic defusing tends to make a *fact* disappear into a metaphoric form. Is this the effect of censorship (often self-censorship) when faced with a growing consciousness of the fact that the relationship of the sex classes is actually *a relationship* of appropriation? We act as if appropriation were one of the characteristics of our anatomy, in the same way as eye colour, or (putting things in the worst light) in the same way as a bad case of flu. We consent to being 'appropriated' on the condition that it remain vague and abstract. Above all, let there be no accusations.

To reappropriate one's body! This body is either 'one's own' or it is not; it is possessed or it is not, by oneself or by someone else. In order to grasp the exact meaning of appropriation and the hypocrisy of this metaphorical game, here is a suggestion: 'Appropriate for yourself' the funds of the establishment where you go to reappropriate your body. Now the meaning of the term appears very quickly in all its crudity. *The physical violence exercised against women* (blows given them by men who do not allow them the least attempt to gain autonomy or to reappropriate of themselves) conveys in the same way the message that women do not have the right to decide their own actions. (...) The owner of the woman tries to prevent her from acting as she wants. And that is his right. 'Satisfaction guaranteed or your money back' could be a good slogan for male divorce.[30] Women cannot make decisions for themselves because they do not belong to themselves. No one can decide what will be the allocation of objects as long as they have an owner. Basically we do not want to see that we are *actually* taken as objects in a well-defined relationship: that *appropriation is a relationship*, and that it requires at least two people.

In other words, we accept in some way — and alas, we even insist upon it sometimes — that we might be naturally 'women': that each and every one of us is the expression (exquisite or formidable, according to differing opinions) of a particular species — the species *woman*, defined by her anatomy, her physiology. (. . .)

And if we are ever oppressed or exploited, it is the result of our nature. Or better still, our nature is such that we are oppressed, exploited and appropriated. These three terms express in ascending order our social situation.[31]

Women in Nature and Nature in Women

Dissymmetry of 'Nature' According to Sex

The idea that there exists a natural finality in social relations is not uniformly applied. (. . .) The imputation of a specific nature is made to the full against those who are dominated, and particularly against those who are appropriated. The latter are supposed to be explainable *totally and uniquely* by Nature: by their nature. 'Totally', because nothing in them is outside of the natural, and nothing escapes it: 'uniquely', because no other possible explanation of their position is even envisaged. From the ideological point of view, they are absolutely immersed in the 'natural'.

The nature of some . . .

By contrast, dominant groups do not in the first stage attribute a nature to themselves. They may, with considerable detours and political quibbling, acknowledge (as we shall see) that they have some link with nature — some link, but nothing more, and certainly not an immersion in it. Their group, or rather their world (for they hardly conceive of themselves in limited terms), is understood as resistance to Nature, as conquest of Nature, as the location of the sacred and of culture, of philosophy, of politics, of planned action, of 'praxis' — but, whatever the term, it is certainly the location of *distancing* through consciousness or creative activity.

The first move of dominant groups is to define themselves in relation to the system which is ideologically decreed to be the foundation of the society. Obviously this varies according to the type of society. In this way the dominant group can consider itself as defined by the sacred (the Brahmins in India, the Catholic Church of the Middle Ages), by culture (the élite), by property (the bourgeoisie), by knowledge (the Mandarins, the Scribes), by their action on the real world (solidarity among hunters, accumulation of capital, conquest of territory), etc. In any case, they define themselves by mechanisms which create history, not by constraints that are repetitive, internal, and mechanical — constraints that they reserve for the dominated groups. In this way *men claim to be identified by their actions, and they claim that women are identified by their bodies.* (. . .)

However, revolts, conflicts, historical upheavals and other reasons sometimes force dominant groups to enter into a problematic which they loathe for themselves just as strongly as they cling to it for those whom they exploit. They may then try to define their links with that very attentive Nature which furnishes them so conveniently and opportunely with living 'supplies'. At this stage they can undertake to develop those 'scientific ethics' (triumphantly liberal as well as Nazi) which proclaim that certain groups have the right to domination by the excellence of their qualities and innate capacities of all sorts.[32]

Nonetheless, they do not abandon the feeling that they are not one with the elements of Nature. And they consider that, as it happens, their capacities give them (what luck!) the possibility of transcending internal determinations. For example, nature gives them intelligence, which is innate but which, as it happens, allows them to understand Nature, and thus to dominate it in a certain measure. (. . .)

In this vision, human culture (technology, prohibition of incest, etc., whatever is said to be the source of human society, varying according to the writer) is the fruit of solidarity and co-operation between males of the species — a solidarity and co-operation that derives either from hunting or from war. In short, once rid of the burdensome females, men, all on their own, like grown-ups, soared to the summits of science and technology. And, apparently, there they have remained, leaving the females of the species behind in Nature (out of the running) and immersed in contingency. And there we still are. This orientation is so totally androcentrist that we cannot even call it misogynist in the common meaning of the term, since the human race appears in it to be composed solely of males. The dialectical relationship to the environment, the 'transformation of Nature', is described in and with regard to the class of men (males) — leaving the rest in an obscurity that would be non-existence if it were not that occasionally a ray of light is thrown on the female: a distant silhouette busy with natural activities, destined to remain in that situation and maintaining no dialectical relationship with Nature. This view is present in almost all social science works. In a still more sophisticated form, it takes the form of a conceptual dissymmetry in the analysis, as Nicole-Claude Mathieu has shown — a dissymmetry which has each sex class described and analysed according to different theoretical assumptions.[33] (. . .)

The second stage of naturalist belief thus implies that the nature of some and the nature of others is subtly different and not comparable — in a word, that their nature is not the *same* nature. The nature of one group is supposed to be entirely natural, while the nature of the other is supposed to be 'social'. 'Basically', one could say (as an analyst ironically commented in a recent text) that 'man is biologically cultural. Woman on the contrary is biologically natural'.[34] Law and architecture, strategy and technology, the machine and astronomy are supposed to be the creations that 'moved' humanity out of Nature. And thus civilisation and society, being the inventions of the group of men as well as the intrinsic and potential characteristics of each male, are supposed to be the dynamic expression of a creation that leads the male of the species to 'dominate', to 'use' the natural environment by virtue of a particular ability, of a quite specific orientation of natural behaviour.

Whereas, conversely, reproduction, child-rearing and food preparation are supposed to be the expression of stereotyped instincts, perhaps adaptive, but in any case expressions of *the permanence* of the species — the permanence carried by women. (. . .)

In brief, if there really is a nature peculiar to each of the groups, one of these natures tends towards nature, while the other tends towards culture (civilisation, technology, thought, religion, etc. — use whatever term is dictated by your choice of theory, be it culturalist, marxist, mystical, psycho-analytic, functionalist, etc.). Whatever it is, the term you choose is likely to imply that nature tends, in THIS group (the group of men), to transcend itself, to distance itself, to transform itself, or to dominate itself, etc. And another nature, the one which is basic, immobile, permanent (that of women and dominated groups in general), appears mainly in activities that are repetitive and capricious, permanent and explosive, and cyclical, but which in no case have *dialectical and antagonistic relationships* with themselves or the exterior world — a pure nature which constantly renews itself.

. . . and the nature of others.

This is exactly the nature attributed to us. Our periods and our intuition, our childbirths and our whims, our tenderness and our caprices, our endurance (in all trials) and our very special recipes, our fragility (unfathomable) and our old wives' remedies, our healing magic, the telluric permanence of the body of *women*. Well, that grates a little — permanence? In fact, our bodies are inter-changeable, and, even more than that, they must be changed (like sheets), because it is youth that is telluric in women. And it is about us as a *species*, not as particular individuals.[35] We believe it for a moment, just as we believe we can say 'I', until reality explodes on us, telling us that it is nothing of the sort.

Each of our actions, each of the actions which we engage in in a specific social relationship (speaking, laundering, cooking, giving birth, taking care of others) *is attributed to a nature which is supposed to be internal to us*, even though that social relationship is *a class relationship imposed on us by the modalities and the form of our life*. And this nature — outside of all relationships — is supposed to push us to do all those things because we are supposed to be 'programmed' and 'made for that', and because we obviously are supposed to 'do it better' than anybody else. Besides, we are ready to believe this when we are confronted with the legendary resistance of the other class to performing such acts as cleaning, *really* taking care of children (and not just taking them out for a treat or having 'a really serious talk' with them), really taking charge of food (every day and in detail), not to mention the laundry, ironing, tidying-up, etc. (which a grown man has no qualms whatever about leaving to a child of ten, as long as the child is female) — all of these being areas in which the amount of co-operation known and observed is close to zero.

Certainly our 'nature' also has sides which are more fantasising and joyful and superficially less utilitarian, but which all the same reinforce the idea that we are supposed to be made of special flesh which is suitable for certain things and not at all for others (like for example *making decisions*).[36] (...)

The idea that we are made of a particular flesh and that we have a specific nature, can be dressed in charming colours. That is not the question. Whether couched in contemptuous or eulogistic language, the Nature argument tries to make us into finite *closed beings*, who pursue a tenacious course, consisting of repetition, enclosure, immobility and maintenance of the (dis)order of the world. And this is exactly what we are trying to resist when, described as 'unpredictable', capricious, and perplexing, we then accept the idea of a feminine nature which, in this guise, seems to be the opposite of permanence. Deviations are willingly granted us, as long as it means that we are outside of history, *outside of actual social relations*, and that everything that we do comes only from the surging forth of some obscure genetic message buried deep in our cells. For thus we leave to the dominant group all the benefits of being the inventors of society and the masters of the great unknown and the gamble of history, the latter being not the expression of a profound fatality, but, on the contrary, the fruit of invention and risk — 'taking chances' suits them better than seeing themselves as 'programmed'.

Two Distinct Species?

Rather than envisage the social process which determines the two 'genders', they prefer to consider either (1) that there exist *two 'natural' somatic groups* which can be considered to be linked by organic ties to complementarity and functionalism, or which can on the contrary be seen as opposing each other in a relation of 'natural antagonism'; or (2) that there are two groups, also anatomical and natural, but heterogeneous enough at the same time, so that one group frees itself from nature and the other remains immured in it. In no case do *class relations* occupy a central position in the discussion. In fact, they are not even envisaged. The real existence of these groups is hidden from view by describing them as anatomical-physiological realities onto which a few social ornaments such as 'roles' or 'rites' have come to be grafted. And in order to be able to consider them in this way and to maintain the affirmation of their natural specificity, one arrives at a division into two heterogeneous species with specific genetic messages, and distinct practices rooted in these messages. Ultimately this interpretation can lead to theorising the relations between the sexes as being ascribable to symbiotic groupings of instinctive exploitation, like ants and their little parasites.

These insinuations, which imply the existence of a male species *and* a female species, are unquestionably *the sign of the real relations* which exist between the two groups. (. . .) But this is not an *analysis* of these relations, for what it is really about is intra-specific social relations, not species-to-species (inter-specific) relations.

The arrogance of these conceptions, enunciated with emphatic indifference, pervades daily life. Educated men — from paid-by-the-word journalists to high school teachers, from armchair philosophers to ivory-tower researchers — enunciate them with explanations, examples, variations, and other rhetorical accompaniments. Professional intellectuals, when they start to think about the sexes, do not consider them as classes but as natural categories dressed up in a bit of socio-ritual cheap finery. (. . .)

Political Consequences

The political consequences of this ideology are incalculable. Apart from the prescriptive aspect of such a discourse (the dominated are made to be dominated; women are made to be submissive, ordered around, protected, etc.), this Naturalist discourse attributes all political action and all creative action — indeed, even all possibility of such action — to the dominant group alone. All political initiative on the part of the appropriated individuals will be rejected or severely repressed, using the classic repressive mechanisms of total power over any challenge or any project which does not espouse the dominant view. But it will also be repressed as a *terrifying eruption of 'Nature'*. Struggle itself will appear as a natural process *without political meaning*, and will be presented as *regression* towards the dark zones of instinctive life. And it will be discredited.

This would not be important if it only affected the opinions of the dominators (generally speaking, political conquests are not made with amenity, and we certainly cannot count on it). But an ideology characteristic of certain social relations is more or less accepted by all the actors concerned. The very ones who are subjected to the domination share it up to a certain point — usually uneasily, but sometimes with pride and insistence. Now the very fact of accepting some part of the ideology of the relationship of appropriation (we are natural things), deprives us of a large part of our means, and of some of our potential, for political thinking. *And this is indeed the aim of this ideology, since it is precisely the expression of our concrete reduction to powerlessness.* We ourselves more or less come to admit that our struggle is supposed to be 'natural', immemorial, a metaphysical 'struggle between the sexes' in a society forever divided by the laws of Nature — in short, nothing but submission to the spontaneous impulses that issue from the depths of life, etc.[37] Thus, hey presto, no more analysis of society, no more political plans, no more science, nor any more attempts to think the unthinkable.[38] (. . .)

Conclusion

Some Aspects of Practice and Some Aspects of Theory

Let us summarise. As a result of the fact that women are actual material property, a Naturalistic discourse is developed *about* them (and *against* them). They are credited with (as certain optimists believe) or accused of (as is in fact the case) being natural beings, immersed in Nature and set in motion by it — *living things* in some sort of way.

And these living things are seen as such, because *in a determined social relationship — sexage* — they are things. We tend to deny it, to forget it, to refuse to take account of it. Or better still, we tend to dress it up as a 'metaphorical reality', even though this relationship is the source of our political and class consciousness.

Men, however, know this perfectly well, and for them this constitutes a set of clearly conscious habits on which they draw every day, *outside of* as well as *within* the legal ties of private appropriation. It is also a set of practical attitudes which range from harassment designed to obtain continuous physical services from women (clearing the table, giving men the right of way on the pavement by clinging to the wall or stepping down into the gutter, leaving them two-thirds of the seats on the subway or bus, passing the ashtray, the bread, the pasta, the tobacco, leaving them the meat, etc.) to the eventual exercise of *de facto* rights over our physical integrity and our lives.[39]

From these habits and attitudes they draw not only political conclusions that have a constant utility, but also theoretical propositions. The latter aim to give a 'scientific' form to the status of appropriated individuals as things, and to *affirm* in this way that this status as a thing is not the product of a human relationship. Leading the existence of a material, manipulable thing, the appropriated group is then *ideologically materialised*. From this comes the postulate that women are 'natural beings'. From this comes the absolutely normal conclusion that their place in the social system is entirely enclosed within this matter.

In this manner, these conceptions eliminate the class relationship between the two sexes: the intra-human relationship. They strengthen exploitation and seizure by presenting them as natural and irreversible. Women are things, therefore they are things — in essence.

The idea of nature is the absolutely daily recording of an actual social relationship. In one sense it is a pronouncement; after all, the naturalist discourse never means quite simply that X (women, for example) are dominated and used. *But* it is a pronouncement of a particular type, a prescriptive pronouncement in all cases, whether it is Aristotle talking about the nature of slaves or the recent colloquium at Royaumont once more expounding the specificity of women's brains.[40] In both cases the pronouncement of the particular place occupied by those called slaves or those called women is associated with the implied obligation to remain in this place since they are 'made like that'. Both forms proclaim that social relations being what they are, they *cannot* be otherwise, and *they must* remain the same. The modern Naturalist discourse introduces a novelty into all this: internal programming of the appropriated individuals, which implies that they themselves work at their own appropriation and that all their actions tend in the last analysis to perfect it.

Species Consciousness or Class Consciousness?

Everything keeps telling us that we are a natural species. Everybody strives to persuade us more and more that we, a natural species, are supposed to have instincts, patterns of behaviour, qualities, and inadequacies characteristic of our nature. Within humanity we are supposed to be the privileged ones who bear witness of innate animality. And our behaviour and the social relationships in which we are involved are supposed to be explainable by Nature alone, *contrary to the other facts of society*. So much so that certain, if not all, scientific theoretical systems openly show their hand. Women are the natural part of the human *socius*; they are only analysed *separately*, and in a naturalist perspective. The more that domination tends toward limitless, total appropriation, the more insistent and 'obvious' will be the idea of the 'nature' of the appropriated ones.

Today we are building up the consciousness of our class, *our class consciousness*, against spontaneous belief in ourselves as a natural species — consciousness as opposed to belief, analysis as opposed to spontaneous social behaviour. We are waging a struggle against the truisms which are whispered to us to distract our attention from the fact that we are a class, not a 'species'; that we are not outside of time; that it is very concrete and very daily social relationships that form us and not a transcendental Nature (which we could only call on God to account for). Nor are we formed by an internal genetic mechanism that is supposed to have put us at the disposition of the dominators.

Notes

1   'Pratique de pouvoir et idée de Nature' was first published, in two parts, in *Questions féministes*, nos 2, pp. 5–30 and 3, pp. 5–28 in February and May 1978. A translation by Linda Murgatroyd was published in *Feminist Issues* Winter 1981, pp. 3–28 and Summer 1981, pp. 87–108.

   This translation has been abridged by the author for the present collection. The full version appears in her collection *Racism, Sexism, Power and Ideology*, London, Routledge, 1995. Cuts are indicated by (...)

2   This is Selma James's formulation in her analysis of capitalist social relations (Dalla Costa and James, 1975).

3   *Sexage* is a new term based on the model of *esclavage* (slavery) and *servage* (serfdom). (*Translator's note*)

4   The fall in the birth rate in Europe in the eighteenth and nineteenth centuries shows that birth control is not necessarily related to *female contraception*, and

that it can occur without this. This drop in the birth rate is known to have depended largely on *male control* (in terms of *coitus interruptus*, terms which include, for us, *political control* of women by men). The violence of the resistance to contraception (or abortion) being actually accessible to women, and to all women, shows clearly that what it is all about is a conflict of power. On the other hand, in some forms of marriage, not providing the husband with children, or the desired children (e.g. sons) is grounds for annulment.

5   The owner of social welfare payments in France remains the husband-father (and as it sometimes happens that he is not present, his dear children may have the greatest trouble in obtaining allowances theoretically intended to render their 'maintenance' less difficult). Equally, the administrator of the potential property belonging to the children and the family community remains the father. This is not without interest in the middle and upper-middle classes.

6   In any case, a custody decision is never final and may be called into question. Custom and judgments confirm that the smaller the children (which means the greater the burden), the more likely mothers are to have exclusive material charge of them; whereas at adolescence, when the children are already raised, the links with the father are strengthened. See Delphy (1976) and de Lesseps (1973).

7   In the diverse forms of slavery known historically, a few (for example, in the ancient world) did not include such extended rights over the physical individual. Certain Athenian slaves had ownership of their children, or more exactly their children did not belong to their master, whereas in modern plantation slavery the master was able to keep the children on the plantation or in his house, or to sell them to another master. The materiality of the slaves' bodies could be manipulated at the mercy of the master, and they could be treated as beasts of combat — as happened in Rome. Serfdom and certain historical or non-western forms of marriage do not imply such extended rights either.

8   The transition from the 'extended family' to the nuclear family is supposed to have profoundly altered family ties and the duties that they imply. However, if the members of the same 'family' no longer live together, this does not imply that the material duties which fall on the women have disappeared. It may be less frequent, but even in Paris women continue to move around the city taking meals to sick or aged relatives, doing their house-cleaning and shopping, and visiting them once or several times a day, depending on how far away they live. The tasks which are supposed to have disappeared (one asks why this idea is so widespread) remain very current.

9   On this point, the abundance of writing, from de Beauvoir to the most anonymous of us, is so great that almost all feminist literature is relevant.

10   *Not to be paid* simply means that the work is completed without a determined quantity of money or upkeep being provided to confirm its completion; while being *non-paid* for a job means that it is part of its character *not to have any relation with any quantitative measure whatever*, of money or of upkeep.

11   We can say quite logically (and not everyone thinks it funny!) that the woman was 'kept' by her husband with the money that she brought in to him (with the price for which she was 'knocked down', as they say in auctions).

12   Two individuals: this dual relationship is specific to the relations of present-day European sex classes, in contrast with other relations of appropriation. For instance, in slavery the relationship is actualised between a *number* of specific individuals (the slaves/the master); similarly for serfdom and for polygynous marriage. Each woman has a personal boss who has only her as a *private* domestic (from *domus* meaning *house*) worker.

13   Fugitive serfs and artisans were, in the urban regroupings of the Middle Ages, at the origin of the commune (free town) movement. The latter developed an anti-feudal solidarity, necessary to resist the attempts by the feudal lords to recapture

or seize the individuals who were trying to take their freedom. There was a contradictory situation between the charters granted to communes in their capacity as profitable economic units, and the pursuit of the private individuals who composed these communes. Also, a time of *de facto* emancipation was fixed: a year and a day of residence.

14 In fact they escape the *institutions*, and only the institutions, which are an actualisation of sexage. The relation of social appropriation of the whole class by the other class remains dominant, and collective appropriation is not overcome even if private appropriation does not take place.

15 See Sullerot (1968).

16 In French this means both a domestic house and a brothel (*editor's note*).

17 Always 'your' children, when it comes to keeping an eye on them, feeding them, or being responsible for their faults and inadequacies.

18 See Hanmer (1978).

19 See *Alternatives* (1977).

20 In 1978 the bus shelters and subways in Paris were covered with a poster whose funny side was certainly not intentional. It said: 'Have "your" photograph put on "your" cheques to be sure that they aren't accepted by shop assistants unless you yourself present them.' The argument for this was security, and to illustrate the point the photograph of a 50-year-old man appeared on the cheque next to the name and address of the owner of the bank account. But then one read the name of the owner of this account. It was Mr *and Mrs* So-and-So. But no photograph of Mrs So-and-So. This is after all normal in sex classes relations — but in these conditions, for security? Could any woman whatever (and it is quite true there are a lot of us) use this cheque book without any hindrance? Or could none of us use it, not even Mrs So-and-So?

21 See Boigeol (1977).

22 This is a *material* interpretation and not a *materialist* interpretation. There is a logical leap involved in *explaining processes* (social processes in the case we are interested in, but they could be of another kind) *by material elements* that are fragmented and imbued with spontaneous symbolic qualities. If in practice this attitude is the line of traditional idealists more attached to the social order and to sound distinctions than to the materialism of which they accuse their enemies, it is sometimes presented as materialism on the pretext that in this perspective 'matter is causal'.

But it is not a materialist proposition, because the properties attributed to matter have a specific characteristic here: they arise *not as consequences* of the relations which the material form maintains with its universe and its history (that is, with other forms), but actually as *characteristics intrinsically symbolic of matter itself*. This is simply the idea of (metaphysical) finality decked out with a materialist mask (matter as the determining factor). We are far fom abandoning a substantialism which is the direct *consequence* of a determined social relation.

23 The religious institutions of the theocentric societies, chiefly the Catholic Church, have been explicitly confronted with this question: first, during the Middle Ages, with women; then later, as early as the sixteenth century but above all during the seventeenth and eighteenth centuries, with slaves. Do women have a soul? Should slaves be baptised? In other words, are they not things? If they are things, it is out of the question to let them enter the universe of salvation. But do they not speak? In which case, must we not consider them as being part of the universe of Redemption? What to do? Can objectification and redemption be reconciled?

24 The ideas of the Victorian middle class are the best known on this subject, and are almost caricatures. Several generations of women were mutilated and crushed by them. But there are other forms. One of them is the morals of the American plantation society. There the wife of the master and the mistress of the master

fulfilled opposite 'functions' as objects, one devoted to reproduction and reputed to be devoid of all sexuality, and the other devoted to diversion and reputed to be unalloyed sexuality. The Fascist and Nazi societies professed an identical view. The common features of these forms — which deny the existence of sexuality in women/wives — is the reduction of their genitality to reproduction. In these forms, reproduction is considered as necessary to the maintenance of 'the line' in the aristocratic classes, or as indispensable to the constitution in the popular classes of a permanent and inexhaustible reserve of workers or soldiers. The very idea of sexuality is unimaginable in these perspectives.

25 Since the expression *marriage by capture* conventionally designates a certain type of marriage whose rules are completely institutionalised, it is in one sense then the opposite of a real 'abduction', which would seem to be more related to ancient mythology and exoticism than to any actual practice.

26 By 'constant symbolic sign' we mean an arbitrary mark which replaces the individual and assigns each individual his or her position as a class member. This sign can have any somatic form whatever: it can be the shape of the genitals, it can be the colour of the skin, etc. Such a characteristic 'classifies' the bearer of it; a woman, who is the child of a man and a woman, will be relegated to the class of appropriate persons. This is a mechanism very close to that by which Jacob built his own flock from that of his father-in-law, Laban:

> And he said, What shall I give thee? And Jacob said, Thou shalt not give me any thing...I will pass through thy flock today, removing from thence all the speckled and spotted cattle, and all the brown cattle among the sheep, and the spotted and speckled among the goats: and *of such* shall be my hire...And Laban said, Behold I would it might be according to thy word. And he removed that day the he-goats that were ringstraked and spotted, and all the she-goats that were speckled and spotted, *and* every one that had *some* white in it, and all the brown among the sheep...' (Genesis, 30: 31–35)

The determination of our class affiliation is made according to the conventional criterion of the shape of the reproductive organs. And thus *designated by the female genitals*, as were Jacob's sheep by the colour of their coats, we *become women*.

27 It is important to determine the *different social relationships* which make use of the anatomical difference between the sexes. In theory there is no reason why the sexes should necessarily be the occasion for a relationship of *sexage* (in the sense in which this term is used in Part I of this article — that of generalised appropriation). And if in practice everyone considers that the dichotomy of sex in the human race is a primordial characteristic, to the extent that all known societies today associate some sort of division of labour with the anatomical shape of the sex organs, as Margaret Mead pointed out in the 1930s, it is nevertheless not an identical social relationship which always overlays the difference between the sexes.

28 See Delphy (1979).

29 *Work*: 'A man worthy of the name keeps his wife at home.' 'But why do you want to bore yourself working; it's enough for one of us to do it.' 'And besides, it doesn't bring in any money.'

   Food: 'I fixed a steak for you.' 'Please give me a pork chop for my husband and a slice of liver for the child.' 'I'm not hungry when I am all alone.' 'The restaurant is too expensive. I'll take a snack with me' — said by a secretary whose husband works in a small workshop. She stays in the office for lunch or buys a cup of coffee. Her husband goes to the small restaurant in the area where he works.

   Decision-making: 'That guy, it's his wife who pushes him' — apparently it is not herself that she pushes. 'Pillow power'. 'Really, believe me, it is the women who dominate.' No, I don't believe you. It is amusing to observe these remarks amount to saying, not that women do the deciding (as their authors insinuate), but precisely that someone else does. Guess who?

30 In so far as divorce can be the sanction resulting from the non-satisfaction of a husband who considers the tool unfit to carry out the tasks for which he acquired it. See Delphy (1978).

31 *Oppressed*. This is the point on which differing interpretations unanimously agree. We all feel that we are hindered and fettered in most areas of existence; that we are never in a position to be able to decide what is fitting for our class and for ourselves; that our right to expression is almost non-existent; that our opinion doesn't count, etc.

Exploited. Although we all feel this oppressive weight bearing down on us, far fewer of us clearly perceive that men get substantial material benefits from it (psychological benefits also, of course, for they go hand in hand); and that a part of our existence (our work, time and strength) is appropriated to assure the class of men a better existence than they would have without this appropriation.

Appropriation. Few of us realise the extent to which the social relationship based on sex exhibits a specificity that makes it very close to the slave relationship. Social status based on 'sex' (we are sex) derives from sex class relations which are founded on material appropriation of physical individuality and not simply on monopoly of labour power, as we saw in Part I of this article.

32 As an analysis of the historical development of racism in France (and doubtless in the whole western world) in the eighteenth and nineteenth centuries shows, the dominant group, although it was fascinated by other groups as groups, spontaneously did not see ITSELF. Not seeing itself, neither did it make any judgment about its own social existence, which was taken as a matter of course. It remains fixed on the idea that it is a group of particular individuals. It also accords only to its own members the right to individuality: a right which is inconceivable for the dominated group. Individuality being a human quality, it cannot be applied to natural groupings. The élitist discourse, centred on itself, proclaiming rights over the world, is *secondary* in time and logic. Gobineau only develops his hymn to the Aryans once racism has crystallised. See Guillaumin (1972).

33 See Mathieu (1978 and 1979).

34 Mathieu (1978, p. 60).

35 See 'The Older Woman: a stockpile of losses', in Atkinson (1974, pp. 223–6).

36 An elegant anecdotal example is the panic of the columnist in an evening paper at the idea that he cannot make the 'right decision' when he finds himself in the situation of arriving at a door at the same time as a woman. For, he says, if you allow the lady to go first, you are a male chauvinist (as women would say); but if you go through first, you are undoubtedly a cad. So (he groans) it's hopeless. But no, Mr Columnist, not at all. It has obviously never entered this man's head that a woman could also take the initiative herself in these areas of daily life, where the heavy burden of the male consists mainly of preventing women from making a move or taking the slightest initiative.

37 This doubtless also explains why traditional politics never recognise that a feminist position is a political position.

38 All science is elaborated in opposition to 'the obvious', by showing what the latter hides/exhibits. To think what has not yet been *thought* with respect to that which is considered to be *known* (and which is considered to have no significance other than 'natural') is the object of a feminist science.

39 The exercise of violence, *always potentially present*, is the root of this fear which is endemic in women's lives — a fear that certain women now brandish *against* feminism, which they accuse of causing an increase in male violence.

40 See Sullerot (1978) and critique by de Lesseps (1981).

Chapter 6

Natural Fertility, Forced Reproduction[1]

Paola Tabet[2]

One thing I have learned in a long life: that all our science, measured against reality is primitive and childlike — and yet it is the most precious thing we have (Albert Einstein).[3]

Besides, domination is denied; there is no slavery of women, there is difference. To which I will answer with this statement made by a Roumanian peasant at a public meeting in 1848: 'Why do the gentlemen say it was not slavery, for we know it to have been slavery, this sorrow that we have sorrowed.' Yes, we know it, and this science of oppression cannot be taken away from us (Monique Wittig, 1992, p. 31).

Human reproduction and women's fertility are often called upon in anthropology to explain, even to justify, the subordination of women and inequalities between the sexes. The way in which they are used is both simple and significant. In the end, women's subordinate position is supposed to be due to the 'natural, biological constraints' weighing them down, i.e. to their 'role' in procreation; and anthropological literature also commonly speaks of women's reproductive 'function' as if it were an obvious and given fact, unchanged across space and time for thousands of years.

Such a fixed and aproblematic presentation of reproduction (which one so often finds in accounts of relations between men and women), the scant theoretical interest anthropology has given to concepts that might help us think about procreation, the place assigned to field data on it (e.g. generally such catch-all descriptions as the 'life-cycle', whose bits and pieces of unsystematic documentation recall older works of folklore), all combine to make procreation simply appear as a biological event — an event we could say somehow outside of social relations. Society does get involved with it, but, it would seem, almost a posteriori, when it reintegrates these natural and seemingly spontaneous events into the social by means of rituals. By referring reproduction to nature, anthropological thought can, on the one hand, base masculine domination in nature, in a more or less complex and sophisticated way; and, on the other, succeed in obscuring effectively the historical and social character of relations of reproduction.

My purpose here is to examine reproduction as a fundamental ground of social sex relations.

One possible way to do this would be to analyse data on the control of the reproductive body and on the agents intervening at different stages in the *sequence or process of reproduction: from the social organisation of coitus and pregnancy, etc., up to the weaning of the child*, since each point in the reproductive sequence is a possible location for decision-making, control and conflict. Such an approach would require systematic and detailed documentation, covering, for many societies, the various stages of the reproductive sequence and the variables that govern its organisation. We could then test the hypothesis that these variables are related to the form of social organisation, the sexual division of labour, the systems of representation, and the forms of relations between the sexes in general. Unfortunately, the available qualitative and quantitative information on reproduction is far from satisfactory.[4]

The state of documentation therefore leads us to question the theoretical field from which and as a function of which the object of research has been constituted and the body of field data elaborated. What concepts are available in anthropology to analyse reproduction? First of all, we have a set of concepts concerning fertility and reproduction that have been fairly well elaborated in demography, but that can be found, in elementary and often less explicit forms, throughout the human sciences.

Demography theory opposes two ideas:[5]

— First, *natural fertility*, which according to current definitions this is that of a couple (or a woman) who practise(s) neither contraception nor abortion, i.e. fertility where no conscious effort is made to space births or to limit their number (see, Léridon, 1973, 1977, Pressat, 1979). In other words, any behaviour not explicitly aimed at restraining fertility is classed as 'natural': as part of the natural conditions of fertility.

— Second, *controlled fertility*, where there is interference on births, or, more specifically, where there is intervention to limit births.

Indeed, so far as reproduction and more specifically fertility is concerned, it should be stressed that the notion of 'control' is generally used only in the sense of *limitation*.[6] Thus, the various forms of intervention on the body are given differential theoretical treatment: it is not assumed in fact that *any intervention*, both that which *limits* reproduction, *and* that which *enforces* it, is the object (is an act) of social management. Current ideas, be they common-sense or academic, choose and privilege certain effects of social relations, and define them, and them alone, as social elements.

This use of the idea of control is not only unilateral and limited. Rather, the dichotomy between 'natural' and 'controlled' (managed) fertility is in fact an ideological product. What we have here is the construction, side by side with current indigenous and popular ideologies, of an academic ideology, which subtly allows power relations — basically here the relationship between the sexes — to be removed from the analysis of reproduction. It separates men from reproduction, and makes fertility an issue of women alone, a property of women, or even indeed a property of women's age.[7] We therefore need to envisage a broader model of the social management of reproduction.

There are some anthropological approaches which might serve our purposes, i.e. theories that link the exchange of women — described by Godelier (1977) as the 'irreplacable producers and means of biological reproduction of the group' — to the control of their reproductive power. But here again we are usually confronted with two distinct sets. In one set, that of nature, there are women with their 'periodic pregnancies', as Godelier puts it (1976, p. 31), where pregnancies seem to be of the same order as menstrual cycles or rain or the seasons. In the other set, that of the social, we find men exchanging these women — the women themselves and their perpetual, sorry, periodic, and even 'handicapping' reproductive capacity — in order to produce alliances and co-operation, culture and society.

This opposition can be found in many authors, maybe nuanced but with little variation even when their theoretical orientations differ. So far as pro-creation is concerned, the exchange of women and 'control of their fertility' seems to be simply a *distribution of women and of their spontaneous products*. Men at the very most intervene to try to limit this overwhelming production, if women themselves do not. Take for example this description by Héritier of the exchange and appropriation of women:

> Women are fertile, inventive, and create life, but men bring order, regulation and political control. This is made possible by the handicap which parallels fecundity: pregnant or nursing women are less mobile than men (Héritier, 1979b, p. 809).

At first sight it might seem that the exchange of women and their fertility is not compatible with the idea of a simple (if weighty) 'natural constraint'. Might there not, in fact, be a link between this biological domain, so procreative and feminine and this social one, so organised and masculine? Alas, writers apparently have felt no need to mention this link. The gap between the two domains is not generally filled in. The 'natural' is astonishingly resistant when it comes to women.[8]

There seems in fact to be a slippage, which is also apparent in the words currently used, between the *capacity* and the *act* of procreation. Instead of the latter being the result of a process which obviously needs two sexes, it has become the essence, the very nature, of women. Not only eggs but also children are produced by women alone, so that the 'exchange of fertile women' seems like an exchange of laying chickens. But this is not an innocent slippage. The gap, the chasm, between the production of eggs (and sperm) and the production of children is not a neutral terrain. There are potential conflicts and contradictions located here, and it is here that the reality of the relations between the sexes (the social organisation of sexuality) is played out. This includes, of course, exchange of women, their appropriation and domination.

However, authors usually resort to generalities when it comes to the actual and direct elements of the management of reproduction.[9]

Thus we have, on the one hand, demographic concepts that tend to remove men from reproduction; which get used (often in over-simplified forms) far beyond the domain of demography. Demographers admit a minimal social treatment of reproduction, in the shape of control, but they think of this control only as restriction of fertility. Anthropological theories, on the other hand, despite their importance, despite the quantity of material they handle, and despite their references to the concepts of appropriation and subordination of women (which have become more and more frequent since the resurgence of feminism), leave a sort of no man's land, an unthought area, between kinship, marriage, the exchange of women, and reproduction: the area of the social exercise of sexuality.[10] There seems no way out.

The object of this article is precisely to locate and analyse some of the mechanisms through which the control and appropriation of women get transformed demographically into reproduction. Thanks to these mechanisms, we move from a simple biological capacity, to an imposed, even, one could say, a forced reproduction.

I propose to reverse the usual concept of 'control of reproduction', so that limitation becomes one particular form of control, and systems of descent one of its elements. I shall argue that human reproduction is entirely social and totally integrated into social and gender relations.

The mechanisms I shall try to clarify *rest on the specific biological organisation of the human species*, and *manipulate it in various ways*.

I shall look at the social manipulations of reproduction on a rising scale of interventions: manipulations by which the imposition of reproduction is established. I shall try to organise the information about forms of control of reproduction along a line of ever more thorough manipulation. Starting from situations of general and socially organised imposition, which may be more or less violent, I shall move to more complex forms of intervention in biology. These (1) empirically *use* biological givens, (2) *manipulate* biological givens, and (3) *transform* the biological givens themselves.

This rising scale of intervention should not be thought to imply a historical evolution, passing from simpler to more complex forms. None of these forms excludes the others. Rather what I am attempting to produce is an *analytic exposition of mechanisms*. And, it must be stressed, certain of these forms of intervention are not universal. Far from it. They may even be specific to certain societies. This is in fact one of the problems facing us. We need systematic research on the forms of social intervention in sexuality, and how these are linked to the socio-economic organisation of the societies involved, the forms of gender relations, and the oppression or the autonomy of women.

Anthropological evidence will be used to *illustrate* the mechanisms, to make them explicit, rather than as demonstration. This implies that something may be absent in other populations, or have completely different characteristics elsewhere, from those I describe here. I shall also not attempt to evaluate the importance of given phenomena nor how widespread they may be, either geographically or in relation to different types of society.

Finally, I shall examine the implications of the proposed analysis for the status of procreative activity. Reproduction is subject to social processing at all its stages. This processing or control takes the general form of a constraint to reproduce, exercised by men over women. The social character of reproductive activity requires that we question its status as an activity and its classification among human activities. Is it work? Can we apply to reproduction ideas of alienated work, exploitation, and appropriation-expropriation of the product?

Interventions into the Capacity to Reproduce

Generalised Intervention:the Social Organisation of Exposure to the Risk of Pregnancy

In a country where there are few illegitimate births, the beginning of the period of exposure to the risk of conception is marked by marriage (Léridon, 1977, p. 17).

Nubility is the average age at initiation of the capacity for conception (Hassan, 1981, p. 128).

Reproduction, obviously, is consequent upon sexual intercourse. Demographers, however, have largely ignored this subject, and anthropologists have seldom given it quantitative treatment (Polgar, 1972, p. 204).

When we consider the ways in which reproduction is controlled, we are confronted by forms of constraint of varying degrees of violence. At the most explicit and obvious maximum, these verge on women being directly used as reproductive livestock, as was often the case with slaves on American plantations or women in the Nazi *Lebensborn* experimentation (Hillel, 1975; Thalmann, 1982).

Beyond these well-known cases, whose status in relation to other forms of reproductive manipulation will be considered later, there is a more generalised constraint to reproduce. This is obtained by a complex series of social, physical or ideological pressures, covering the entire reproductive sequence. The most important will be considered here.

Directly related to the tendency, noted above, to pose fertility as a property of women, very little attention has been paid to the means by which it is socially assured that women will be regularly, or even maximally, exposed to risk of pregnancy.

To situate this question correctly, we need briefly to mention certain biological facts about human reproduction. The human species is *relatively infertile*. For example, while a single artificial insemination of a cow has a 75 per cent probability of being effective, for women one must calculate three to four cycles with three artificial inseminations in each (during the fertile period of course). For humans, the probability of conceiving with a single coitus is therefore limited: statistically, one act of coitus is not sufficient to produce a pregnancy.[11] Potter and Tietze's calculations give 'a minimal probability [of conception for a given menstrual cycle] of 28 per cent with a coital frequency of 6 per cycle, and a maximal probability of 45 per cent with a frequency of 12 per cycle' (see Short, 1978, p. 198). (This assumes the length of the fertile period is 72 hours, which actually seems too high, see below.) On the basis of the results of recent research and studies of historical demography, Léridon has estimated the average probability of conception per month (the 'fecundability') of a married woman of (around) 25 years at about 25 per cent (Léridon, 1973, pp. 37, 40 ff and 80).

To this relative infertility of the human species must be added the specific characteristics of sexuality among human females. First, women's sexual drive is not tied to procreation by a regulating hormonal compulsion. In other words, *there is no synchronisation of the moment of ovulation* (hence, of fertility) and *sexual drive*. Sexual drive is intermittent and not cyclical or seasonal (unlike other mammals). Second, the fertile period is not signalled (there is no external manifestation), nor is it indicated by a particularly intense sexual drive.

Hence the difficulty — unlike other mammals — of determining the moment when conception is possible; or, as is said, when the female (woman) is 'fecundable' (can be impregnated).[12] This difficulty in determining the moment when conception is possible is further accentuated by the marked variability of the ovulatory cycle. This involves:

   (i) the (average) duration of the cycle from one woman to another (which can vary from 10 to 45 days);
   (ii) the length of successive cycles for the same woman;
   (iii) the location of the day of ovulation within the cycle; and
   (iv) the age of the woman (Léridon, 1973, p. 15).

In addition, a large proportion of cycles are anovular. In other words, the ovulatory cycle varies to such an extent that, even in a cycle defined as 'normal' (i.e. with a duration of 26–30 days), 'ovulation can occur between the 10th and the 18th day of the cycle: *the zone of uncertainty therefore covers 25 per cent of the cycle*' (Léridon, 1973, p. 15, stress added).

Conception 'results from the combination of a "calender" of the cycle and a "calendar" of sexual relations' (Léridon, 1973, p. 40). But without a sexual drive leading women to copulate when conception is possible, and without a precise knowledge of the fertile period, the maximum coverage of the possibility of conception can only be assured by *regular and frequent exposure to coitus*.[13]

This frequency and regularity seems precisely to be best and most often assured in human societies by marriage. Marriage thus appears as the social response to the specific characteristics of women's sexuality: to the inter-mittent character of female sexual drive and to its not being necessarily tied to reproduction. If women are not *biologically constrained* to reproduce, how can reproduction be assured? Beach notes that it is not correct to describe women as always 'receptive' (though many do). Rather, he says, they are 'always copulable' (Beach, 1974). (Note the implicit or unconscious theorisat-ion of rape.) And marriage does seem to be the basic agent that transforms 'not always receptive' into 'always copulable'. Marriage is therefore not only an institution that creates kinship through the exchange of women, which ties men and women together in a division of labour, which legitimates children and gives them a social mother and a social father, and which controls the destination (allocation) of children. It is primarily, for our present purposes, the institution which seems to guarantee the greatest chances of fertility. Through marriage, generally speaking, *permanent exposure to coitus, hence permanent exposure to the risk of pregnancy,* is assured.

Statistical data seem to confirm this role for marriage. In Martinique, for instance, legitimate fertility in marriage is 7.9 children per woman, while the mean number of children per woman is 5.4 (Léridon, 1971, and Léridon, Zucker and Cazenave, 1970. See also Nag (1971) for a similar situation in Barbados).

Demographers attribute this 'low' fertility (which Léridon calls 'apparent subfertility') to 'marital customs'. The instability of marriage or the presence of free unions seem to play an important role in this apparent subfertility. Think of the many societies studied by anthropologists where couples can separate easily and women may spend considerable periods outside marriage — periods which provide, among other things, the possibility of a lack of regular exposure to the risk of pregnancy (see Howell, 1979); and think also of the presence of free unions, concubinage and sexual friendships, which occupy years of women's lives (as in the case of the Antillais, see Léridon, 1971) and which most probably do not carry the same regularity and frequence of coitus as marriage.

Society may nonetheless try to 'remedy' such 'inconvenient' non-exposure to impregnation of some women. For instance, among the Diola there is:

> the practice of *budji*, or *bayankatetin* [which] periodically required all the widowed or divorced women to choose a husband in the village (whether for a few nights, a few months or longer) so that their wombs should not stay on holiday for too long (Journet in Echard *et al.*, 1981, p. 384, and in Mathieu (ed.), 1985, p. 25).

On the other hand, regular exposure to the possibility of impregnation (to risk of pregnancy) means that in some populations of so-called natural fertility, women — being incessantly overtaken by a cycle of pregnancy-lactation-and-new-pregnancy — have no menstrual periods from the time of their first pregnancy up to their menopause. These include the famous Hutterites, the measure and favourite example of demographers, a model society constantly used to theorise about natural fertility:

> The Hutterites are useful as a standard of comparison for fertility achieved by other populations — a calibrated yardstick — against which to measure the ways in which other populations fail to achieve maximal levels of fertility (Howell, 1979, p. 154).

In this North American, Anabaptist, sectarian population, women who spend all (or almost all) their reproductive life married, have a mean of twelve children (Eaton and Mayer, 1954; Sheps, 1965). This is very close to the maximum biologically possible.[14]

Such a reduction of women to reproductive machines does not produce the same quantitative results everywhere, but the mechanism is the same. Thus, among the Manus converted to Christianity, 'that woman who never menstruates because she is always either pregnant or breast-feeding a child is regarded as most patriotic and virtuous' (Mead, 1956, p. 328).

We must therefore ask how such perpetual child-bearing is achieved. Is regular exposure to the risk of pregnancy (the fact that women are permanently exposed to it) just a feature of marriage in itself, a 'natural' fact, present everywhere in the same manner? This means assuming marriage is (from the point of view of reproduction) nothing more than the optimal place for the *spontaneous* realisation of sexual drives. Or, at most, the place assigned to the *natural* and symmetrical desire of the two people involved; where desire could manifest itself, albeit with some compromises, in the place destined to lodge it. Maybe a little corner of paradise, where you might suppose each partner realises his or her sexual drive with reciprocal equality to choose the forms of expression, timing, etc.? As if men's domination over women did not exist, and as if one could imagine sexuality and marriage to be hallowed ground, where power relations were off-limits?[15]

The anthropological and historical record shows clearly, however, that this is not the case. Consider, on the one hand, not only the many societies in which marriage is (or was) a relationship imposed on one or both partners, but also the forms of training (not to say 'breaking in'[16] and use of force) around sexuality; and, on the other, the huge variation that exists in the regulation of relations between men and women in marriage (including, among other things, the presence or absence of rules requiring the execution of 'conjugal duty'), and hence women's different margins of autonomy to manage their body, sexuality and reproduction (the management of sexual relations, contraceptive practices, abortions, etc.).

In fact, if marriage represents the potentially optimal place for women's permanent exposure to impregnation, this can be effected only by a complex (and variable) apparatus of ideological pressures and physical and psychological coercion. What interests us, therefore, are the means used to allow marriage to actualise its function as a reproductive institution — the means which assure the appropriation of women's bodies for reproductive purposes. I shall separate out specific 'moments': 'apprenticeship' or training for coitus; physical and psychological constraints to conjugal duty; and, finally, surveillance of conception, pregnancy and childbirth. But it should be stressed there is no break between these moments, and that the training of women aims at both the collective submission of women to men and the submission of each woman to a particular man in a marital relationship.

Training for coitus; let us pause here a moment. I want to make it quite clear that I am not suggesting that women do not experience desire, nor that they have less strong sexual impulses than men, nor that their desire is addressed towards men only because of coercion. What is at issue is a quite different question. It is, on the one hand, how women's sexual impulses are channelled, by socialisation, towards one single type of sexuality, that of coitus (see below); and, on the other, the ways in which they are coerced into it, even when they feel no desire, once again by psychological and physical means. Acts of power which thus have nothing to do with sexuality.

I do not intend in any way to examine the forms of women's (or men's) sexuality. What is at stake is rather the political relationship between the sexes; the question being whether one can, or cannot, constrain the other, and expropriate the very person of the other: whether 'sexuality . . . for women [is not] an individual and subjective expression, but a social institution of violence' (Wittig, 1992, p. 19).

This means abandoning any explicit or implicit conception of coitus as self-evidently consisting of penetration and ejaculation, and as something that happens 'naturally' in human societies: and instead paying systematic attention to the forms by which sexuality is conditioned and/or limited to this exclusively genital and reproductive form. I shall return to this point later.

Coital 'apprenticeship'

I shall not dwell on the ways in which girls are socialised to accept coitus, and particularly coitus when their husbands demand it. Such rules are the subject of both general and informal education as well as direct and formal lessons, for example, during initiation rites and marriage, etc. (see, Richards, 1956; Wilson, 1957, 1977). This is well known, too, for Western societies, both ancient and modern (Flandrin, 1976, 1981). Along the same lines are ideologies that define women as made for procreation; maternity as women's true function and, in contrast, sterility as abominable; or the vagina as the only, or true, wealth of women (see, for example, Echard *et al.*, 1981; Schneider, 1955).[17] All these forms of psychic pressure are well-known and widespread enough for it not to be necessary to labour the point. But we should also consider — as necessary training for the acceptance of conjugal sexual relations and reproduction — the many and diverse forms of institutional apprenticeship to sexual relations (see below).

Even so, psychic training would not be sufficient to obtain the general submission of women. The threat of violence and use of force complete the conditioning. Using various degrees of constraint and violence, men take it upon themselves to compel to conform those who do try to escape the rules at any time. This can be seen, for instance, in the widespread forms of rape, or barely disguised rape, such as the practice of *moetotolo* in Samoa, and *motoro* in Mangaia, or worse still the collective rape used in Mangaia to make 'haughty' girls submit to boys — all of which occur, let us note, in what are thought of as the paradise zones of sexuality (see Mead, 1975; Freeman, 1983; Marshall, 1971, and on Polynesian sexuality generally, Ortner, 1981).[18]

For it is indeed by 'shock treatments' (Roheim, 1933) that they 'break down [our] resistance' (Berndt, 1962, p. 170); treatments and procedures 'explicitly aimed at domesticating the recalcitrant spirit' (Williams, 1969, p. 163) of women in many societies.[19] Collective rape in some New Guinea societies, for instance, is 'designed to give [a girl] a liking for intercourse, to break down any resistance on her part and to make her feel at home' (*sic*), according to one author (Berndt, 1962) who provides a detailed description of the treatment.[20] Rape is also used against all forms of women's insubordination (see Murphy and Murphy, 1974), and the threat of rape looms overhead to forestall resistance. This also applies to initiations based on sexual mutilation of girls, as with Australian rites where a girl is forcibly carried away by a group of men, deflowered with a stone knife, and then submitted to copulation by several men, in order to make her 'quiet' once and for all (Roheim, 1933, pp. 234–6; also Spencer and Gillen, 1927; Roth, 1897).[21]

Individual, socially codified, violence, like rape, is also widespread in nuptial ceremonies, such as those of the Tikopia, Gusii and Hima (see Firth, 1963; LeVine, 1959; and Elam, 1973), and, with more or less variation, those of many other societies. The procedures are multiple. For instance, Spencer describes in detail a Samburu marriage, that of Nirorol, a girl about 16 years old, with Darapul, aged around 50 years.

> within less than 48 hours [the girl's] relation with her lover was completely broken, she was circumcised... subjected to a long and exhausting harangue by the elders, made to leave her mother's hut to which she had been attached all her life, in a slow procession, which after her circumcision looked both painful and exhausting, and from that moment onwards she had to associate closely with unknown men, who as elders she had been taught all her life to avoid (Spencer, 1965, p. 248).

In fact, a Samburu girl is already terrorised before being handed over to her husband (who is generally 10–40 years older). In the case above, Nirorol quickly realises everything is in the hands of the elders and that

> her only way of retaining a place in society and even of surviving at all is to accept her change in status and transfer to a new social group as inevitable (Spencer, 1965, p. 248).[22]

Whether these treatments are preparatory to coitus and/or marriage, as in the Aranda rites and in the other forms of sexual mutilation; whether they are carried out by individual agents but socially sanctioned or directly collective (carried out by men as a group); and whether they occur during the marriage ceremony or as a punishment for women whose preceding training has somehow failed, is not the point here. (There are many forms whose socio-cultural context could be analysed.) So far as we are concerned, they are all variations on the same model and pursue the same goal: the deadly taming of women to make them 'tool-bodies' for reproduction.

Forced conjugal duty

Not all societies use such methods to 'develop the sexuality' of women. But submission (subjection) to a husband's sexual will is obtained in innumerable populations, not only by psychic pressure and economic and affective blackmail, but also by blows. This is considered perfectly legitimate — the right of a husband. The severity of beating is quite variable, but the husband's right can receive social support, at least from men (in diverse ways according to the society), even in instances of torture. Thus, in a case presented by Berndt, a woman, inherited by the brother of her deceased husband, refused to have coitus with him, and, after several attempts, he surprised her when she was asleep:

> 'he parted her skirt and taking a piece of bark from the fire, put it into her vagina.' She awoke and the man 'then pulled out the bark and copulated with her.' Hearing the woman's cries, some men rushed up. 'Some of the men were very angry with him and asked why he had burnt her. He replied that he wanted to have coitus with her, but she did not care for him. "So I burnt her vagina. Leave it, there is no need to fight. If she dies, you may cook and eat her." The others then turned on Nigibi and scolded her: "Have you no hole? Why are you afraid of Jonao? You're not a little girl!"' (Berndt, 1962, p. 141).

More 'moderate' Mangaian men consider that marriage 'gives you the right to copulate with your wife any time that you want', but since women are in any case less interested in coitus than men, this may mean having to 'beat the wife into submission'. 'When husbands wish to copulate they must keep after the wife until she gives in even if this requires beating her' (Marshall, 1971, pp. 142 and 124).[23] Among the Kgatla, many women bitterly told the anthropologist that their husbands imposed intercourse on them however tired they were, and 'if they refused or resisted, they were usually beaten into submission'. As a young wife told the anthropologist, 'if she had known what was before her, she would rather have remained single, for then she could at least have chosen her own times for sexual intercourse' (Schapera, 1971, p. 162). The threat of blows looms large in the life of !Kung women (Shostak, 1983, pp. 150ff, pp. 311ff and *passim*) and of Buka women (Blackwood, 1935, p. 105). Among the Baruya, refusal to make love with a husband, like all other forms of insubordination and resistance by women, is met with repression: with psychic and physical violence (blows and wounds) from men, in this case directly exercised by the husband himself (Godelier, 1982). These few examples illustrate a phenomenon so widespread that any attempt to provide adequate documentation is likely to fail. The blows can lead to murder, which from time to time is noted in the anthropological literature (Wilson, 1977, p. 128; Shostak, 1983, p. 311).

Violence and blows are also among the means used against women who want to leave their husbands. A Guidar girl who has an *oudaha* (primary) marriage, 'has "a dowry on her back" until she gives birth to a child. She can be compelled to stay by force until then' (Collard, 1981, p. 9). If she escapes before this happens, the father will search for her and chain her up

> on his plot of land and put pieces of broken pottery onto her temples, attaching them firmly so they cause her pain and break her obstinacy. He also deprives her of water and food for some time (Collard, 1979, p. 62).

Nor should one think this is a description of an individual unfortunate case. The anthropologist is quite clear about this:

> Almost all our women informants of mature age had been subject to this mistreatment, which was still sanctioned in 1971 by all the older fathers of family (ibid).

Keeping women married is the sure way to get maximum fertility from them, as Chagnon also seems to show for the Yanomano.[24] On the other hand, the best way for husbands to keep wives, is often to get them pregnant as early and as often as possible (Collard, 1979, p. 63; and for the Rukuba, see Muller, 1981, p. 13). As they say in Virginia (USA), 'keep 'em barefoot and pregnant', and in the south of Italy, 'To keep a woman at home, hide her shoes and get her pregnant.' The same model of immobilisation by repeated pregnancies was also found in the Tuscan countryside (Arezzo). The programme announced and carried out at the beginning of this century by the grandfather of one of my students (personal communication) was 'Un anno poccia, un anno trippa, cosi è bell'e sistemata' ('One year breast, one year belly, will keep her cornered'). He had 'given' his wife 12 children, at regular two yearly intervals, until her death at 43 years of age in the epidemic of Spanish flu of 1917, after about 24 years of forced reproduction. So, immobilise women to make them breed, and impregnate them to immobilise them.

Surveillance of conception, pregnancy and childbirth
Once conditions for women's regular or maximal exposure to the risk of pregnancy are guaranteed, and their submission to coitus (their 'copulability')

obtained, other measures are still needed to assure the success of the act of impregnation. Women have to be watched to make sure they do not try to defend themselves and escape its possible consequences. First of all, the use of techniques and means of contraception must be prevented or limited (or indeed knowledge about them withheld, as we know from our own recent and past experience in the West, see Himes, 1963); once a pregnancy has begun, recourse to techniques of abortion must be prevented; and finally there must be surveillance to prevent women eventually freeing themselves of a child by infanticide.

It should be stressed here that there are enormous differences between societies, as is well known, and probably between types of societies. Some, notably, though not exclusively, hunting and gathering societies, allow women a certain (even considerable) control of abortion and infanticide as well as contraception (Devereux, 1976; Himes, 1963). I shall not dwell on this management by women, which has already been focused upon by other researchers (Cowlishaw, 1978, 1981; Hayden, 1972; Leacock, 1978). I want to stress, however, that the weak demographic growth of hunter-gatherer societies in prehistory is attributed largely to such techniques; and that it is to the so-called 'slackening' of such forms of 'control' (would this mean that 'women are obliged to keep (all) the products of (all) pregnancies'?) that the population growth of the Neolithic is largely attributed (Hassan, 1981).[25]

Though the anthropological literature documents some sanctions on abortion, and hostility towards contraceptive practices, it is rare for these sanctions to be seen as one of the elements of a *continuing* surveillance of wives: of their menstrual periods (see, for example, Echard, 1985, pp. 41–2) and their pregnancies. The methods of surveillance exercised on the wives of the king of the Ganda, as in other analogous situations (see Hrdy, 1981), are extreme instances that usefully magnify a phenomenon which, in its common forms and modalities, may remain, if not unnoticed, then insufficiently remarked.

The king's wives were subject to periodic inspection by his maternal aunts, who acted as royal midwives. When they noticed one of the wives was pregnant, she was conducted to the house of the Nabikande, the chief midwife, according to a ritualised procedure. There she was not only guarded by the Nabikande, but also strictly watched by a maid, 'whose duty it was to wait upon her and to see that she took her medicine, and did nothing that would be likely to injure her baby' and who 'was not allowed to go away or to leave the woman for more than a few moments, by day or by night, until the child was born'. Her behaviour, and that of the other servants in charge of the pregnant wife, 'was like that of a prisoner's maid, because the condition of their mistress was termed "Being a prisoner"' (Roscoe, 1911, pp. 50–1).

Surveillance on behalf of the husband's patrilineage, 'because it was the patrilineage especially which was concerned about the pregnancy', was also exercised on other Ganda women. Some of the husband's elderly relatives would move in with the wife to watch her until the child's birth, or else the wife herself was transferred to live with one of them.

The birth was a moment of heightened control:

> if a woman disliked her husband or if she had any quarrel with him, it might happen that she would try to kill the child during the time of delivery either by crushing it, or by sitting on it. The midwives, at such times, threatened the woman, and went so far as to whip her if she did not remain in the best position for the delivery (Roscoe, 1911, p. 54).

Birth is usually a 'charged' moment, partly because of the dramatic risks for mother and child, but partly also from the point of view of control over women and procreation. Whether or not there is surveillance is an important difference between societies. Who the specific agents of surveillance are, for example, whether the women present are from the husband's or wife's kin, may indicate different conditions of control or management. The same pertains to the liberty of women in a menstrual shelter or separate birthing place. Even if it is linked to representations of women as polluting, isolation does provide some space for female management — sometimes minimal and contradictory, suspect and restricted — but a margin of control all the same. (On Baruya women's management of childbirth and their supposed or real infanticides, see Godelier, 1982, pp. 223 and 235).[26]

But this margin may be almost totally absent. Chagga women are excised at puberty:

> The girl has her ornaments removed and is laid on the ground, the old women crowding around, and some holding her down. The operator, a woman renowned for her skill, cuts away the labia majora and clitoris with a special knife. She begins on the inside of these parts and in the end holds a ring of bloody flesh in her hand. The wound is treated with herbs to stop bleeding and cause speedy cicatrization (Raum, 1940, pp. 306–7).

This form of excision makes childbirth dangerous and extremely painful, especially the expulsion phase, which can be prolonged, producing physical injury to the mother and child and a high perinatal mortality. A successful birth and the courage of the mother are saluted by cries of victory — the *kyulilili* used by women to celebrate a hunt or raid, women's courage being exalted like that of warriors (Raum, 1940, pp. 81 and 85). The birth is attended by the mother of the husband, while the husband listens outside. A woman in labour 'is responsible for the life of the child, because her unruliness during labour could cause its death'. Incidents during labour are in fact attributed to a lack of control by the mother. She is told that if she cries during the birth, her husband will hate her, and if her child dies he could divorce her. A man can groan when he is in pain, but a woman must not yell or cry during childbirth.

She may only make a *ngrk* like a ewe when its throat is cut. This is what girls are taught about good behaviour during labour:

> But you should know the womanly way, my granddaughter. We are
> sheep. . . . My granddaughter, even though you suffer such severe pain
> as to make you think that you are dying, control yourself and go *ngkr*
> like the sheep. A sheep doesn't scream when the knife is being stuck
> in. It only goes *ngkr* until it dies (Gutmann, 1932, p. 217, HRAF
> translation, p. 123).[27]

Clearly a great distance separates these forms where women are completely dispossessed of the very experience of childbirth (Rich, 1976), from modalities where the woman is alone, aided by at most another woman, as in many nomad societies (see Shostak, 1983 for childbirth among the !Kung), or surrounded by a group (see the detailed account of a birth in Pukapuka in Beaglehole and Beaglehole, 1938, or for the Buka, Blackwood, 1935). Variation in the autonomy of women, and their possibilities for managing this moment in the reproductive sequence — as well as other moments — is enormous.[28]

To go further, however, we need precise and systematic analyses of the relationship between what is demographically necessary for various social formations, different modes of production, and the forms of social control of sexuality and reproduction — and such work still largely remains to be done.

> What has to investigated . . . are the conditions under which women
> are forced, or socially programmed to accept, the role of intensive
> breeders, and the conditions under which some women become
> 'surplus', either segregated into productive undertaking and not
> allowed to reproduce, or killed at or near birth (Edholm, Harris and
> Young, 1977, p. 114).[29]

Such analyses will allow us, amongst other things, to address a problem of great interest: to what extent is the imposition of reproduction (with its variable apparatus and instruments of control) indissociable from, and structural to, marriage?

Specific Interventions into the Capacity to Reproduce

Determining the fertile period

> Knowledge of the female menstrual cycle is of major importance,
> because it is known that an ovum can only be fertilized during a very
> short period of time, estimated by different authors at between 48 and
> 24 hours (Léridon, 1973, p. 14).

One of the main problems in technically controlling human reproduction is, obviously, precisely knowing women's fertile period. We need only look at the amount of reflection devoted to this in societies past and present. First, it is not foreseeable (except with modern techniques, such as those based on examining a temperature chart, but then only on condition that the cycle 'is not too irregular', see Léridon, 1973, p. 15) and we have already seen how 'the zone of uncertainty may cover 25 per cent of the cycle', given the marked variability of the ovulatory cycle. Second, its length is uncertain. Even recent research leaves an important margin of imprecision (even indetermination). As to the exact number of hours when a woman can be fertilised, estimates have varied from 12 to 48 or even 72 hours, i.e. from a half to three days! (Léridon, 1973 and 1977; Bourgeois-Pichat, 1965). (Precision is however possible with laboratory analyses — such as are used, for instance, in artificial insemination and *in vitro* fertilisation.)

The interest of the issue (of exactly determining the fertile period) is undeniable. It would make it possible to regulate coital activity according to whether or not fertilisation was desired; hence, *a more economical and precise technical management of reproduction*. Instead of a system of generic coverage of all the possibilities for fertilisation, such as we have seen above, there could be directed interventions, either to fertilise or to abstain so as to achieve the opposite effect.

This topic features in many societies' representations, with the fertile period usually located around the time of the menstrual period, or during the period itself — just as it was also in western medicine (and popular thinking) for a long time. Masai girls, for instance, have, or should have, sexual relations with warriors during the time before they get married, but they should not get pregnant. They are therefore recommended to avoid intra-vaginal sexual relations during the four to six days following their periods (see Merker, 1910; Leakey, 1930). Akamba girls, on the other hand, avoid the days of their period so as not to conceive, but married people 'always cohabit during the wife's period' (Lindblom, 1969, p. 40).

What often is at issue is acquiring an understanding of individual menstrual cycles, so as to be able to fertilise a woman at a chosen moment. Thus, among the Chagga, during the part of the initiation concerned with education for married life, young men are taught how to determine empirically (it could be said, experimentally) the time in the cycle when conception is most likely. If the elder giving the lessons judges a young husband worthy, he will receive

> precise directions to determine the day on which the particular woman can conceive. He is told to experiment during the course of the months, until conception occurs, beginning with the first day of menstruation and continuing, if necessary to the last. He is to remember the proper day during the cycle carefully, and to adjust to it as soon as they want a new conception. Then he must stick to it. This

conduct is called: *ititsya nweri*: testing the month (Gutmann, 1932, pp. 38ff., HRAF translation, pp. 24–5; and see also Raum, 1940).

I want to stress the considerable technical competence as regards reproduction in general, the stages of formation of the foetus, and the anatomy of the genital organs, which many pastoral populations have acquired (for example, the Masai and Chagga, etc.) — probably through cattle breeding. A striking example is the Zulu technique of 'closing women's wombs' by inserting little pebbles into the uterus — a technique also used with female camels — when major changes of location were about to take place (Kitzinger, 1978). This contraceptive method in some ways prefigures modern intrauterine devices (IUDs). Alongside this competence there was a problematic and practice of reproduction management, of strict demographic regulation-manipulation of the human group, directly tied to that of the herd. A review of the anatomical/reproductive technical knowledge and the representations of reproduction in pastoral groups would be interesting.

Breaking the sequence of reproduction
The choice of the fertile period is thus a *simple form of technical management* of reproduction. Research on and knowledge of the fertile period just uses certain biological characteristics of the reproductive process in a less uncertain way. There is, however, another form of *manipulation* where one *intervenes directly* in the reproductive process: by interrupting it. By the reproductive process, I mean the whole sequence from coitus to the weaning of a child, at the moment the child is able to survive. (The timing varies from one society to another in relation to the possibility of other food substituting for maternal milk and the existing hygiene and medical conditions.) In this process, nourishment of the foetus, first assured by the placenta, is transferred to the breast, and some even speak of an *'extero-gestate foetus'*: a foetus part of whose gestation is accomplished outside the uterus (Harrell, 1981; Jelliffe and Jelliffe, 1978).

The process is *biologically complete* when a child can do without its mother's milk. From the biological point of view, it is therefore *a process that constitutes a unity*, even if it is made up of different stages. A new cycle does not begin, in principle, until the preceding one has been completed. This biological organisation of reproduction, common to all mammals, is linked to the fact that there is a certain degree of protection against risk of a new conception (which could be deadly for the already-born child): i.e. there is a more or less lengthy period amenorrhoea and without ovulation. The biological mechanism inhibiting ovulation, its efficacy and length are still under debate. Different interpretations have been proposed about the relative importance of such elements as the intensity and frequency of suckling (lactation itself releasing hormones), the woman's weight, etc. (see Cohen, 1980; Frisch and McArthur, 1974; Harrell, 1981; Hassan, 1980; and Howell 1979). However, the process itself is well attested, and breast-feeding is used, with more or less success, as a means of contraception in peasant societies.

But it is known that interrupting breast-feeding, whether by premature weaning or the death of the infant, ends the anovular period, and the woman can then conceive again after a fairly short delay. Demographers have calculated the difference in the intergenetic interval according to whether the preceding child survives or dies, and it is quite striking. For instance, a longitudinal enquiry carried out in Senegal to study the correlation between fecundity, infant mortality and breast-feeding, found that the interval between births increased by '12 months on average when the age at death [of the preceding child] went from less than three months to over eighteen months' (Cantrelle and Léridon, 1971; and see Léridon, 1973, p. 86ff.).

I shall discuss here two quite different instances of direct intervention in the reproductive sequence, both based on this same biological mechanism: (1) selective infanticide of girls among the Eskimos; and (2) wet nursing in fifteenth-century Florence.

(1)   Eskimo infanticide

> Infanticide has many social implications. It is labelled often as a population control device, and I hope to show that this label is unsuitable (Cowlishaw, 1978, p. 262).

Anthropologists have long been interested in the preferential infanticide of girls among the Eskimos. It is so frequent that some authors have suggested it could actually endanger the survival of the group in the long term (Rasmussen, 1931).[30]

The imbalance in the sex-ratio of difference groups of Eskimos attests to female infanticide:

	Girls	Boys	Girls per 100 boys
Cape Smyth, Alaska 1902	14	27	52
Netsilik, Eskimos 1902	66	138	48
Quernermiut (Barren Grounds) 1929	11	24	46
Aivilingmiut (N.E. Coast, Hudson Bay) 1902	15	27	56

(Source Balikci, 1967, p. 616)

Rasmussen's well-known data (1931) give a measure of the situation. After an enquiry in which he questioned women one by one, he established a list that showed that out of 96 births (in 18 marriages), 38 girls had been killed.

The preference for male children is explained (by the people and by the anthropologist himself, see, Rasmussen, 1931, pp. 139ff.) by rules governing the sexual division of labour and marital residence. Only males can hunt and only males will be able to provide for the needs of elderly relatives. Girls, then, are a useless burden and parents consider they 'cannot afford to waste several years nursing a girl':[31]

They hold the view that if a woman is to suckle a girl child it will be two or three years before she may expect her next confinement. But if she has not to suckle, she may expect another child comparatively soon after; so *they encourage the number of births — when it is a girl that is born* — either by killing it or giving it away immediately after birth, and then hope that the next will be a boy (Rasmussen, 1931, p. 140, stress added).

The girl is given away in adoption as an alternative solution to infanticide, but the point is that in both cases the child is separated from the mother to make her 'susceptible' to fecundation, i.e. so she can be impregnated again.

Similar procedures are used in animal breeding. For instance, the same form of intervention is currently used by breeders of chimpanzees in captivity. There are not many chimpanzees and they serve well as guinea-pigs. The problem is that chimpanzees reproduce slowly both in captivity and in the wild, the average interval between one birth and the next being about five years. But also among chimpanzees, if a baby dies (or is taken away from its mother and fed artificially in breeding conditions), the female is soon copulable (in oestrus) and fecundable, and the interval between births is reduced (Teleki *et al.*, 1976). Breeders therefore remove babies from their mothers and so accelerate the rhythm of reproduction (Bourne, 1972).

Other forms of infanticide are certainly known: e.g. infanticide of handicapped infants; infanticide due to 'extreme ecological pressure' (famine, lack of game, etc., see Balikci, 1967 and 1970); infanticide due to the impossibility of feeding and carrying two children at once when births are too close (among nomads in particular there is an absolute need to have a long interval between births, as noted by Carr Saunders already in 1922 — an explanation often repeated since, see Cowlishaw, 1978, 1981; Lee, 1972, 1979, 1980; Tindale, 1972); and infanticide due to a refusal of maternity.[32]

Selective infanticide among Eskimos differs from all these cases first of all because of its long-term demographic effect. It is a more effective means of limiting demographic growth. But the fundamental difference between Eskimo selective infanticide and other forms of infanticide is at a sociological level: at the level of gender relations and the social manipulation of reproduction. In the other cases, the resumption of ovulation, and hence the possibility of conception, are secondary and even unwanted effects of the interruption of the reproductive process. One does not kill a child to swiftly get pregnant again.[33] But this, on the other hand, is precisely the aim of female infanticide: the elimination of 'time wastage' due to breast-feeding (when the woman is not fecundable), to get the good product, a male, as quickly as possible. It is therefore not enough to see it as limitation of reproduction, since the 'limitation' in fact involves an *intensification* of women's procreative work through destroying some 'defective' products.[34]

We can therefore see the selective infanticide of girls as a technical intervention in reproduction: an intervention that approaches stock-breeding techniques, and this differentiates this form of infanticide from the others mentioned. We could also say this intervention differs from the others because of its management. In the other cases, infanticide is mostly a practice controlled by women, and directly by the woman giving birth, with variable agreement on the part of men, and sometimes against their wishes (see for example, Warner, 1937, p. 96). Whereas this infanticide of girls is mainly controlled by men — 'the father mostly makes the fatal decision' (Balikci, 1970, p. 149) — even if it is often executed by women. The child may be killed against the wishes of its mother, as is shown by Van de Velde, who gives an account of a mother killing a baby on the orders of her husband: 'There was no way to do otherwise, because in those days we were really afraid of our husbands' (Van de Velde, 1954, p. 8).[35]

(2)   'Mercenary' breast-feeding (wet nursing)

> Since the breast is a less effective organ than the placenta, and also must provide for the needs of a larger child, lactation appears a weaker point in the process of reproduction than gestation. Lactation thus becomes a limiting factor, able to control a certain number of other mechanisms in the reproductive function of women (Short, 1978, p. 201).

If lactation is a weak link in the process of reproduction, and if it controls and limits reproductive possibilities, this is a stage where one can intervene to increase the yield from the procreative machine and to speed up its 'rhythm' and output. This is indeed what is done in various societies, and what is possible for part of the population, in a more systematic fashion, in hierarchical or class societies.

This 'weak point' of lactation has indeed attracted societies' attention, and they have resolved the problem of a necessarily long interval between two births in various ways. The first necessity is for the health of the mother, given the burden feeding and carrying a child impose on her. It is also known that in precarious conditions, at a strictly biological level, 'priority goes to the infant at the expense of the mother. A cattle breeder knows only too well how nursing can wear-down an under-nourished cow' (Short, 1978, p. 202).

In addition, as the !Kung say, 'women who have one baby after another like animals, always have bad backs'; and Lee has calculated the relationship between the length of the genetic interval (birth spacing) of women and the weight per kilometer they carry (Lee, 1972, pp. 331ff.; 1979, pp. 313ff.; 1980, pp. 324ff.). Tied to the objective impossibility of keeping two children when they are born too close together, there is, in many nomadic societies, some female management of abortion, infanticide and sometimes also of contraceptive techniques. There are also taboos on sexual relations during breast-feeding (which lasts two to three years) and eventual responsibility for their application may return onto men (for example, among the G/Wi, see Silberbauer, 1972, p. 307).

Knowing the danger of premature weaning for a child, many (especially agricultural) societies establish a period of one to three years of *non-exposure* to the risk of pregnancy for a new mother, until the child is viable.[36] If a child is to survive, there seems no possibility other than prolonged maternal breast-feeding, except individual cases of adoption (though this again takes place mainly after weaning and not before).[37]

So is there no social management of nursing other than imposing a long post-partum taboo on women,[38] and less often on men, to accompany and allow prolonged breast-feeding?

On closer examination, we can see there are in fact several forms of intervention and management of nursing. These turn out to be precise technical manipulations of reproduction, by which nursing as a limiting factor is partially overcome. One way to achieve this has been the veritable 'Taylorisation' of reproduction seen in some hierarchical or class societies.

This technical manipulation is clearly used in the rearing of animals. We have seen the example of chimpanzees. Similarly among Banyankole cattle-breeders, if a cow does not go into oestrus and conceive after a 'suitable' delay, they try first to act on the mechanism that connects lactation and ovulation, by reducing lactation through milking only once a day. If that is not enough, they put juice from irritating herbs into the cow's vagina, 'this set up irritation and caused the cow to seek the bull at once'. In this population, mothers always nurse a child for two or three years, except when 'the man is anxious to have another child soon'. In which case the infant is taken away from its mother and fed artificially (Roscoe, 1923, p. 113). Please note here the superiority of the human species. As women are 'copulable' without 'oestrus', there is no need to put irritating juice into their vaginas to make them breed. This society nonetheless does take care to discipline women, by such measures as forced fattening (gorging) — to such an extent that a girl 'will lose the power of walking so that she could only waddle' (Roscoe, 1923, p. 120).[39]

Consigning the second part of the cycle (breast-feeding) to a second woman — so freeing the first one either for sexual service or a new pregnancy — is the form of interruption of the reproductive cycle preferred by hierarchical societies. For instance, among the Ganda, if the king was especially attached to one of his wives, when she was in labour they would seize a nursing mother who happened to be passing, and keep her as a nurse for the king's child, so the favoured wife could sleep with the king again. (The child of the nurse was raised on cow's milk, Roscoe, 1911, p. 53.)

Some modern European societies have similarly overcome — for part of the population — the inconvenient obstacle posed by extended nursing. This has two effects. First, it has freed some women from part of reproductive labour, making them available for sexual relations (NB using a nurse to this end is recommended by theologians, see Flandrin, 1981, pp. 189ff. and passim) as well as for other activities. The latter can be social activities, as in the case of the bourgeoisie, or work in the husband's workshop or shop, as among silk workers and shop keepers in Lyons in the eighteenth century (Garden, 1975).

Second, there is a much greater fecundity, since in the absence of nursing the interval between births shortens considerably. This process can be seen, for example, among the Florentine bourgeoisie in the fifteenth and sixteenth centuries (Klapisch-Zuber, 1980).

Women were married in Florence before they were 18 years old, and they conceived their first child on average five months after marriage. Thereafter, 50 per cent of births followed at an average interval of about 17 months (the average interval is generally 20.85 months). Babies were sent to a nurse one after another, immediately after birth. The father had complete control of the nursing. It was he who decided to whom to entrust the child, when to send it and when to get it back, how much money to pay, etc. As Klapish-Zuber shows clearly, the contract for wet-nursing was a contract *between men*: it was made between the bourgeois father of the baby and the husband or father of the wet-nurse — the latter being called the *balio*, the masculine form of *balia*, 'wet nurse'. (The language of the *Ricordanze* expresses this totally male management: 'I entrusted the child to *him* to nurse', '*he* no longer gives it the breast'.) The merchant's wife who was not subject to the permanent constraints of nursing, certainly benefited, but at the price of a higher fertility. She had a 'respite' from reproductive labour: she gained a period of eight to twelve months 'free' between the end of one pregnancy and the start of the next.

This is technical 'progress': a division of labour and Taylorisation of reproduction shared between two specialised machines, tied to one another by relationships of sexage and of class in the everyday sense. The reproductive body of the bourgeois wife produced one child after another for the husband's lineage, and the nursing body of a lower class woman assured the second, longer, phase of reproductive work.

The 'weak link' in the reproductive sequence, which in large part controls the rhythm of reproduction, was broken.

But it would be wrong to think that interventions in procreation, like wet nursing, function smoothly and 'rationally'. For what was an intensification of reproduction in the case of Florentine merchants, and a certain respite from reproductive work for their wives, could become under the combined effects of sex and class domination, a massacre of women and children. This can be seen in the case of silk workers in Lyon (Garden, 1975).

In Lyon, silk workers had a particularly high fertility in comparison to rural France of the same period. As Garden shows, this did not stem from early marriage — this was actually delayed, the average age of girls being 27.5 years at first marriage — but rather from the reduced interval between births due to sending children to wet nurses (with associated high infant mortality). A third of families had more than ten children.

Fertility rates were exceptional during the first ten years of married life. A rhythm of annual births was present in almost all families for at least three consecutive children . . . the frequency being sometimes much greater . . . As one got further from the date of marriage, the number of still fertile (or living) women diminished yearly . . . Only after fifteen years of marriage and fertility did births become more and more spaced.

Take 'the average demographic profile of a Lyonnais woman silk worker of the 18th century': she had '7 or 8 children during the first ten years of marriage, 4 in the first five and 3 or 4 in the following five'. And record: 'a woman gave birth every year for twelve consecutive years' (Garden, 1975, pp. 53–4).[40]

Women's high fertility in both cases was of interest: for the power of the lineage among rich Florentines, and to produce labour for the workshop in Lyon. The mortality of children who were farmed out to wet nurses outside Lyon seems extremely high, but the dispatch was necessary, as it was impossible for women to work in the workshop (where they were indispensable) and look after their children at the same time. Hence the infernal cycle of births and deaths of children and deaths of mothers.[41] But was there no margin of reproductive 'gain', no increase in the number of descendants acquired, even with the squandering of lives and despite the losses linked with baby farming? Or should we see in this only the effects of men's total and blind recklessness in a period when birth control was beginning in the French countryside? The data give no clear reply on these points.

We have seen there are two different mechanisms for manipulating reproduction: first, empirical research on the favourable period for fertilisation; and second, forms of intervention in the reproductive process that involve cutting it in two, to eliminate 'time wastage' through breast-feeding and the associated anovular period. (Really 'idle time' in relation to an intensified exploitation of the reproductive machine!) These mechanisms have in common that they are specific *technical moments of directed intervention* in the reproductive sequence. They intervene in the economy of reproduction and its efficacy: they repair 'mistakes' (a female born instead of a male); extract more profit from the machine (specialising two different machine–persons for successive phases of reproductive work); and reduce hazards of timing in production (with useful knowledge, and hence choice, of the fertile period, which allows better technicality in coitus — it can become a technical act of insemination with maximum probability of success). As *directed technical interventions*, these mechanisms have a different status from the first mechanism considered: the *institutionalised* exposure of women to risk of pregnancy through marriage, with the associated complex forms of control/training and surveillance that compose the very basis of social organisation. If we can therefore speak of a *rising scale* of manipulation of reproduction — as regards the intensity of manipulation and degree of specialisation (or technicality) of intervention in the biology of reproduction (which is the line I have chosen to present this account) — the importance and the very forms of the different mechanisms set to work, also lead us to distinguish them at a theoretical level. On the one hand there are the fundamental and very general forms of control of reproduction; and on the other, specific mechanisms of technical intervention which may accompany them.

Increasing control, sought and obtained through such a variety of elements, involves the reproductive agents and their qualities, as well as the quantity and quality of their products. All these elements slowly bring to light and allow us finally to see a grandiose project of domestication of reproduction.

Of utmost importance in this operation of domestication is the last mechanism of intervention in, and transformation of, reproduction I shall now consider — the separation of reproductive and non-reproductive sexuality. We have here perhaps the ultimate form of technical manipulation of human biological organisation as regards sexuality and reproduction; and at the same time a general and institutional form of intervention.

The Domestication of Women's Sexuality

The forms of manipulation of biology I shall now consider, concern (and have multiple solutions for) a distinctive characteristic of human biological structure: the absence of a constraining hormonal link between ovulation and sexual drive. This involves two elements: (1) women's ovulation (the moment of possible fertilisation) is not necessarily accompanied by a sexual drive leading them to copulate (or be 'receptive'); and (2) their sexual drive is *inter-mittent*, independent of their ovarian state, and moreover '*situation-dependent*' (Hrdy, 1981, pp. 136 and 144ff.).

We have already seen forms of social intervention on the first point: the coverage of possibilities for fertilisation being assured by socially organised and regulated (and hence potentially flexible with the demographic needs of the time and the form of society)[42] exposure of women to coitus and risk of pregnancy. This implies fundamentally that copulation and impregnation can take place in the absence of any sexual desire on the part of women, and that a totally imposed reproduction can be established.[43]

What I shall try to show here is a still more complex and extensive form of intervention, a 'second degree' one in relation to the first. This is the socially elaborated response to the other constituent of the potential divorce between reproduction and sexuality — the presence of *a sexuality which is not conditioned by reproduction, not ruled by the rhythm of reproductive hormones, and which is even completely detached from procreation*.

It seems important to stress that the two forms of institutional control, of systematic and extensive manipulation of reproduction — i.e. marriage and those we are about to examine — both address the same central problem of human biological infrastructure: *the potentially free and social character of sexuality, the potentially non-constraining character of reproduction.* The evolutionary tendency towards a separation between sexuality and reproduction — at its initial stage among the higher primates — reaches its maximum development in human beings.[44] Hence a radically important consequence: the possible expansion of a sexuality theoretically open to any expression, having broken all necessary relationship with reproduction; an extremely *flexible, non sexed sexuality*, not dominated by sex distinction, tendentially *undifferentiated*, and multiple in its forms as in its objects.

Recent research shows manifestations of such polymorphous sexuality in some higher primates too (see work by Chevalier-Skolnikoff and many others; and for an overview Hrdy, 1981 and Symons, 1979), but its latent potentialities seem much wider in the human species. The astonishing plasticity of human sexuality allows extremely varied cultural elaboration. What interests us here is the specific elaboration human societies give to the problems posed by a sexuality that has passed from a hormonal cyclic organisation to one tied to the cortex, where socio-affective elements win in importance over strictly bio-reproductive behaviours. Or, to put the question differently, if human biology allows great flexibility to sexuality (that of women, among others), how can sexuality be constrained to specialise for reproduction?

I shall touch on the vast and important subject of human sexual flexibility only as regards the forms and techniques of social control of reproduction. How do different societies behave in regard to the latent cleavage between reproduction and sexuality? Do they reduce or increase it?[45] For indeed it seems that the dissociation of sexuality from reproduction is socially accentuated in most societies, and in fairly precise ways.

We are faced in fact with *a specifically oriented control of this dissociation.* The divide is (1) deepened and institutionalised by distinguishing situations (partners and times, etc.) where reproduction is acceptable (or required) from those where sexuality must not lead to procreation; and (2) at the same time re-elaborated in many ways so as to limit the polymorphous potentialities of human sexuality and channel them towards heterosexuality and obligatory reproduction. These forms somehow regain (or even impose at another level, social and cultural) the strict union between sexuality and procreation that human sexual structure precisely allows (and which it often tends) to surpass.[46]

But to frame the question this way is still partial. It would erase a simple and obvious but very important fact: namely that there is no symmetry in the reproductive roles of the two sexes, and that in most known societies men and women occupy different positions in power relations. This makes it very unlikely that social interventions on sexuality will be *neutral* in regard to relations between the sexes.

The process we will examine seems, in fact, to involve principally the sexuality of *women*, and it ends up producing an actual specialisation of their sexuality for reproductive ends. Training and integral, complex manipulation of the psycho-physical being of women, is accomplished through direct action on sexuality (of which we shall see various examples), and through these means, the optimal conditions for the exercise of control and imposition of reproduction are realised, of which marriage seems to be the supporting beam.

The different and even divergent forms through which this intervention into sexuality is realised, will thus constitute important variables in the analysis of sex relations.

Here I shall look only at the social machinery that structures forms of heterosexual relations, stressing again that it is the break which is initially introduced into a sexuality which tends towards indifferentiation, that constructs the possibility of channelling it exclusively towards genital hetero-sexual practice, i.e. reproductive sexuality.[47] I want to stress the scarcity of anthropological documentation on different forms of homosexuality, from the point of view of both the quantity and quality of data. And that lack of data is particularly acute on the sexuality of women (Davenport, 1977).[48]

Very broadly, we can say that the elaboration and institutionalisation of a divorce between reproductive and non-reproductive sexuality — especially for women — takes two very widespread forms, shown in many historical and ethnic variations.

However, these forms are by no means present, nor present in the same way, in all societies, and some even appear to be tied to specific types of social organisation. This, once again, calls for systematic research, specifically on relations between forms of socio-economic organisation, forms of gender relations, and social manipulations of sexuality.

The First Form of Dissociating Sexuality and Reproduction: the Division between Categories of Women

One of the institutionalised ways of dissociating reproductive and non-repro-ductive sexuality is what could be called a 'vertical' separation. This model seems to be linked to hierarchical and class societies, where a distinction or division, which is often extremely rigid, is established within the group of women between those engaged more or less professionally in the exercise of sexuality, and those (the majority) engaged in (even 'consecrated' to, see Michard-Marchal and Ribéry, 1982) reproduction.[49] This division between categories of women produces, for example, the stereotypes, dear to our western societies, of the courtesan or whore and the madonna or holy and desexed mother, to which the Victorian era gave an extreme and well-known form. Staying with Western civilisations, the Greco-Roman world also showed a marked separation in its social practices, mythology and rituals, between reproductive and non-reproductive sexuality. But this division affected the two sexes so differently that we could ask if, in reality, it did not apply only to women, because a man could have non-reproductive sexuality, i.e. amorous passions and/or homo- or heterosexual physical relations, and at the same time reproductive relations with his wife. For women, on the contrary, there was a clear dissociation between the only two forms of sexuality permitted them: reproductive sexuality (for wives) and non-reproductive sexuality (for courtesans). Though mutually exclusive these are in fact complementary patterns of a subjugated sexuality, assigned to different categories of women in the service either of men's will to procreate, or of men's pleasure.

Recall here the words of Demosthenes: 'Courtesans are for pleasure, concubines for everyday care (of the body), wives for legitimate children and to be faithful guardians of household things' (in *Contra Néera*, quoted in Vernant, 1974, p. 60). Or, again, the opposition between the mythology and rituals of the feasts of Adonis and those of the Thesmophories, an opposition structured through a multiplicity of codes (food, astronomical, and plant, etc.). Detienne (1972, p. 154) underlines the differences which on some levels (for example, that of aromatics and perfumes) even 'take the form of a declared antagonism' between actors of the two rituals: on the one side, the seductive and debauched women of Adonis, the courtesans and concubines; on the other, married women and mothers, the matrons of Demeter. Demeter was the goddess of agriculture and marriage, and 'by and through marriage' a wife became 'cultivated, cereal-bearing land', producing 'valuable and welcome fruits, legitimate children, where the father could recognise the seed he himself by ploughing had sown' (Vernant, 1972, p. xii). The antinomy between procreation and desire, erotic conduct, is clearcut. Marriage is not aimed at pleasure but at the procreation of legitimate children. Erotic seduction is fundamentally foreign to it, and even seen as a threat. A wife who 'abandons herself to the call of desire rejects her matronly status to assume that of a courtesan, leads marriage astray from its normal ends to make it an instrument of sensual pleasure'. Indeed 'one of the striking traits of Greek civilisation in the classical period was that strictly amorous relations, heterosexual as well as homosexual, took place outside the domestic domain' (Vernant, 1972, pp. ix–x).

In Rome, for 'norm conforming' male sexuality, both women and boys were 'sexual tools' and held to be passive, because 'what is important is being a swashbuckler; the sex of the victims is of little matter'. The pertinent opposition for men in Roman society lay not between loving women and loving boys, but between activity and passivity, and between 'free love and conjugal exclusiveness'. For men, and for the relevant legislation, 'what mattered was not being a slave, and not being passive'. In any case 'to be active is to be a male, whatever the sex of the so-called passive partner... A woman is passive by definition.' Finally, 'illegitimate, immoral and moreover infamous relations' were those where free men were passive, where there was 'infamous willingness by women', and, of course, 'female homophilia especially on the part of the active lover. A woman who takes herself for a man is the world upside down. Equal in horror, says Seneca, to women who "ride astride" men' (Veyne, 1982, pp. 26–31).

Hence, for men, there was what Philippe Ariès calls 'a swashbuckling bisexuality' (which tended to be transformed into reproductive sexuality even before Christianity);[50] and for women a role of passive submission to the pleasure of men or to reproductive requirements.

It is certainly ironic that the Christian ideological endeavour, which in admitting only a procreative sexuality strove towards a spiritual behaviour far removed from animal instinctuality, should have ended up re-establishing (regressively and through the repression of pleasure) the tight union of procreation and sexuality characteristic of the less evolved species, from which humanity has distanced itself. The repression so introduced, in reality, succeeded neither in completely cancelling the dissociation of sexuality and reproduction (and the history of ideas shows compromises and changes in attitudes towards sexuality), nor in cancelling the multiform character of human sexuality. It did, however, succeed in producing female individuals specialised in reproduction and mutilated of their sexual potential.[51]

On the other hand, it by no means suppressed the other specialisation of women — that of sexual service, i.e. prostitution. For this a category of women was recruited — particularly from the poor class, for whom in principle no right or duty of procreation was recognised — through more or less institutionalised channels, such as forms of collective public and degrading rape, etc. (see Flandrin, 1981; Rossiaud, 1982).[52]

However, even for this category of women, the sole admissible sexual conduct has been the genital-reproductive one, because — and this is fundamentally important — the reproductive claim marks and delimits the field of possible sexuality (more or less rigidly, it is true, according to period).

There is a tendency to underestimate a rather important element — which is explicit in the discourse and regulation of prostitution in the last century (see Corbin, 1982), but older and more widespread — that prostitution is a necessary evil for social order (according to the Augustinian tradition), a means of avoiding 'unnatural' sexual practices, and indeed any practice which is not potentially procreative. The system of surveillance and punishment of prostitutes set in place in 1800, aimed at understanding prostitution better, in order to

> limit its growth and, above all, to prevent 'unnatural' sexual conduct developing within it. We should not forget that the function of the vile but necessary underworld of regulated prostitution is to channel extra-marital sexuality, and, above all, to make sure somehow that it continues to conform to nature (Corbin, 1982, p. 30).

Thus, the sexuality practised in prostitution, even if in principle it should not lead to procreation, must be exercised according to 'normal', reproductive forms and techniques, and it should not stir up other desires, interests and experiences. For example, in the first half of the nineteenth century, 'a [brothel] prostitute would not practise fellatio; for the other girls would have obliged those who did to "take their meals separately"' (Corbin, 1982, p. 187).[53]

According to projects of the time, officially 'tolerated prostitution should be a society of women destined to satisfy male sexuality under the direct control of the administration' (Corbin, 1982, p. 27). An isolated society, a 'seminal sewer' as one author called it at the time, a brothel, with bars and frosted glass in the windows and a double door entry system, isolated if possible also by 'altitude' (i.e. not on the ground floor or mezzanine) (ibid, p. 26). But

> throughout the century it was never the 'receiving' rooms (*chambres de passe*) which attracted the anger of observers and administrators, but the 'cabinets' (*bahuts*) where the girls gathered together when not working. It was here that anarchic promiscuity of bodies, and worse bodies of the same sex, was created (ibid, p. 128).

It was in fact the 'morality' of the prostitutes themselves that was directly surveilled. Authors of the first half of the nineteenth century thought prostitution 'could lead to the lowest depths of degradation', i.e. to homosexuality. 'The public woman risks above all eventually becoming a "tribade"; and because of this she casts, let us repeat, a terrible threat to the sexual order of which she is otherwise the surest guarantee' (ibid, pp. 19–22; and on the isolation of 'vicious' girls in prison, see ibid, p. 22).

The second form of dissociating sexuality and reproduction: the separation of life stages
The other form of institutional practice which dissociates sexuality from reproduction can better be described as a 'horizontal' division. Here the distinction is not between persons or categories assigned once and for all to some aspect of sexuality, but rather separates out two periods, or stages of life, for each individual. One takes place around girls' puberty (either pre- or post-puberty depending on the society) and is dedicated to more or less 'free' sexuality. Girls and youths engage in often multiple love relationships, where procreation is usually forbidden. The other period is characterised by conjugal sexuality aimed at reproduction. Women are thus divided not by categories of persons, but by age groups. Note that (as with 'vertical' separation) this distinction of periods is only entirely valid for women, because for men the break between the two periods is often less clear cut, and the 'juvenile' period may be prolonged after marriage and even after fatherhood. But this is just one aspect of the asymmetry that exists between the situations of men and women in these practices.

Often it is institutional structures that organise this pre-marital sexuality: for instance, to choose from many possible examples, the forms of sexual apprenticeship within the framework of the Muria *ghotul* (Elwin, 1959) or the Hausa *tsarance* (Echard in Echard, *et al.*, 1981); the relations between girls and young warriors in the Masai *manyatta* and their equivalents among other East African pastoralists (Leakey, 1930; Merker, 1910; Spencer, 1965, 1973); or some Polynesian practices (Ortner, 1981). The appearance of sexual 'liberty' should not make us forget, however, that, as Héritier says of the Muria, 'it is not just that one has the right to make love, it is a crime to refuse' (Héritier, 1976, p. 8) — a crime which may be punished by various forms of ostracism and social rejection as well as by measures involving physical coercion of girls (such as the forms of rape already mentioned, see above, pp. 118), depending on the society.[54]

One immediate question to be asked is, how old are the girls during this period of 'liberty' and sexual initiation? Does it occur before or after puberty? From the point of view of reproduction, there is a considerable difference. With pre-pubertal girls, there is a sexual apprenticeship, but, by definition, they are not removed from reproduction. Since they are not yet fertile, there is no 'loss' of usable time for reproduction. It is just a matter of a sexual use of girls. In the other case, a variable fraction of reproductive possibilities will be cancelled: that is to say, X fertile years will be removed from reproduction (see below),[55] with the same demographic effect as the late age of marriage in Europe before the nineteenth century. This can be seen therefore as a model of sexuality that fits a need to limit reproduction — or that, at least, seems to be its effect. We need to analyse the context of these various practices to see if they are coherent with the demographic objectives of the societies concerned: with an inclination to limit population or, on the contrary, to maximise reproduction.

But then another problem arises, deriving from the frequent asymmetry of men's and women's rights and duties in these practices, a problem needing specific research and analyses for its resolution. What is the place of women in the game? How far is it a question of the (pre- and/or post-pubertal) sexual use of girls, which refers to, or is just *one of the possible transformations of, the bodily specialisation of woman* into those 'for pleasure' and those for reproduction? (The specialisation being realised in this case on the basis of age groups.)

It may, for example, be a way for the elders to keep political and economic control in society, by allowing young men access to nubile women, and so diverting them towards pleasure and play, etc. This seems to be the case in Polynesian societies, where young men are encouraged to have a 'hyperactive but non-reproductive sexuality' (Ortner, 1981, pp. 401ff.); also in Micronesia (for the Yap, see Schneider, 1955, p. 226); and in an analogous but different way, among some pastoral and warrior societies of East Africa.[56] Such a 'political' use of women and of sexuality is well-known, and frequent, in western societies. Rossiaud shows how in fifteenth century French society, the authorities favoured 'youth abbeys' (*abbayes de jeunesse*) 'with the aim of containing violence whilst giving youths the means to express their resentments and allowing free play to their "follies"', and institutionalised municipal brothels: 'big houses' or 'town halls' with an 'abbess' and 'beautiful and amusing girl whores' which the youths were encouraged to seek out. The girls were there 'for the benefit of the commonwealth'. As Rossiaud says, public prostitution served as an 'institution of peace. A "good house" is an instrument of "good law and order"' (Rossiaud, 1982, pp. 76–8).

But let us look closer at some of the many possible ways in which this separation between juvenile non-reproductive and reproductive conjugal sexuality is structured.

As we have seen, a series of oppositions distinguishes the two periods, the major and fundamental one being between prescribed procreation in marriage and (often rigorously) forbidden procreation during the pre-marital period. If pregnancy is mostly avoided in the latter, either because these sexual relations exclude full coitus in principle (Lallemand, 1977), or because coitus is practised with some precaution; or because of the young age of the girls, what concerns us here is the social response to eventual pregnancies in societies that forbid pre-marital procreation. These pregnancies are *socially annulled* by various procedures, of which the most common are abortion and infanticide *imposed* on the pregnant girl (see, for the Chagga, Gutmann, 1926; for the Hausa, Echard in Echard, *et al.*, 1981; for the Muria, Elwin, 1959; for the Samburu, Spencer, 1965; for the Rubuka, Muller, 1976; and for Tahiti and Polynesia in general, Ortner, 1981, p. 385). In fact, according to Devereux (1976), societies that most rigorously impose abortion in the case of pre-conjugal conception are the ones which prescribe and institutionalise (or at least permit) juvenile relations.

As Mathieu has clearly shown, it is not always enough to bear a child to become a mother. For a young woman to 'be a mother in the physical sense does not imply that she may be a social mother.' In fact 'it is not so much the generative function but the social role attributed to the mother which underlies the idea of maternity' (Mathieu, 1979, p. 235).

An example will show how this social manipulation of biology is a function of power relations. The Rukuba have an institutional system of pre-marital relations. These are regulated in terms of acceptable partners, forms of approach, duration, the 'love price', etc. The relationship is only pre-marital for girls; married men can contract liaisons with non-married girls, but not the other way round. Men can have several partners simultaneously, but girls only one lover at a time, though they can change every six months. The child conceived from pre-marital relations must be immediately aborted or, if not, killed at birth. The few children that escape this fate belong to the opposite moiety to that of their mother, i.e. to the moiety into which she is supposed to marry. The exchange of women thus concerns obligatorily the total reproductive capacity of the woman (Muller, 1976, pp. 74ff.). 'All the children born to a woman of a moiety belong to the opposite one, whoever is the father' (ibid, p. 76). But in this society, which so rigorously prescribes abortion and infanticide in case of pre-conjugal pregnancy, men *know about, but do not use, coitus interruptus* because 'it spoils the pleasure'; they know about condoms, but use them only sometimes and only to avoid gonorrhoea in casual relationships in town. As regards marriage, 'men say one of the best ways to keep a wife is to make her pregnant as quickly as possible' (Muller, 1981). When they heard that a girl working in town had talked about the pill, men fell into a panic. ' "Male" contraceptives were not to be feared', but 'the pill put everything in question because men did not control it.' Some of the 'anxious husbands' sought out information about the pill from the anthropologist. Reassured that he had not talked about it to their wives (although 'one wife in particular complained of four successive births'), they forebade the anthropologist ever to tell the women. 'Male solidarity closed ranks once again', says Muller (ibid, p. 20), including well and truly, it would seem, the male anthropologist.[57]

An alternative procedure to abortion and/or infanticide is to make pregnancy the end of the period of juvenile sexuality. This can also be interpreted as a negation of pre-marital procreation. Among the Samo, for instance, girls at puberty choose a lover who cannot be their husband (Héritier, 1976, pp. 10–11). The end of this relationship is marked by the approach of the birth of the girl's first child:

> At the birth, the husband takes possession of his legitimate wife and the child, which is considered to be his . . . . There are unhappy wives who do not accept the break-up [with their lover] nor the physical proximity of the husband to whom they have been delivered, against their will, and who flee. They are brought back by force.

But anyway, the pre-marital relationship is socially annulled and obliterated: 'its memory is swallowed, and it is never referred to in public again'. Even if the mother leaves, the husband has the right to keep the child she has conceived with the lover.

When conception puts an institutional end to the juvenile period, girls' opposition to marriage may also be expressed through abortion. (Its sociological meaning is then quite different from the cases of abortion cited above.)

Among the Yap (of the Caroline Islands), the period of juvenile sexuality, of fun and variety in amorous relationships, can last quite a long time — even after marriage, which is initially marked simply by cohabitation. (The girl agrees to live with her lover but assumes the specific duties of a wife only after some time and a particular ceremony.) Marriage can be quite easily broken off *whilst there is no child*. Social pressure in favour of procreation is, however, fairly strong. Men do not tolerate contraceptive methods, nor abortion. A woman who 'gets rid of her child' is viewed very badly. If she is married, she may be beaten and/or exposed to divorce.

In marriage, the obligation to procreate is expressed in economic terms as an exchange between the children the woman produces and the land of the husband's patrilocal group. Woman do not have access to land, and they say on Yap that a woman has '*her land in her legs*', meaning not only that she has to change residence on marriage, but that she herself, although landless, has 'a kind of "land", her reproductivity — that she could exchange for the land a man held' (Labby, 1976, p. 28). Thus 'in exchange for the land itself, she had to produce children', and also 'equally important, to repay the *magar*, or invested labor of the husband's clan group, she and the children she bore had to work for them on the estate' (Labby, 1976, pp. 19–20).

The birth of a child thus greatly changes the freedom of a young woman (but not that of a young man). From that moment, she is completely tied to the child (Schneider, 1955, pp. 219–22) and obliged to do the agricultural and domestic work of the household. The birth of children also makes divorce quite difficult (and, in fact, infrequent): children must stay with the father, and, in addition, it is thought very bad for a woman to leave her children.

But abortion is very widespread on Yap. It is even considered one of the causes of the marked depopulation of the island (Hunt *et al.*, 1949). It is a means by which young women can keep a certain autonomy, and *they practise it frequently, up to the age of 30*. They perform abortions in secret, using several techniques, and against the wishes of lovers and husbands.[58]

Abortion thus shows resistance to marriage: to its productive and reproductive obligations.[59]

The antinomy between juvenile and reproductive sexuality is structured on a multiplicity of levels: variety of partners, difference of age, relations of power, choice of partner, possibility of ending relationships, etc. A few cases, among the dozens possible, may illustrate these points.

Spencer stresses that among the Samburu, girls and *moran* (young warriors) 'tend to treat each other to some extent as equals', the relationship between lovers (where procreation is prohibited) is 'formed and maintained largely out of sexual attraction with a variable element of mutual affection' (Spencer, 1965, pp. 215ff.). One or the other may terminate it at will. In this relationship, girls have on the whole 'an unusually high status'. The result is that even *morans* who 'love' their young lovers 'a lot' and would be able to marry them, admit they 'have no desire to do so' because in a family 'the husband should be the undisputed master'. And this position of power is based on violence — 'the normal way in which an elder keeps his wife under his control is by beating her as he thinks necessary' (Spencer, 1965, p. 220) — and on the wife's economic dependence: women neither own nor control cattle, the principal means of production of the group. The husband's power is set up from the very start of the conjugal relationship. The whole wedding ceremony — which is preceded by excision and followed by departure with the husband — immediately establishes the power relation, by breaking all the young woman's resistance (see above).

Many practices specifically affirm the power of the husband and train young women to submission. Among the Rukuba, 'up to the time of her marriage, a girl belongs sexually to her lover, and sexual relations with her future husband are considered evidence of very bad conduct on her part'. But men's 'favourite game' is to try to rape their fiancée just before marriage. 'Men believe this instils respect in the girl, and that she will thereafter treat her husband with all the deference due to him' (Muller, 1976, pp. 96–7).

The very forms of sexual technique may accentuate the opposition between pre- (and eventually extra-) marital relations and marriage.

On Yap, the preferred form of non-marital sexual relations is *gichigich*, which centres on women's pleasure: multiple orgasms are obtained by stimulating the clitoris prior to penetration. This practice is abandoned as soon as possible after marriage, with the husband substituting a 'regular style of intercourse, man on woman', i.e. what is called the missionary position. In marriage '*gichigich* is deliberately not done', otherwise (it is said) 'his wife would insist on it all the time, and he would not be able to work like other men. Neither would his wife want to work as she should' (Hunt *et al.*, 1949, p. 189).

Among the Hausa of Ader, Echard has shown the process through which the institutionalised sexual initiation of girls (the *tsarance*) leads to a 'monopolising of their reproductive power, transforming their body into a tool which is manipulated as such' (Echard *et al.*, 1981, p. 353). 'Once the little girl is considered a *budurwa*, her sexuality is the object of orientation towards strictly heterosexual relations with socially authorised partners, accompanied by an education in submission to male desire' (ibid, p. 349). This is accomplished within the framework of the *tsarance*, where a group of girls of the same age class is united under the direction of a 'Master of Girls' and where each girl must constitute herself 'a clientele of male partners'.

During the *tsarance*, 'boys and girls have a "good time" together, that is to say, they play at jostling ... and fondling each other, the girl "massaging" her partner's shoulders, he "kneading" her buttocks and sex' (Echard *et al.*, 1981, p. 350). Coitus is not forbidden within recent practice. The girl cannot avoid the demands of young men who present a gift to the 'Master of Girls' and ask to spent a night with her. 'At the end of the night, the man gives the girl a present or a small sum of money' (ibid, p. 349). This period is, in short, as Echard says, 'an apprenticeship in good sexual manners'.

The second stage of the process is marriage:

> from the multiplicity of partners — even though to begin with they were largely imposed; from the 'games' of chat and caresses — even though they are limited; and from a quite relative and restrained capacity for bodily expression, there follows a conjugal relationship which requires singularity, avoidance and passivity. From a very young girl little by little obliged to submit to men, transformed into a girl constrained to heterosexual relations ... within ten years, the society produces a young married woman. Within the framework of marriage alone, her body is henceforth assigned to coitus and reproduction, to 'women's work' as the Ader women themselves say (Echard *et al.*, 1981, pp. 352–3; also Echard, 1985, pp. 37–60).

In the Mossi *rollendo*, young people sleep together, but female and male anatomies are 'symbolically divided up into permitted and prohibited zones ... the *rolle* can only caress the shoulders of her partner; he has right to her entire upper body' (Lallemand in Echard *et al.*, 1981, p. 367). The caresses of the *rollendo* are followed by marriage and coitus with an imposed husband, coitus which is experienced and practised as violence. 'You cry for a month. When the husband calls you to come to his hut, you flee. When we have periods, we hope they will never stop.' Escapes are followed by forced returns and struggles to avoid coitus. Finally, the woman is overcome and raped (ibid, p. 369). Thereafter, reproductive coitus will be the only sexual manifestation and expression for the girl.

A final painful physical mutilation (in addition to excision) — that is a train of violence experienced as such — irreversibly completes the transformation of a young Mossi woman into a reproducer. This is the squashing of the mammary gland, the *peebo* ('milking'), 'aimed at insuring abundant lactation.' For a whole week after the delivery, the breasts are stretched downwards with an iron tool used for carding cotton. This transformation of the breasts of young women into 'breast bags' or 'fallen breasts', marks them as reproducers. 'In Mossi country, one glance suffices to put a girl into one or other of the two categories', and 'those who have endured it, feel that they have been made irredemiably ugly' (Lallemand, 1977, p. 235; and Echard *et al.*, 1981, p. 363).

The first pregnancy is experienced with despair. When she learns she is pregnant, a girl 'bursts into sobs . . . She feels shame, pain and, they tell us, anger at having been tricked.' Sometimes the husband does not go home, to avoid 'the fury and *despair of the one he is going legitimately to make a mother*' (Lallemand in Echard *et al.*, 1981, p. 362, stress added). 'She went into her hut and cried. She delivered the baby, and the man (her husband) passed in front of the hut. She felt like throwing away the child and killing the man with a gun!' (interview in Lallemand, 1977, p. 230).

Psychic training, coercion, physical mutilation; the forms of intervention into women's sexuality, of traumatisation, are many and varied. With more or less persistence, work and violence, the problem is to remodel the organism in order to specialise it for reproduction. One of the means to assure the success of this operation of domestication and subjection, is the destruction or the reduction of sexual potentialities.[60] The practices of excision often expresses this explicitly, with some constant features to be found even in very different societies. What they try to obtain is a better reproducer. By eliminating too strong and autonomous a desire, a dangerous sexual indifferentiation, they construct the 'true' female sexual nature; in brief, they create a *a woman*. The price paid by women at the level of their health varies according to the operations they endure, but as recent medical research has shown, it is extremely high (Hosken, 1979; Minority Rights Group, 1980; and on representations of excision, see Sindzingre, 1977, 1979).

Sexual mutilation (like the forms of psychic training that are the functional equivalents of physical mutilations) is meant to produce a reduction or even an elimination of women's sexuality. Just think of the widespread forms of inhibition and destruction of women's sexual drives in Christian civilisation, and also of 'frigidity' — the partially researched but nonetheless extreme result of (and possible resistance to) a situation of oppression and of subjection to reproductive sexuality. The control of reproduction thus necessarily passes through the control of women's sexuality. We are so removed from any 'natural' sexuality that reproduction is organised through pure and simple imposition, totally separate from desire — or, even more, through the suppression of desire. Hence, probably, by a complete reversal of hominid inheritance.[61]

Reproduction thus becomes the pivot of all relations between the sexes and all sexual relations; not as a biological fact, but as a system of control and manipulation of all female individuals (and males too, though to a lesser extent). To the point where hetero- and homosexuality could, at the limit, be seen as by-products of the division between reproductive and non-reproductive sexuality that I have just described; or rather of the control and imposition of reproduction.[62] The establishment of the obligation to reproduce (the domestication of reproduction) would thus seem to be the key operator that has blocked the unfolding of an unrestricted and polymorphous human sexuality, and has led to partial — determined and constraining — forms of sexuality.

The different interventions into sexuality seek *to produce a female organism specialised for reproduction*. This process constitutes the strongest and most complex transformation of the biological conditions of reproduction, and correlatively, the strongest and most complex sociological manipulation of the biological conditions of human sexuality.

The Exploitation of Reproduction

[A] class system was revealed, a system so perfect that it has long remained *invisible*. (Guillaumin, 1984, p. 38)

Reproduction as Work

It is currently argued that women are restricted in productive work by their reproductive biological function. But isn't the production of human beings itself work?

Procreation, as fundamental to the species as the production of the means of subsistence, is an activity which likewise requires a measureable expenditure of energy.[63] However, since expenditure is common to all organic processes (digestion, sleep, etc.), the criteria of expenditure of energy alone does not suffice to define procreation as work. What does, however, distinguish reproduction from other organic processes is: (1) on the one hand, it is not essential to the preservation of the *individual* who is the reproducer; and (2) on the other, it leads to the creation of an *external* product, which is not waste material from another process, but rather a product *programmed for its own sake*: a new being.[64]

These characteristics apply to the whole animal kingdom. The peculiarity of the human species in this domain is its not being physiologically subject to reproductive constraints: the fact that human sexuality is not synchronised with, or determined by, the ovulatory cycle. This opens up a possibility of choice and individual decision. Reproduction can be intentionally engaged in, sought after, or refused — the margin for manoeuvre depending on technological conditions.[65]

According to Marx's well-known definition, labour is

'a process in which both man and Nature participate', in which man 'opposes himself to Nature as one of her own forces, setting in motion arms and legs, head and hands, the natural forces of his body, in order to appropriate Nature's productions in a form adapted to his own wants. By thus acting on the external world and changing it, he at the same time changes his own nature' (Marx, 1887/1974, p. 173).

We can look at the characteristics of the reproductive process in the light of this definition.

In reproduction, as in work, human beings 'set in motion . . . the natural forces of their body'. But rather than appropriating external products of nature, reproductive activity sets forth the production of the human species itself.

The reproductive process engages the biophysical nature of the human species:[66] (1) at the level of the species, as an activity that modifies certain of its characteristics; and (2) at the level of reproducing individuals, as a process internal to their own bodies.

(1) The different forms of intervention, choice and regulation of reproduction (and sexuality), and the forms of reproductive care during pregnancy, childbirth and breast-feeding, constitute work on the nature of the human species, on the forms of perpetuation of human groups. As such, they are part of the process of domestication of reproduction, some of whose aspects were described above.

Through the management of reproduction — from its very beginning and from even the simplest forms of intervention, starting with intentionality itself — the natural activity it was becomes *non-natural*; and procreation *becomes* work. Hence, also, the socially organised *social character* of reproductive work. By this work, humanity directly modifies the very nature of its species, and in the full meaning, transforms itself.

(2a) In reproduction, the object of work is not part of a physical world distinct from the labourer, outside her, but part of her very body. The process takes place inside the body, with materials metabolised by the maternal organism, on the foetus (the object of work), which achieves its genetic programme through the work of the maternal organism. Up until breast-feeding, when the breast takes over from the placenta, energy expenditure is used to produce modifications within the body, rather than on the external world, as in manual work.

(2b) A long evolution has lead the human species to the externalisation of gestures, functions of the hand, muscular strength and certain functions of the brain, and to their integration into machines and tools separate from the human body (Leroi-Gourham, 1965, pp. 41ff.). This evolution has allowed humanity to master many natural processes, but it has not yet really affected reproductive work.

In reproductive work, tools are not detached from the female body: person and tools merge together. As a consequence, in reproduction the appropriation of the instruments of labour (the power or capacity to procreate, and, up to a point, the product, the child) consists purely and simply of the seizure of reproductive persons themselves. The tool here is, however, certainly more than a tool: it is a biochemical machine of formidable efficiency, such as no human activity has yet created. Once it has received the impulse of a 'fertilising insemination', which needs an agent and external matter, this machine 'works' on an object with internal materials (produced by the metabolism of the reproductive organism itself) to carry the process of procreation to its biological end (to childbirth, or expulsion of the product, and lactation).

Let us now look at reproductive activity in relation to one final element in the marxian definition of labour: that of intentionality. In 'every labour-process, we get a result that already existed in the imagination of the labourer at its commencement.' Man subordinates his will to realise 'a purpose of his own that gives the law to his modus operandi'. This application of will is not a momentary act, but expresses itself in a 'close atttention' that 'the process demands . . . during the whole operation' (Marx, 1974, p. 174).

In reproduction, will or intentionality is present in some measure in the programming and individual and collective control of each gestation (of each whole reproductive process), but not in the unfolding of the process itself. Once set in motion, this process continues without requiring the conscious participation of the (female) reproducer, and often even against her will. In this sense it could be said that reproductive activity is not identical to manual work.

However, if we take intellectual work into account, the distinction between work and procreation diminishes considerably.

(1) If we consider intentionality or voluntary control in its (perhaps most simple) aspect, as a capacity to start or stop a process, then we cannot stop the brain's activity either. We know from common experience

that the brain works, intentionally or not; that ideas 'think' themselves; that we cannot necessarily produce an idea at a chosen moment, nor always stop mental activity, which continues without the intervention of our will, at non-conscious levels.

(2) Like procreation, intellectual work is accomplished inside the body, with internal 'instruments', materials etc., and sometimes with the brain as the *only* 'instrument'.

What element would allow us to discriminate between what is and what is not work? One of two things: either we deny the qualification 'work' to intellectual work as much as to reproduction; or we question the common meaning of 'work'.

It has often been shown that ideas and representations of work are historical products, tied to specific forms of productive relations.[67] So might the excluding of reproduction from the conceptual field of work not also be an ideological expression of certain relations of production and reproduction? Or rather, could it not be that the *notion of work itself* is constructed on '*the initial exclusion of women as producers-reproducers of the species*' (Vandelac, 1981b, p. 70)?[68] (For a critique of the exclusion of reproductive work from Marx and Engels's analysis, and that of their followers, see also O'Brien, 1981, pp. 158ff. and passim.) From this point of view, the concept of work could, therefore, turn out to be a function of existing historical relations between the sexes.

Reproduction as Exploited Work

Like all work, reproductive work can be *free or the object of exploitation*. In the latter case, procreation is then alienated work, and the reproductive agent is dispossessed of herself.

Unlike other relations of production, the management of reproduction implies a relationship of particularly close physical proximity between the woman who brings to term the creation of a new human being, and the man who participates solely in the constitution of the basic cell; between the woman who works on the gestation and the man who doesn't work on it, but can impose it. All relations which so directly affect bodily territory are particularly charged. All forms of access to another's body have a heavy import and imply a rigorous codification of bodily proximity and distance in the animal kingdom — humans included. Access to bodily territory puts in question identity itself. Hence the specific character of relations of reproduction. Hence the possibility of a tie of material appropriation; the most material thinkable, a material appropriation that reaches the very integrity of the person. This specific character of the relations of reproduction is also redoubled by bodily co-existence with the foetus: the long symbiosis with an unborn child, making imposed pregnancy particularly intolerable:

There is no way a pregnant woman can passively let the foetus live, she must create and nurture it with her own body, a symbiosis that is often difficult, sometimes dangerous, uniquely intimate. However gratifying pregnancy may be to a woman who desires it, for the unwilling, it is literally an invasion — the closest analogy is to the difference between love making and rape (Ellen Willis quoted in Pollack Petchesky, 1980, p. 669, note 17).[69]

Exploitation may consist not only in the general imposition of pregnancy, but also in:

- depriving the reproducer of the management of her conditions of work, i.e. of her choice of (1) partner, (2) time of work (when to have children), and (3) rhythm of work (the space between births and the quantity of work: the number of children);
- imposing the type (quality) of the product (the sex, legitimacy, 'racial quality', etc.);
- depriving the reproducer of the product; and
- depriving her of her reproductive capacity and work at a symbolic level.[70]

The techniques cited above for training women and imposing reproduction on them, aim precisely at accomplishing this exploitation. They are veritable rules for the use of the reproductive machine, to ensure it functions well, for setting it in motion and adjusting its rhythm. 'Reproductive power' being an internal biochemical mechanism makes it possible both to exploit and to hide this exploitation. Procreation has been represented as so 'natural', or automatic a process that it has been possible to deny it is work, and even that it is a specifically human and social activity.

But not only is reproduction an entirely social activity, *it is part of the general process of evolution that has lead to progressive externalisation of the capacities of the human body.* The process described in such an illuminating way in relation to manual and intellectual work by Leroi-Gourhan, also affects different stages of the reproductive sequence. Reproduction is gradually being taken over by this process.

Externalisation (or liberation, in Leroi-Gourhan's words) touches the function of lactation first. Maternal feeding is replaced gradually. But well before the move to totally artificial feeding, agricultural and pastoral societies had tended to reduce the length of breast-feeding and the frequency of feeds by introducing cows' or goats' milk and cereal porridges.

The problems posed by the externalisation of other elements of the reproductive sequence — from conception to the end of the pregnancy — are much more complex, and their evolution has only just begun. Procedures destined to confront 'urgent cases', such as premature births, develop first, from the most simple (for instance conserving the body heat of a baby by wrapping it in absorbent cotton) to the most sophisticated techniques, which allow a 'naturally' non-viable foetus to survive outside the womb and partially replace reproductive work. Henceforth a foetus can survive after less than 24 weeks of gestation. Moreover, research on genetic engineering seeks to artificially produce other elements of the reproductive sequence outside the body. For example, artificial insemination and *in vitro* fertilisation, where fertilisation is dissociated from copulation, and, in the case of *in vitro* fertilisation, the fusion of gametes is effected outside the human body. The recent attempts to produce an artificial placenta, if and when they are successful, will achieve the full externalisation of reproduction.[71]

The politico-economic interest of this sector of research is obvious. Like all other production, artificial reproduction outside the body could be organised according to political and economic requirements, not to mention allowing intervention into the 'quality' of the human product.[72]

Reproduction is thus following the same evolutionary logic as the hand and the brain. But — and this is centrally important — it is not only at the level of technical evolution that the production of human beings has a place analogous to that of other forms of work: the same holds for the level of social relations. *Relations of production and relations of reproduction have followed parallel and structurally homologous lines of evolution*. And in both cases technical evolution and social relations are intertwined.

The structural homology of the two processes has remained invisible for two reasons. On the one hand, there is a certain time-lag between the two processes; and on the other, ideologies have tended to assign fecundity and even women's whole being 'to nature'.[73]

Nevertheless, the transformation of relations of reproduction underway in industrialised societies show this parallel well. We are witnessing a phenomenon in some ways quite close to that produced with the development of capitalism and the transition from relations of serfdom (direct appropriation of the worker) to capitalist relations of production (where the worker is a free individual). There is an analogous evolution in relations of reproduction: from private appropriation of reproduction within the tie of personal dependence constituted by marriage, to the current emergence of relations where global appropriation of the reproductive (female) individual is not the condition for reproduction itself. I shall return to this (see below).

Just like technical evolution, the transformation of relations of reproduction has been gradual and it has not taken place at the same time for different phases of the reproductive cycle.

Breast-feeding
The relations of production for breast-feeding have taken various forms:

First, where all mothers breast-feed. Generalised maternal breast-feeding can be found in different relations of reproduction, ranging hypothetically from those where the reproducer performs free (non-exploited) work, to those where reproductive work is imposed/exploited to an extreme degree.

Second, where some women are exempt from this part of reproductive work (in the same way as some men were freed from manual work because this was done for them by slaves or serfs — though the two situations are not identical, see below). The centuries-old custom of wet nursing allows breast-feeding to be clearly seen as work, even if it were to consist only of the metabolism producing milk and some time for suckling (and not also care of the child). Women who do mercenary breast-feeding, do it within various work relations: from situations where they are dispossessed of their person and belong to a master as a slave, to those where a 'free' nurse (free at least *vis-à-vis* the purchasers of her milk) sells her capacity to lactate in a paid work relation.[74] This may have a parallel at the level of gestation and the uterus, in 'womb renting' (see below).

At the extreme limit, milk is sold like ordinary merchandise whose production is organised in a 'rational' fashion. In India, for instance, mechanised collection of mother's milk and its commercialisation has been envisaged (see below).

Finally, where artificial milk largely, if not totally, replaces human milk. Henceforth, the work of feeding is not necessarily carried out by the/a mother, nor even by a woman. Because of this, it changes character. It no longer involves a biological function specific to the female body. It is no longer part of reproductive work *sensu stricto*, but rather of domestic work (the raising and care of the children), which the sexual division of labour allots to women.

We have, therefore, on one side, historically variable relations of reproduction; and on the other, a technical evolution leading to the 'liberation' of the breast and the transfer of lactation to production completely external to the body.

But we should not, however, imagine an unavoidable, almost automatic, technological evolution, without conflicts and without retreats; a liberation 'offered' to women by disinterested scientific progress. Things may go in quite the contrary direction for women. A clear example of an apparently neutral action, humanitarian in its purpose to safeguard babies' health but with specific effects on women, is the campaign to maintain or return to breast-feeding, particularly in Third World countries. Artificial feeding has, in fact, two major inconveniences: (1) if it is not practised in rigorously sanitary conditions, it provokes real damage; and (2) it costs the consumers too much. There have, of course, been attempts to introduce health or economic measures on a vast scale, to lower the price, to distribute the product free of charge, to improve the production of cow's milk, and to create medical, health education and contraceptive information centres.

But a much more economical solution has been found — or as some researchers put it, at last 'changing awareness may be indicated' (*sic*). Women are there, with their ability to lactate. Women's milk — considered for the first time *as production* — has become the object of economic calculations and of a big campaign of scientific, medical and political pressure. Breast-milk is evaluated as 'potential production', and above all as virtual 'loss' and 'unrealised production' — with catastrophic results for national economies. Calculations have therefore been made: 'the yield of human milk in developing countries is about one quarter of that produced by cows' (Jelliffe and Jelliffe, 1978, p. 295) — about 18 out of 66 million tons. In India, if women were to abandon breast-feeding, this 'would require the immediate development of an additional herd of 114 million "lactating cows"'. In Chile, where breast-feeding involves only 6 per cent of women, it has been calculated that, in 1970, 84 per cent (about 78 600 tons) of 'potential breast-milk production was unrealized' and that 'the output of a herd of 32 000 Chilean milk cows would be required to compensate for the 1970 loss of breast-milk'. Or again, the waste or loss in breast milk is said to be equivalent to two-thirds of the national health budget (of Kenya during the 1970s). These are obviously not the only examples that could be cited (see Jelliffe and Jelliffe, 1978, pp. 133ff. and 294ff.).

The price of 'double cycle' food products (i.e. products of animal origin, such as skimmed cow's milk, the base of artificial milk) increases day-by-day because of the rising costs of agricultural and industrial work and the price of cattle food. When they are imported they become too costly. It therefore comes to mind: (1) that 'human milk forms part of the usual (earth to animal) food chain, with the mother acting as the last link in the chain, as biological transmuter' (Jelliffe and Jelliffe, 1978, p. 133); and (2) that 'by contrast there has been no rise in labour or production costs in the maternal processing plant, even though the price of the extra foods needed by the lactating woman has increased with inflation' (ibid, p. 136).

The solution has thus been found. But (careful!) it should not be thought, as it was previously, that pregnant or lactating women need 'overly expensive foods, particularly animal products'. All they need is economical food:

> appropriate mixtures of less costly, locally available, and culturally acceptable everyday foods (particularly using the principle of 'multi-mixes', based on cereal-legume mixtures) together with inexpensive vitamin supplements, if necessary (Jelliffe and Jelliffe, 1978, p. 134).

No is it necessary to increase the cost of food for nursing women in well-to-do classes (and/or in rich countries). Their appetite may be sharper during lactation, but it has an 'automatic adjustment': these women need only content themselves with 'somewhat larger helpings of usual foods, which may already be available and wasted' (ibid, p. 135).

The advantages of this solution are clear. There are no extra costs of feeding a milch woman, nor any costs of clearing her stable: she does her own housework (and that of the family as well) and prepares her own 'multi-mixes'. All this (and many things besides) are included within the framework of unpaid domestic work, but not within agricultural or industrial work, which has to be paid for. The profitability of 'milking women' is thus guaranteed.

To such a point that in India it has been proposed to promote mechanical milking of women and the commercialisation of their milk, which could be pasteurised and even dried: 'cattle in India produce only 250 litres of milk per year, whereas it has been estimated that poorly nourished Indian women can secrete almost 200 litres of milk in the first year of lactation. Such women could receive part of their earnings in food and meals and part as cash.' This 'would only institutionalise and mechanise the age-old wet-nursing principle', and would, we are told, 'conform to the concept of *using human resources* as a national economic asset, especially in highly populated, less industrialised circumstances'! (Jelliffe and Jelliffe, 1978, pp. 140–1, stress added).

The uterus

The evolution of the function of generation and its progressive liberation has also been effected in several stages, of which the last (complete externalisation of gestation) has not yet been achieved. The relations of reproduction involving gestation take several forms:

First, where all women bear children or should do so (the counter-part of this for the milking function being generalised maternal feeding).

Second, where certain women are 'exempt' from the obligation to procreate and freed from the whole or part of the work of bearing children (parallel to the employment of wet nurses or mercenary breast-feeding). For example, hierarchical relations in some societies allow some of the work required for biological reproduction of the dominant groups to be done by women from other groups or stranger groups. For instance, Mbaya women practice abortion and infanticide 'in an almost normal fashion, so the perpetuation of the group occurs by adoption much more than by generation; one of the principal aims of warrior expeditions being to procure children.' At the start of the nineteenth century, '10 per cent at most of the members of a Guaicuru group belonged to it by blood', which Lévi-Strauss attributed to 'a lively distaste for procreation', 'a horror of nature', which the Mbaya also expressed in their face painting (Lévi-Strauss, 1962, pp. 156–62). We should view some cases of Oceanic and African adoption in the same way: richer or hierarchically better placed groups (or individuals) benefit from supplementary children whose production is not effected by women of the group itself.[75]

There is thus a parallel with the situation of mercenary breast-feeding. However, the work is not here divided between one woman who gestates and one who suckles, but between several women who are differently situated in relation to the beneficiaries of their reproductive work.

In cases of sterility, we know the reproductive work of one woman can be wholly replaced by that of another. There is evidence of this in the history of Sarai and Hagar:

> Sarai Abram's wife bare him no children: and she had an handmaid ... whose name was Hagar. And Sarai said unto Abram, Behold now, the LORD hath restrained me from bearing: I pray thee, go unto my maid; it may be that I may obtain children by her ... And Hagar bare Abram a son: and Abram called his son's name, which Hagar bare, Ishmael (*Genesis*, 16: 1, 2 and 15).

This episode condenses three aspects of what could be called 'womb substitution': First, a woman of an inferior class is used in place of a higher class woman. In principle, Sarai has Abram's child through Hagar. Second, the effective beneficiary of this replacement is not directly the woman of the higher class. The real beneficiary of the operation is Abram: Hagar bears Ishmael for him. What exists between the women here is not a simple class relation, such as exists for example between a man and his slaves, where the owner is freed of certain work and derives benefit from exploiting the work of other men. Sarai herself does not derive benefit from the reproductive work of her slave Hagar, nor from her own (unchosen) exemption from breeding. Finally, the status of substitute reproductive agents may present certain ambiguities. Hagar despises Sarai and does not seem to accept being reduced to just a womb.

In the many societies where one finds practices of this kind (including various forms of woman-to-woman marriage), we need to look closely at the status of the partners. These range from contemporary situations, where one reproducer comes to replace another as a new wife, without there having been a divorce or repudiation of the first wife (see Astuti, 1988); to those where, in fact, only the reproductive function (only the womb) is replaced, and where the reproducer does not have an effective status of wife (see, for example, Krige, 1974, p. 20). These forms are analogous (at the level of generation) to some forms of employing wet-nurses. Let us look at a very recent form, that of 'womb-renting'.

Current Transformation of the Relations of Reproduction

In the West we have recently witnessed a transformation of the centuries-old relations of reproduction in which the female reproducer's whole person, and not just her reproductive capacity, was privately appropriated. From now on, the bond of private appropriation is in question. I shall examine two aspects of this transformation, one very particular, and the second more general.

Womb-renting

Procreative capacity or power can by itself be the object of an exchange. We have therefore seen associations multiplying in the USA that organise the 'renting of wombs'. For a sum of money (US$10–15 000 in 1980), women agree to be artificially fertilised and to produce babies for other people — for couples where the wife is sterile or does not want to be pregnant. The man, the 'tenant of the womb', is thus directly and in an undisguised way the employer of the reproducer. Artificial insemination eliminates the personal relationship between the partners, and somehow renders the waged work relationship aseptic.

'Womb-renting' could be seen as just an extreme case of market logic finally reaching the most 'private' domain of personal life. But it is really more *a sale, in which procreative power is exchanged in the same way as labour power.*

In 'womb-renting', if production of a child is directly assimilable to production of a commodity (even though it does not look like that to the 'tenant'), it is because procreative power is, in marxian terms, 'offered and sold by its owner'. The woman who agrees to have the child is the free owner of her labour power, of her own person. She and the purchaser of the womb are exchangers 'on the basis of equal rights, with this difference alone, that one is the buyer, the other the seller; both therefore equal in the eyes of the law.' Further, and this is an essential point, the buying and selling of reproductive capacity is done for a *fixed time*, the length of the pregnancy — the measure of time being what distinguishes a temporary assignment of a capacity (of which the owner stays the owner) from a total transfer of this capacity. For

> if [s]he were to sell it rump and stump, once for all, [s]he would be selling [her]self, converting [her]self from a free [wo]man into a slave, from an owner of a commodity into a commodity (Marx, 1974, p. 165).[76]

'Womb-renting' can thus be distinguished from both plantation slavery (where reproduction was imposed on women to produce work-hands and/or slaves for the market), and from the numerous forms of marriage, where this transfer of reproductive capacity is limited neither in time nor in the quantity of production.[77]

Towards the dissolution of ties of private appropriation?
Womb-renting is just the tip of an iceberg, the visible part of a process in which the solid structures that have controlled reproduction for centuries are crumbling.

I envisage here a much more general phenomenon than procreation for payment, namely 'single-parent families'. Sociologists so designate — by a name that hides both the meaning and reality of the phenomenon[78] — the situation where women assume the burden of reproduction and responsibility for children on their own, either because they are divorced or have stopped living with a man, or because they have chosen to have children alone. The meaning is the same, whether they have or have not chosen the situation, and whatever their degree of political engagement or consciousness: women's tie of personal dependence in marriage is dissolved and *private appropriation of female reproducers is no longer a necessary condition for reproduction*.[79]

We are thus faced with a structured transformation of relations of reproduction, comparable in some respects with the dissolution of the ties of serfdom in Europe, a dissolution that allowed the appearance of 'free' workers, the modern wage-labourers.[80]

The rapid rise in numbers of supposed 'single-parent families' shows a transformation of the relations of reproduction is indeed underway, even if its course sometimes appears uneven and contradictory. In France, for instance, between 1962 and 1975, while the number of single mothers living alone increased by around 20 per cent, divorced women heads of families increased by 77 per cent [two-thirds of divorce petitions coming from women], and the progression for the same period was 280 per cent *among those aged under 35 years* (Fine and Lalanne, 1980, p. 90).

In Quebec, women heads of single-parent families 'numbered 132 515 in 1976, 8.5 per cent of families with children. . . . There will currently [1980] be close to 160 000', and their number constantly increases (Dandurand, 1981, p. 104). The breakdown of marriage, long considered peculiar to urban slums and shanty towns in under-developed societies, has lashed industrialised countries. This breakdown does not appear inconsistent with the tendency to empty the family of some of its former functions (both as to productive activities and to the rearing of children), nor the tendency to reduce the birth-rate (see Laurin-Frennette, 1981). The dissolution of marital ties may even be made possible or facilitated by these elements.

It is perhaps too early to understand the meaning and concrete scope of this transformation and to decide if it is a transformation that would *question male domination*, or if we are seeing *a new version of the same domination*. We can, meanwhile, already ask ourselves who is carrying the load and who is receiving the benefits of this transformation.

The history of capitalism reminds us that its establishment was, essentially, paid for by the working class — in misery, in material insecurity, etc. Similarly, when the old relations of reproduction are in a process of transformation without anything changing in the socio-economic relations of the sexes — women's wages are still lower, their access to work unequal, etc. — we can ask ourselves if women alone are not paying the whole price of this transformation.

In Canada, for instance, 'in 1976, nearly 55 per cent of families on social security were women-headed single-parent families'. The poverty risk rises steadily with the degree of 'autonomy' of women:

when they are married, 9 per cent of women risk living in a situation of poverty, while the same risks among women 'without husbands' are as follows: unmarried single, 34 per cent; women heads of single-parent families, 44 per cent; widows and other single, divorced or separated women, 54 per cent (Dandurand, 1981, pp. 104 and 101).

The weakening of the marital institution thus produces a deterioration in the situation of women. Henceforth men will be exempt from the material and psychic costs of reproductive labour, from which they will continue to profit collectively and often individually. Separations and divorces, 'serial monogamy' (where wives remain alone with 'their' children to feed, raise, and care for, etc.), and the frequent indifference of fathers with regard to their progeny, show clearly that the economic and material load of reproduction is left to women. This reproductive work (which also, of course, includes the rearing of children) is essential to perpetuate the human group. But its burden is assumed neither individually by fathers *nor collectively* by society. We thus might be faced with a new form of exploitation of women, more crushing than the one before. In any case, the break-up of private ties of reproduction does not, apparently, bring an end to male domination any more than the breakdown of relations of serfdom at the end of the European middle ages brought an end to class relations. Rather there is a substitution of one form of exploitation for another.

Nonetheless, this process has another aspect: the contradiction 'between the (social) appropriation of women . . . and *their reappropriation by themselves*: their objective existence as social subjects' (Guillaumin, this volume, p. 82). Situated within this reappropriation is the *choice* many women make to have children on their own, not to live in relations of serfdom. In it too are *objectively* the other women who find themselves in the position of single mothers in charge of children. Produced by internal contradictions of the patriarchal system, produced by choices, by women's struggles and by their class consciousness, these situations seem to be the crest of a wave and the dawn of a transformation. Notwithstanding the conflicts, the costs, and the contradictions, they partake of a possibility of liberty, a possibility of leaving behind a long prehistory.

Meanwhile possible developments are hard to discern and uncertain. But nothing will be given to us for free.

Notes

1   To the precious and inextricable contradictions in my relationship of knowledge and love with Gaoussou and Ken Thai.
2   'Fertilité naturelle, reproduction forcée' was first published in Nicole-Claude Mathieu (Ed.) *L'Arraisonnement des femmes: essais en anthropologie des sexes*, Paris: Éditions de l'École des Hautes Études en Science Sociales (in the 'Cahiers de l'Homme' collection), 1985, pp. 61–146. This is the first English translation, by Diana Leonard.
3   These words of Einstein's are cited on the back cover of Dukas and Hoffman (1972).
4   This has often been asserted (cf., Nag, 1962 for the general situation; and Raphael in Saucier, 1972, p. 261 for data concerning lactation in the *Human Relations Area Files*). Documentation on different stages in the reproductive sequence is unsystematic, and there have been few ethno-demographic enquiries.
     Sometimes this lack of interest in procreation rests on ordinary sexism, redoubled by racism, with authors reproducing stereotypes, such as that women in 'primitive' societies do not experience pain during labour because they are more 'natural' — whether or not it is also implied they are 'like animals' (see on the contrary Blackwood, 1935, pp. 153ff.). As a result, we have very little detailed description of childbirth, and little on maternal mortality. We know, however, that it was as important in prehistory (Acsadi and Nemeskeri, 1970; Angel, 1975) as in

European populations in past centuries (cf., *Annales de Demographie historique1*, 1981). According to a study, in Bas-Languedoc at the end of the seventeenth century, for instance, 'one married woman in ten died giving birth to a child' (Gelis, Laget and Morel, 1978, pp. 94–5). The fear of death in childbirth is certainly present in populations studied by anthropologists. In Truk, for instance,

> the dangers of childbirth were formerly emphasized rather dramatically in a feast held by the woman's closest relatives near the end of her pregnancy. . . .This ceremony, which was performed only during her first pregnancy, was phrased as a farewell feast in the event that she died in childbirth; the cloths [offered to her on this occasion] would then form her shroud. If she did not die, they were saved in case she might die in a later birth or her baby be born dead (Gladwin and Sarason, 1953, p. 134).

5 What is given here is a fairly simplified sketch. Though a considerable contribution to knowledge (including knowledge of reproduction) has been made by studies of historical demography, paleo-demography and the demography of anthropological populations (see for instance the important research of Howell (1979) on the !Kung), I think demography's conceptual apparatus — its constant use of such concepts as 'natural fertility' and 'idle time' (see note 37) — does require a profound epistemological critique.

6 This is very evident in the work of Nag. He speaks of elements *affecting reproduction*, but refers only to factors limiting it. For instance, he says

> The only society where the fertility level seems to have been affected by the frequency of coitus is that of Yap. Their fertility level is very low and their average coital frequency is also low (Nag, 1962, p. 76).

This implies a 'spontaneously' high fertility can be expected when there are no voluntary factors (such as abstinence and abortion) nor involuntary ones to upset this natural mechanism.

7 For current definitions of fecundity, fecundability, etc., see Henry, 1961; Léridon, 1973, 1977; or Pressat, 1979. For a brief critical history of the key concepts relating to fertility used in demography, see Le Bras, 1981, who shows the cultural and political context of their emergence.

For example, regarding procreation as a property of women, he says:

> Until the end of the 19th century, great confusion reigned in this field. Sometimes the fecundity of men was measured, sometimes that of women, and sometimes that of couples, depending on the age of the spouses or the length of the marriage. . . . Geneticists and biometricians don't have these hesitations. There is no marriage among flies, so the new biological nature of man made it possible to make a parallel lopping off. First men were separated from reproduction. Time was ripe for women to be specialised within maternal and domestic roles. Demography confines them there. They are the ones who make babies from the 1900s onwards. No more need for men, no more need for marriage. The reproductive power of women develops according to age, from 15 to 50 years . . . and as the biological idea gets reinforced, a predominant role tends to be attributed to the age of the woman. The number of children she produces at a given age appears less the result of multiple social constraints relating to the age of marriage and to the wishes of male family heads, than a demonstration of biological capacity (Le Bras, 1981, pp. 94–5).

8 For an analysis of discourse of Nature as an ideological aspect of the material

appropriation of women (i.e. of the relationship of 'sexage'), and as the ideological justification for other relations of domination also (for example, discourses of 'race'), see Guillaumin (1978a and b, in this volume, and also 1977, 1980, 1981c and 1995). The dichotomous treatment of the two sexes in sociological and anthropological accounts, as well as the ways in which women are constantly attributed the category of natural and negated as subjects, has been shown by Mathieu (1971, 1973, 1977). Michard-Marchal and Ribéry (1982) provide a linguistic analysis of anthropologists' discourse, showing that, even within statements, a process of reification of women is at work, which is characteristic of the dominant naturalist ideology.

9   We thus find in anthropology the same tendencies as we saw at work in demography, which tend to separate men and social relations of sex from procreation. For instance, as Nag notes, although

> it is generally recognized that sexual practices differ in a variety of ways that can be directly attributed to cultural learning . . . very little attempt has been made to study the relationship between sexual practices and human fertility (Nag, 1972, p. 23).

(See also Polgar, 1972, p. 204.) In this context, it is not by chance that one of the least studied elements of the reproductive sequence (to date) has been the frequency of coitus (cf., Nag, 1972; Polgar, 1972). Coitus is the single moment in the sequence where men (males) are directly and clearly involved, on as much a biological as a social level.

10   This no man's land is occupied in an interesting and very specific way in the social sciences by socio-biology. The latter tries to legitimise scientifically the ideas and acts of (what are for our societies) the most traditional forms of male sexual behaviour — with all their constituent parts: reproductive imposition, including aggression; a 'natural tendency' to polygyny; jealousy; etc. — and to imprison women within behaviour which is complementary to that of males. All this to increase *adaptive fitness* and *reproductive success*.

Is it just by chance that so many legitimising studies in this genre — whether the authors declare themselves completely socio-biological or not (see, for example, Symons, 1979) — have been produced in the years since forms of male domination, including the sexual appropriation of women's bodies, have been called in question? Here, as elsewhere, the political colours of socio-biology are fully illuminated (see Sahlins, 1976; Haraway, 1978, 1981; and also Guillaumin, this volume).

11   This phenomenon is explained by Short as follows:

> Normal human sperm contains a very high proportion of morphologically abnormal spermatozoids, often more than 40%, while other primates (with the exception of the gorilla) have remarkably uniform spermatozoids (Short, 1978, pp. 99ff.).

Genetically defective spermatozoids, of which, as we have seen, there are a high proportion, are either incapable of uniting with an ovum, or 'if they were able to fertilize the ovum, would produce abnormal embryos'. This causes most of the extremely high embryonic mortality (calculations say up to '63 per cent of fertilized eggs are spontaneously eliminated', Léridon, 1973, p. 80) and above all early abortions.

12   An analysis of the very vocabulary used for procreation, as much by demographers as in everyday speech, may make clear its strongly ideological character. The words to 'impregnate', to 'fertilise' or to 'fecundate', and 'impregnation' and 'fecundability', all imply and express a representation of biological

events where male gametes (spermatozoa) and female gametes (ova), whose fusion produces the embryo and which each carry an equal store of genetic information, have a differential status. The male gamete is 'active' and accomplishes the 'fertilisation'; while the female is 'passive' and submits to fertilisation: it 'is fertilised'. We thus have, not terms expressing 'scientific' concepts, but an obvious, if trite, metaphor for real power relations. It is but one of many symbolic representations of procreation known from anthropological literature and the history of ideas. (On the history of the concept of 'fecundability', introduced by the demographer Gini, and the demography of the fascist period, see Le Bras, 1981.)

I may use the same words in the remainder of this paper, but with a sociological meaning: as descriptions of the imposition of reproduction, as reproduction taking place in specific conditions of domination.

13   This is shown by the calculations presented in the following table:

The probability of conception during a cycle, by the length of the fertile period and the number of sexual relations (n)

n	Fertile period (in days)						
	0.25	0.5	0.75	1	1.5	2	3
1	0.010	0.020	0.030	0.040	0.060	0.080	0.0120
2	0.020	0.040	0.059	0.078	0.116	0.154	0.226
3	0.030	0.059	0.087	0.115	0.169	0.221	0.319
4	0.039	0.078	0.115	0.151	0.219	0.284	0.400
5	0.049	0.096	0.141	0.185	0.266	0.341	0.472
6	0.059	0.114	0.167	0.217	0.310	0.394	0.536
7	0.068	0.132	0.192	0.249	0.352	0.442	0.591
8			0.216	0.279			0.640
9			0.240	0.307			0.684
10			0.263	0.335			0.722
11	0.105	0.199	0.285	0.362	0.494	0.600	0.755
12	0.114	0.215	0.306	0.387	0.524	0.632	0.784
13	0.123	0.231	0.327	0.412	0.553	0.662	0.810
14	0.131	0.246	0.347	0.435	0.580	0.689	0.833
15	0.140	0.261	0.367	0.458	0.605	0.714	0.853
20	0.182	0.332	0.456	0.558	0.710	0.811	0.922
25	0.222	0.397	0.533	0.640	0.787	0.876	0.969

(Source: Léridon, 1973, p. 42, Table A8)

For other approaches to the probability of conception (according to the day of the cycle, the distribution of sexual relations throughout the month, etc.), see Léridon, 1973, pp. 40ff. and Bourgeois-Pichat 1965, pp. 406ff.

As regards not the theoretical model but the real situation:
(1) 'there are few observations of delays in conception';
(2) analysis of the situation is problematic because of the number of badly understood and little studied intervening variables, such as (a) the length of the female fertile period: 'often said to be 48 hours, but in fact the duration has never been precisely determined for a large population' (Bourgeois-Pichat, 1965, p. 408; and see Léridon, 1973); (b) the frequency of sexual relations, on which 'we are not much better informed' (Bourgeois-Pichat, 1965, p. 410). On the lack and/or the unreliability of data on the frequency of coitus in anthropological

populations, see Nag, 1972. Not to mention the probable (and unconsidered) heterogeneity of attitude of couples (and both sexes) towards reproduction in the groups studied.

To take just one example, on the monthly frequency of coitus in a group of white American women, the frequency ranged from 14.8 relations per months for women aged 20–24 years, to 6.8 for those of 40–44 years (data from Kinsey, cited in Bourgeois-Pichat, 1965, p. 409, table X). Léridon notes the impasse in which demographers find themselves when using such unreliable and variable data as those at their command for the analysis of 'fecundability' (Léridon, 1973, p. 41). The derisory slightness of the data relative to the importance of the phenomena being studied, is, to all evidence a product of the theoretical — and political (see Moreau-Bisseret, 1982) — orientations of studies of fecundity which were referred to earlier.

14   According to the calculations proposed by Léridon, a woman who married at 15 and was fertile until 45, who did not breast-feed, could have an average of 17.5 children (Léridon, 1977, pp. 115ff.). Taking account of the variables of sterility (high or low), the age at marriage, lactation, 'idle time' ('non-susceptible', anovular periods where there could be no conception, and please note that this includes the duration of pregnancy!) for the population, Léridon considers there would be a variation between an average of 12.8 children (if there were low sterility, marriage at 19, and no breast-feeding) and 4.7 children (in cases of average sterility, marriage at 25, and prolonged breast-feeding).

In the same theoretical line, Howell has made comparative calculations on the fecundity of !Kung women and those of the Hutterites (Howell, 1979, pp. 165ff.).

15   We can criticise such definitions of marriage and the family as 'the privileged place for the exercise of sexuality between authorized partners' (Héritier, 1979a, p. 7) for implicitly assuming that: (1) there is a natural sexuality, a natural sexual drive, in known human societies; (2) this drive leads naturally only to heterosexual coitus; and (3) societies provide a place for it to be exercised. Hence marriage only intervenes (as regards sexuality) as a 'receiving structure' for such natural forces.

This definition (and others like it) does not take account, or at least does not take sufficient account, of either the training which fashions the modalities of sexuality, nor the psychic and physical coercion and violence which oblige individuals to conform to it.

In this sense, it does not seem possible to support the suggestion that 'the sexual instinct which pushes towards reproduction, and the instinct which pushes towards protection of the new-born, are natural phenomena for both sexes'; while also arguing that 'the maternal instinct' 'is an acquired phenomenon', produced by education, etc. (Héritier, 1979a, p. 15). All the 'instincts' known in human societies must be put rigorously on the same level. They are all social phenomena, tied to political relations between the sexes. Moreover, they are phenomena where it is difficult to envisage a symmetry of situations for men and women.

16   The French term 'dressage' means both 'training' and the 'breaking in' of animals, as well as carrying a sense — for English speakers — of the mincing performance of riding school horses [translator's note].

17   Among the Hausa of Ader, the lack of economic autonomy for women is such that only literate and employed women 'escape . . . the brutal and general assertion in Ader, according to which "women have only their sex to live by" ' (Echard *et al.*, 1981, p. 346). Similarly, 'On Yap a woman's genitals are likened to a man's land: they are her real asset in terms of which she maintains her position in the all-embracing Yap hierarchy of rank and prestige' (Schneider, 1955, p. 231). This

economic dependence is nicely confirmed, with no evasion of the issue, in: 'a woman was said to "have her land in her legs"', and in exchange for the land belonging to her husband and the group (the *tabinaw*), she had to produce children (Labby, 1976, pp. 28ff. and 19ff.).

Affirmations about maternity and sex as women's function are not just ideological: *their reality is indeed material*. The sexual division of labour, with its unequal forms of access to the means of production and to tools (see Tabet, 1979), the unequal division of resources and unequal wages, all, in different ways in different societies, constitute the base of an unequal exchange whereby women surrender not only their labour power (their productive labour) but also their capacity to procreate (their whole body). I shall discuss the status of this 'surrender' later (see below) and for other forms of 'sexual-economic exchange', see Tabet (1987, 1989).

18 I do not agree with Ortner's interpretation of rape in Polynesia (Ortner, 1981, p. 377). She says: The girls behave in a way corresponding to their valued kinship status: they behave as people who can choose their partner or 'voluntarily withhold sex altogether'. This can appear 'stuck up' and haughty to the men, who therefore 'tame' them by rape. But the girls also show an 'enhanced sexual attractiveness'. According to Ortner 'it is the combined and contradictory message transmitted by the girl — "come hither/go away" — that is so provoking to the men'.

This interpretation is much too close to the one we have heard used so many times to defend rapists on trial, as well as in everyday accounts in our own society. 'She asked for it.' Ortner says, moreover, (with Carroll) that rape for Polynesian women is 'less psychologically traumatic than it is for us' (Ortner, 1981, p. 405, note 20)! By contrast, see Freeman's account of the fear and shame of rape among girls in Samoa, and how rape is 'intrinsic to the sexual mores of Samoan men', one of the 'major elements in their sexual behaviour', involving 'culturally transmitted male practices', like a punch in the stomach and the rape of an unconscious girl (Freeman, 1983, pp. 245-7).

19 Williams, talking of young wives who run away to their parents, describes 'a very severe and brutal way of breaking [their] spirit, a custom which could be called communal rape. It may be adopted at the instance of the husband himself' (Williams, 1969, pp. 163-4).

It should be noted that here, as in many other cases, there is no evident contradiction between the collective appropriation of women by a group (the class) of men, and the private appropriation of one (or several) women by one man. The one guarantees and is the condition of the other, and their deep structural solidarity is thus fully illuminated.

20

> A young Ifusa woman named Hagarisoja was negotiated for by Kaᶜeavu, father's brother to Tegenopi of Kogu to whom she eventually went as wife.... Hagarisoja was put into her own hut. That night Tegenopi came down from the men's house to visit her, but she was afraid and refused his attentions. This occurred several times, the girl finally saying that he was a 'no-good' man and was not to copulate with her. Tegenopi then grew angry. He went to Kaᶜi, his elder brother (father's brother's son) and told him that the girl was afraid of him; they could take her into the bush and copulate with her and then return her to him. Kaᶜi got together a number of men ... Kaᶜi took hold of the girl and carrying her on his back brought her to the others, who copulated with her one after the other. Then they told Gumevi, a young man, to take up his position in front of the girl with penis erect. Kaᶜi then stood above him with a stick of sugar cane.... Resting it on Gumevi's shoulders, he

called out invocations to the ancestors . . . On calling the last name Ka^ci broke the sugar cane over Gumevi's shoulders, and he plunged his penis into her, while all the other men called out 'ei! ei! ei!' and crowded behind him, pushed, released, and pushed, with regular movements, until he had ejaculated . . . Ka^ci then heated his penis over a warm fire to make it very hard and pushed it into the girl 'like an arrow' so that she cried out and defecated in fear. 'Thus my brother Tegenopi can copulate with you', said Ka^ci. Then he took Hagarisoja back to Tegenopi' (Berndt, 1962, p. 170).

The commentary by the anthropologist, with his calm and unquestioning identifying of rape with marriage, gives a measure of his integration into the men's group. Cultural relativism does not mask adhesion to, and legitimation of, the suppression of women:

This was partially punishment for a wife who consistently refused the attentions of her husband. She was young and afraid, not so much of intercourse but because she was in an alien district. The treatment was designed to give her a liking for intercourse, to break down any resistance on her part, and to make her feel at home. The special form this takes differs from that in previous examples. It is more *in the form of a rite* [!], symbolic of a husband's right of access to this wife. The sugar cane is likened to a penis which, like it, should 'taste sweet'. . . . Here is a woman from another district who must be assimilated, and this is done through intercourse. Men and women can be adjusted to one another only through intercourse, for this is the basis of their relationship. This important truism is echoed throughout the period of socialization; there is fundamental antagonism between the sexes, and *this can be overcome only through sexual relations, as crystallizing the dependence of one sex on the other*' (Berndt, 1962, pp. 170–1, stress added).

21 The operation which the Aranda girl experiences, the *atna araltakama*, consists in an enlarging of the vagina by an introcision with a stone knife, followed immediately by copulation with several men (Roheim, 1933, pp. 234ff.). Roheim interprets this ritual by recalling an initiation myth (ibid, pp. 235ff.). In the myth, a 'too tight' girl is 'opened', and 'after the operation they all copulate with her and make her *nguanga* (quiet)'. According to Roheim, for Aranda men 'there are only two kinds of women: those who grant their desires and those who refuse to do so — i.e. *alknarintja* (*aninpa*) and *nguanga*, "wild" ones and "quiet" ones.'
It is rape that makes women subdued, as Roheim confirms with a story from an Aranda woman. As a girl she worked for a white boss: 'He locks all the girls into a room and rapes them, i.e. makes them "quiet".' Roheim adds, 'The ritual applies a shock treatment to the under-developed sexuality of the female in order to break her resistance' (ibid, p. 236).
So what does the sexuality of Aboriginal girls in central Australia consist in that it must be developed by such a ritual?

Before marriage every girl is in a certain sense an *alknarintja*, or, at least, it is regarded as the proper thing for her to behave as if she were an *alknarintja*. Of course, there is plenty of prenuptial intercourse, and homosexuality also plays a conspicuous part in the life of a young girl (ibid, p. 238).

This wild, and wildly polymorphous, sexuality is unacceptable, above all to Roheim. It must be subdued — an opinion happily shared by the psychoanalyst anthropologist (who has just equated the white boss's rape and local men's ritual) and his indigenous male informants:

> In order to be transferred from an *alknarintja* to a *nguanga*, from frigidity to object erotism, from homosexuality to heterosexuality, the female must be subjected to force: raped, conquered, castrated (ibid, p. 237).

22 Spencer shows the shock treatment endured by girls is analogous to the training of dogs in Pavlov's experiments (Spencer, 1965, p. 248). The dogs are submitted to mental and physical techniques (castration, digestive problems, excessive fatigue, etc.) that cause depressive states. In these 'transmarginal' states, the dogs can be conditioned and acquire new models of behaviour. He says the same procedures are used in political torture: to confess and accept may be the only way to survive. The training/breaking in of prostitutes who are put to work by pimps, uses the same methods (Barry, 1979).

23 The Mangaian male 'judges potency by his ability (or that of others) to get the same woman pregnant twice in a year' (Marshall, 1971). It is certainly not only in Mangaia that being-a-man, being virile, is identified with being able to impregnate women, to 'blow up their bellies' (in everyday speech in Tuscany). The everyday language of European countries is rich in expressions currently used by men to boast of their capacity to impregnate, and with threats to do so.

24 In a study of fertility, of 'reproductive success' in 'egalitarian' societies, particularly the Yanomamo, Chagnon asks the following question: why do the most fecund men of the group have more children (an average of 5.43) with wives from the numerically dominant lineages, than with wives from other lineages (average 3.3)? He replies that this is due to the stability of marriages, or rather to the 'social pressures' that tend to maintain more stable marriages between individuals from dominant lineages — given their political implications (Chagnon, 1979, p. 394; and also 1974).

This is the example Chagnon offers to demonstrate his thesis. Two heads of villages and members of the two dominant lineages exchanged their sisters. The sister of one formed a relationship with another man, and her brother tried to dissuade her from it. 'The woman refused to follow the advice of her brother, and he consequently killed her with an axe.' Higher and political fertility is thus imposed on some women, and if they do not know where their real 'reproductive interest' lies, they may pay dearly for their lack of socio-biological clairvoyance!

25 This is not the only type of explanation put forward for the weak growth of prehistoric populations and modern groups of hunter-gatherers. Other hypotheses privilege physiological and socio-biological mechanisms of population limitation.

According to Frisch, for instance, a mechanism whereby lack of food affects the reproductive capacity and level of fertility (under-fed populations tend to have a lower fecundity than better nourished populations) seems to be a less wasteful mechanism of ecological adaptation than a limitation of population by higher mortality (Frisch, 1978, p. 29). For an account of this form of 'automatic' control of excess population in groups of hunter-gatherers in difficult situations, see Howell, 1979, p. 205.

For general hypotheses taking account of this type of mechanism since the Pleistocene, see Cohen, 1980; and also Lee, 1980. For a critique of the model according to which mortality and natality would have had to be 'very high' constantly from prehistory to industrialisation, and the idea that a very high fecundity would have been indispensable to prevent the extinction of human groups, see Polgar, 1972.

26 Tilly and Scott show the atmosphere of suspicion surrounding child-birth in

Europe in past centuries. A woman in labour would call in her women neighbours, not only so they could help her, but also so they could witness, in case the child died, that the mother did not kill it. See also Flandrin (1981, pp. 172ff.) on the importance of 'involuntary' infanticide in Europe from the Middle Ages to the nineteenth century, and the repeated attempts by the Catholic Church to put a stop to it.

27 Gutmann considers the fact of not crying during labour

> all the more remarkable since even a normal Chagga birth is much more painful than the average European birth. This is due to the fact that the circumcision scars reduce the elasticity of the vagina. The most torturous pains for a Chagga woman begin after the child has passed the pelvis. Women who have their first child, as a rule experience a dangerous obstruction of the delivery, and the obstruction occurs where there is normally no more obstacle (Gutmann, 1926, pp. 203–4, 179–80 in the English translation).

28 The management of childbirth, its direct monopoly by men doctors, and its medicalisation (along with all 'reproductive care') is one of the most studied aspects of reproduction, including the feminist literature (see, among others, Rich, 1976; Oakley, 1976).

For the history of childbirth's passage from the competence of midwives and wise-women to accoucheurs and obstetricians in France over the last centuries, see Laget, 1977; Gelis, 1977; Gelis, Laget and Morel, 1978; and Knibiehler and Fouquet, 1983. Historically the introduction of instruments in technical care of delivery also marked the limit between work accessible to women and that of men, since midwives were forbidden to use forceps. (See, Tabet, 1979, for a general discussion of women's access to tools and the sexual division of labour.)

29 For an attempt at a demographic analysis of the relations between management of reproduction and social forms, see, Hassan (1980, 1981); Cohen (1980).

30 This thesis has more recently been taken up by Schrire and Steiger (1974) and used in a computer simulation. The program developed does not always take account of the compensatory effects of the reduction of genetic intervals following infanticides (see the critiques of Acker and Townsend, 1975; and Chapman, 1980; and below). According to Schrire and Steiger, even appreciably lower rates of infanticide than those known for Eskimo groups would doom these groups to extinction in a few hundred years. Hence, they suggest, the available facts on systematic infanticide of girls among the Eskimos are incorrect or non-representative.

31 This kind of infanticide involves mainly the *quality* of the child, but there is also infanticide linked to a change of partner, where a woman kills the child of an illegitimate father or a late husband so as to be able to make a child with the (new) husband (see Howell, 1979, p. 242 and Gutmann, 1926 for examples among the !Kung and the Chagga).

Balikci classifies similar cases among the Eskimos as being due to 'purely social causes', as against the infanticide of girls which, he says,

> can only be explained *as a survival response*. Women did not hunt, they were not self-sufficient and they were less independent than men. The hunter had to feed the girl for many years and when she grew up she got married and left the family (Balikci, 1970, pp. 151ff.).

For Balikci obviously this is not the description of a purely social situation! Everyone knows women are biologically incapable of providing for their own needs, and biologically forced to marry and leave their families! Therefore they (or at least some of them) must be killed at birth, or better still, kill themselves, like the widow of the hunter among the Ammassalik, forced to drown herself and her children in the sea — for the survival of the family and the group (Gessain, 1969). '[W]e assume . . . female infanticide was an adaptive measure increasing the survival chance of the Netsilik family', says Balikci (1967, p. 624). In any event, it certainly seems to have assured the survival of a system of male domination.

32 If biological mechanisms and social measures (like post-partum abstinence, see Howell, 1979, p. 120; Silberbauer, 1981, p. 156) fail, nomad women meet the impossibility of raising two children at once by abortion or infanticide.

Working on Australian materials, Cowlishaw (1978, pp. 266-7) has shown the importance and diffusion of infanticide due to refusal of maternity and its links to forms of sex relations and oppression suffered by women. This infanticide very often involves a woman's first child or children. Analogous situations are found elsewhere, and also lead to abortion of the products of first conceptions (for the Mbaya, see Boggiani, 1895; Azara, 1809; and in general, Devereux, 1976). It is a form of women's resistance, analogous to those described for Baruya women (Godelier, 1976, pp. 19ff.; 1982, pp. 223 and 235). A case of resistance and refusal of maternity among the Arapesh, that of Amitoa, is described in detail by Mead (1935).

The open or secret, individual or collective, character of this practice, and the degree to which it is tolerated or accepted at group level, needs equally to be studied in relation to the 'problem of how population size and density affect and are affected by particular forms of productive regimes and socio-political organisation' (Edholm, Harris and Young, 1977, p. 112).

33 Need we point out that ovulation reestablishes only the necessary, not the sufficient, conditions for conception? *Exposure to risk of pregnancy* resumes only if all other conditions remain the same: if exposure to coitus, and in particular the possibility that it will be imposed, remain the same.

As Harrell has said, the discourse concerns solely 'coitally accessible reproductive aged women' (Harrell, 1981, p. 803). Potter's calculations, cited by Léridon, apply to these women permanently exposed to the risk of pregnancy, and are correct but absurd from the point of view of women:

> the number of induced abortions necessary to avert one live birth in the absence of accompanying contraception is 2.5 [in the case of prolonged breast-feeding with a long period of amenorrhea] . . . with no breast-feeding the number of abortions necessary would be just under 2 (Léridon, 1977, p. 127).

These calculations start from the base that abortion does not reduce, but rather *increases* 'the degree of exposure to the risk of conception.' How come? Simple. A woman who carries a pregnancy to term spends a period of 20 months not exposed to the risk of conception, due to the pregnancy and amenorrhea resulting from breast-feeding (or more if the breast-feeding is lengthy). 'If she interrupts her pregnancy her *idle period* [!] is reduced to 4 or 5 months and she is thus exposed sooner to the risk of a new pregnancy' (ibid, stress added, and see also note 35).

The same (modified) calculation could be applied to infanticides. It takes 1.5-2 infanticides to avoid a living child. In conditions of permanent exposure to the risk of pregnancy, one escapes being impregnated only by already being involved in the reproductive process (i.e. pregnant). You have to be dead to no longer be able to die.

34 This fact is underlined by Rasmussen and taken up again by Acker and Townsend (1975). Chapman has integrated it into a computer simulation on the possible rates of infanticide (Chapman, 1980). He shows that *even with 30 per cent infanticide of*

girls, a group will not die out. There is in fact a stronger (and compensatory) fecundity subsequent to infanticides, with a considerable reduction in the length of intergenetic intervals.

35 Freeman sees the infanticide of girls as also linked to the need for explicit assertion of male domination (Freeman, 1971, p. 1015).

The elements specific to Eskimo infanticide — its being a technical intervention, directed by men, which imposes intensified reproductive activity — is also found in other cases of selective infanticide of girls. Among the Arapesh, for instance, the father decides whether or not to keep the new-born: 'Arapesh prefer boys because they stay close to their parents. . . . A family which already has one or two girls and decides to keep another will considerably reduce its chances of having a boy.' The father will therefore probably give the midwife an order not to wash the girl, that is to say, to kill her (Mead, 1935, p. 31).

36 According to Saucier, the substitution of a post-partum taboo, a 'burdensome, complicated and unreliable means of spacing children', for the 'very simple and very reliable' traditional pre-neolithic technique of infanticide, seems 'to be closely related to the low status of women in these societies' (Saucier, 1972, p. 263).

37 The concern for procreation in these cases is with having a living child, with its survival — which is the difference between this and the point of view of demographers who talk of pregnancy as an 'idle period'. The latter is considered one of the 'fundamental factors' in so-called 'natural' fertility. Henry, who introduced this term, defined it as follows:

> A pregnant woman cannot conceive again for a certain period of time, whose end, which is obviously after the end of the pregnancy, is marked by the reappearance of ovulation (if sexual relations have already been resumed) or by the resuming of sexual relations (if ovulation has already reappeared). Each conception thus marks the beginning of an idle period (Henry, 1964, p. 485).

He draws analogies with other *idle times*, e.g. with a machine which breaks down, whose repair is analogous to a pregnancy, and the period after the repair analogous to the anovular period. But the real underlying equivalence comes through clearly when the text is taken word for word:

> [a] *A machine which breaks down* enters a period [b] where *it cannot break down again*; this period is [c] *at least as long as the length of the breakdown,* but it can be longer if the repair eliminates the risk of breakdown for a while (ibid, p. 487, stress added).

This is the same as saying:

> [a] *A pregnant woman* [b] *cannot conceive again* for a certain period of time, whose end is, [c] *obviously after the end of the pregnancy . . .*

Falling pregnant is equated with breaking down. This might sometimes be the way impregnated women feel. But the parallel is not proposed from the point of view of women. Rather it is the point of view of copulatory success.

The other example of idle period Henry puts forward, the 'queue for a telephone line', confirms this. 'A telephone call to an engaged extension . . . must be re-established.' Henry decrees that conversation = 'idle time', which is not true for the people talking, nor for the productivity of the telephone company. It is only true for the arrogance of the dominant. If he is not immediately put through, if he cannot instantly demonstrate his 'power', then it is a loss: it is idle time.

This is a theory of fertilising ejaculation rather than fertility. In it the period when human beings are produced is disclaimed. It is idle time or breakdown. Hence, the more women are involved in reproduction (gestating and breast-feeding), and the more children they have, the more their lives are filled, paradoxically, with 'idle time':

> Boston women spend on the average 7 per cent of their fertile life in idle time, *while Punjabi women spend around 40 per cent of their fertile life in idle time* (Léridon, 1973, p. 89, stress in original).

An analogous example can be found in Bourgeois-Pichat (1965). He establishes, first, that 'there are two groups of women, those who assure the reproduction of the species, and the others'. But, alas, the 'group of fertile women who participate in reproduction' have some problems: 'They pass through periods of temporary infertility. Such as pregnancies.'

A French *Dictionary of Demography* confirms this (Pressat, 1979). Here are some of its definitions:

> *Sterility*: 'inability to *procreate*' (the antonym being fertility, and *procreation* being defined as 'bringing a child into the world. Generally including only children born alive.') Note that Pressat stresses the difference between the medical definition of sterility (inability to conceive) and that of demographers (inability to procreate) (ibid, p. 203).

> *Temporary sterility*: 'Period of sterility in women followed by a return to fertility. The most typical example is the period of idle time which follows a conception and which includes the period of gestation.'

Only repeated conceptions *without pregnancy* perhaps establish full reproductive 'efficacy' and complete fertility, or rather, give these gentlemen the uninterrupted pleasure of impregnating.

38   Even though there can be an opposition between a husband's established right to coitus and concern for the life of the child and the woman (which we are certainly mostly not told about it). Anthropological accounts also show us cases where, in a conflict between the two rules, the reason of the stronger prevails (see Blackwood, 1935, p. 156) and even reaches violence and sometimes murder (Wilson, 1977, p. 128).

For discussions in the Catholic Church on abstinence during nursing over the centuries, see Flandrin (1981, pp. 151ff., and 1982). In the first centuries this was preached as being for the good of the child, since a new pregnancy brought 'bad' milk, hence premature weaning and a risk of death for the infant. But successive decisions of theologians subordinated the physical well-being of the child to the husband's conjugal rights and the salvation of his soul. Continence might push him to adultery, a mortal sin more to be feared than the consequences for the child's life.

39   In preparation for marriage, Banyankole girls are confined and gorged with large quantities of milk, so their mobility is almost totally restricted:

> By the end of the year of confinement, the girl would lose all desire for any form of activity and even lose the power of walking, so that she could only waddle. The fatter she grew the more beautiful she was considered, and her condition was a pronounced contrast to that of men who were athletic and well-developed (Roscoe, 1923, p. 120).

This immobilisation also constitutes a preparation for the collective sexual service to which Banyankole women are subjected after their marriage (see Roscoe, ibid, pp. 123ff; Elam, 1973; and below note 56).

40   An exceptional and even higher fecundity existed in another occupational category in Lyon, that of butchers. Their wives worked in their shops and babies were sent to wet nurses. One butcher's wife had 21 children during the first 24 years of her marriage (Garden, 1975, p. 52).

41   The mortality was such that large towns like Lyon grew, not through a positive internal demographic balance, but from constant contributions from outside.

> Children's stay with a wet-nurse in the country was the main thing responsible for the human deficit in the towns; with *the conditions of life and work of young women in particular* the second element in the high mortality (Garden, 1975, p. 352, stress added).

Lyonnais women had more children than country women, but could not raise them,

> They live like men constantly in the workshop and shop, at the same rhythm as the men, *but not at the same level*. Women's work is indispensable but entirely dependent: married or single, women are perpetual servants (Garden, 1975, p. 351, stress added).

And servants were quickly replaced if they died, as can be seen from the figures on remarriage for men:

> 90% married again 'less than a year after the death of their previous wife and in 80% of cases less than six months after the death. The average time which elapsed was less than four months, and 30% of widowers contracted a new marriage *less than two months* after the break up of the first' (Garden, 1975, p. 59, stress added).

These are the figures for the parish of Saint-Georges, one of the poorest in Lyon, where silk-workers formed about 70 per cent of the working population.

42   A flexibility assured by variations in age at marriage, by the greater or lesser importance of voluntary or imposed celibacy, and also by many prohibitions of a ritual or religious character against intercourse. See, for example, Flandrin (1981, 1983) for the imposition or raising of prohibitions of this kind within the history of Christianity; and Firth (1963) and Borrie, Firth and Spillius (1957) for mechanisms for adapting population to resources in Tikopia, through the imposition of celibacy, *coitus interruptus* and infanticide. We also know from studies in historical demography, that variation in age at marriage was one of the most supple mechanisms for regulating exposure to risk of pregnancy (and hence natality) in demography prior to the nineteenth century. During periods of crisis the age at marriage rose, and with relative abundance it fell.

43   Of course, there can be sexual desire but at the same time refusal of maternity, with a consequent pregnancy imposed on someone who did not refuse the sexual relation from which it results. But shouldn't this form of imposition also be considered a form of rape? It is, after all, bodily integrity which is at stake (see below, pp. 147 and note 69).

44   On the evolutionary tendencies in sexuality among primates, see Butler (1974) and Hrdy (1981). These show that the biological organisation of human sexuality is not separated from the sexuality of some higher primates by quite distinct characteristics (as used to be thought until a few years ago). However, things, like 'the separation of sexual receptivity and reproduction so that sexual behavior becomes an important part of the complex social behavior of primates' (Butler, 1974, p. 31), do assume an importance and particular development among human beings.

45   It is quite difficult to picture what an undifferentiated sexuality would be, given we

have no concrete examples, and hence to grasp the extent of social intervention into human sexual flexibility. For an attempt to 'think the unthinkable' (a 'thought experiment'), i.e. a society without gender and without obligatory ties between sexuality and reproduction, see Cucchiari (1981).

46 Modern contraception perfects the separation between sexuality and procreation, and establishes the *non-necessity* to procreate into biologically reproductive relations themselves. It thus allows women mastery of their bodies (albeit at considerable cost), a point to which I shall return. But this incalculably significant fact does not necessarily contradict the process I have described, which channels all sexual expression towards potentially procreative conduct. If we look at the broad situation in contemporary western societies, we see that 'sexual liberation' led more to multiple and accelerated use of girls — according to the obligatory forms of *male consumption* sexuality (see also Vandelac, 1981a) — than to a multiform erotic flowering (which is also made possible with the complete separation of sexuality and reproduction due to effective contraception).

47 Adrienne Rich has shown that the constraints on women to be heterosexual (compulsory heterosexuality) have not been properly analysed, and that even in feminist literature, women's heterosexuality has been considered, implicitly or not, a presupposition that does not require explanation, a very obvious given. Rich suggests (1980, p. 637) that 'heterosexuality, like motherhood, needs to be recognized and studied as a political institution'. See also Rubin (1975).

48 In relation to this, we must remember the well-known fact that sexuality has suffered, and still suffers, some of the most destructive interventions urged on by colonisation and missionary activity.

For instance, a curfew in several Oceanic islands prevented anyone going out after 9 or 10 o'clock in the evening, in order to avoid (repress), among other things, adultery in general and sexual activity outside of married couples. The following are a few scattered pieces of information I have come across. For Truk, see Gladwin and Sarason (1953, p. 108), for Mangaia, see Marshall (1971, pp. 129 and 149) and for Samoa, see Freeman (1983). In Mangaia, the deacons

> had the equivalent of police powers to enforce an early curfew and to fine those who offended against church-inspired laws. There is still a rigid nine o'clock evening curfew, and all unmarried people must remain indoors or be taken to court (Marshall, 1971, pp. 148–9).

As regards especially extra-marital and non-procreative sexuality, homosexuality, etc., this produced, at a factual level, the result noted by Meillassoux (1975, p. 27) in relation to incest: 'presumably, as with other practices which Christianity considered "shameful" they were quickly suppressed' (Meillassoux, 1981, p. 11). See also Etienne and Leacock (1980), in particular the text by Leacock (pp. 30ff.).

In addition, most importantly, data on sexuality, and particularly studies specifically devoted to it, have been mostly produced by men, based on information given by men — which, as Davenport notes, introduces 'a clear masculine bias both as to subjects and outlook of the observer' (Davenport, 1977, p. 122). Data on homosexuality are few, often 'of dubious quality', and sometimes difficult to interpret. They also concern almost exclusively male homosexuality (ibid, p. 153). The general descriptive framework of the practice of heterosexuality is thus subject to distortion, and the sexuality of women ignored to the highest degree. From time to time some authors (for example, Gladwin and Sarason, 1953, p. 254; and Marshall, 1971, p. 107) acknowledge in passing the partiality and 'masculinity' of their data — while a recent and otherwise interesting French publication on 'western sexualities' (*Communications*, 1982) does not even do this.

49   For this as for the other 'bodily specialisation' of women, wet nursing (i.e. work as a breast-feeder), we need to examine the correlation between this 'vertical' division of sexual labour between women (i.e. some women being specialised full-time as sexually servicers of men) and the demographic size of groups in which it occurs (and obviously also the overall economic structure of the society). Do some societies tend towards a complete Taylorisation of women's 'machine-bodies' — for use in procreation, or sex, or as milk machines?

50   There were in fact various different theoretical and moral positions in the classical world that were not without influence on Christian thought.

The followers of the Pythagorian sect, for instance, whose chaste and virtuous women certainly had a duty to bear legitimate children, and to renounce any form of abortion, also equally preached natural moderation and sexual continence for men: sperm should not serve pleasure, it was reserved for the reproduction of the species. Or again there was a moral of moderation 'according to nature' among the Stoics, for whom all amorous passion (even passionate relations between a man and his wife) were reprehensible — an expression of immoderation (see Veyne, 1982; Detienne, 1972; Flandrin, 1981). See also Etienne (1973) for the relationship between moral attitudes, medical practice, and laws on contraception, abortion and infanticide.

51   For example, according to gynaecological literature of the period, the average sexual experience accorded married women in the nineteenth century in France was limited to acts of coitus giving 'an impression of great monotony and still greater brevity', meaning here an average duration of coitus 'neighbouring that of soft boiling an egg, say three or four minutes' (Corbin, 1982, p. 289). Of course, it was also theorised at the time that a weak sex drive was specific to women's 'nature' (Corbin, 1982; Knibiehler and Fouquet, 1983).

For the history of sexuality in European populations, see the works of Flandrin (on the attitudes of theologians towards procreation and sexuality and on actual behaviour). A résumé of this problematic can be found in Flandrin (1982).

52   This has not in the past, and does not today, prevent many prostitutes from having children. On prostitution in some African countries and its particular characteristics (among others, that of being an often temporary situation between one marriage and another), and on procreation among prostitutes, see Bujra, 1977; Vandersypen, 1977; Vidal, 1977; also, Tabet, 1987, 1989, 1991; and White, 1990.

53   This is evidently in line with 'the sexual order': with the repression of non-genital-reproductive sexual patterns. But it could also be interpreted as a refusal of further alienation on the part of prostitutes; a refusal to offer a service they resented, which was culturally defined as particularly humiliating. See also Pheterson, 1989; Tabet, 1991.

Be that as it may, the idea of avoiding 'unnatural' sexual practices in prostitution was one of the aspects on which the regulatory project was defeated in the second half of the nineteenth century. The wealthiest brothels offered the privileged all manner of practices: erotic shows, tortures and bestiality, etc. (Corbin, 1982, pp. 182ff.). But this obviously did not imply any 'liberation' of the person of prostitutes (nor of their sexuality). On the contrary, in deluxe establishments their lot seems even to have deteriorated (ibid).

54   This applies particularly to women, though there are examples of rape and physical violence exercised, generally by men, towards boys (within the course of initiations, see for example, Godelier, 1982). This shows again that men have a monopoly on violence.

55   This is shown clearly by data on contraceptive measures, abortions (see, for example, data in Elwin (1959) on the number of abortions among girls in the *ghotul* — not that rare in sum total) and infanticides, even given girls' relatively low fertility due to adolescent sterility.

For a summary of the data and anthropological discussions of adolescent sterility, see Nag, 1962, pp. 107–13. For discussions and hypotheses on the minimum critical weight necessary for periods to begin, and for the establishment and maintenance of ovulatory cycles, see Frisch and McArthur, 1974; Frisch, 1975, 1978; and also Short, 1978 for a swift overview of the hypotheses and discussions. See also, Howell, 1979 for applications of Frisch's hypothesis to the demography of the !Kung.

56   A case of sexual usage of this kind, which is also fairly specific because it concerns not girls (for whom sexual relations are forbidden) but married women, is that of the Bahima of the former Ankole kingdom (Bonte, 1976; Elam, 1973; Roscoe, 1923).

After marriage (where the first sexual relations with her husband 'are dramatised and conceived as a rape', see Bonte, 1976, p. 49), a woman must submit to sexual relations with her husband's father, brothers and general agnatic group (she may be constrained to do this by force), and also with his friends and the men with whom he has co-operative economic relationships.

> [T]he reciprocity of sexual access to wives in fact constitutes one of the foundations of the social order . . . The function of these sexual relations is to create, or maintain, social relations which benefit the husband (Bonte, ibid).

The 'sexual freedom' of Bahima women (Elam, 1973) is thus in fact one of the strongest and most explicit forms of men's collective bodily appropriation and manipulation of women for economic and political control.

57   There is here a question of professional ethics (see Mathieu, 1981). The anthropologist gave information to one half of Rukuba society only — to the men — and withheld it from the women, although they needed it. He therefore took a very specific position: in support of the imposition of reproduction and oppression of women. But this is neither the only possible, nor the obligatory position. Cf. Schneider's opposite procedure in 1955 (note 58).

58   Schneider in his research on the causes of depopulation on Yap, was confronted by the following question: should the authorities (the American administration after the war) take action against abortion, since the inhabitants, 'particularly the men, feel the need to do something about the low population'? Schneider said no — 'eliminating abortion and providing no substitute method *would work counter to the felt needs of women under thirty*'. And, he added, 'To challenge this motivation directly would be futile. *It would also be unethical*, in the writer's view.' He therefore approved of the introduction onto Yap of a form of contraception which was less dangerous for women than abortion (despite probable opposition from the men), and said it is 'of prime importance, the technique must be in the hands of women, not men' (Schneider, 1955, pp. 227–9 and 233–4, stress added).

59   For Polynesian societies, see Ortner, who notes that women often lose

> 'both status and freedom' in marriage. This, together with their lack of 'political' interest (women identify with their own kin), could contribute to the widespread abortion and infanticide in these societies (Ortner, 1981, pp. 390–2).

See Devereux (1976, pp. 361ff.) for an attempt to classify abortions according to motivations, attitudes, sanctions and techniques, etc.

60   I use the term domestication in the technical sense of 'a transformation to adapt better to an end or given need'. As Barrau says, the effects of domestication are

on the one hand, a progressive elimination of everything that stands in the way of utilisation by men; and on the other, an accentuation of all those characteristics favourable to utilisation by men . . . (Barrau, 1978, p. 60).

61 Examining the most recent studies of primate sexuality, and partially taking up Sherfey's theses (1973) on the repression and forced elimination 'of women's inordinate sexuality', Hrdy asks: 'If we assume that women have been biologically endowed with a lusty primate sexuality, how have cultural developments managed to alter or over-ride this legacy?' (Hrdy, 1981, p. 176). Considering the systematic forms of suppression of women (infanticide, clitoridectomy, infibulation, forms of confinement, etc.) she notes:

> Only in human societies are females as a class systematically subjected to the sort of treatment that among other species would be rather randomly accorded to the most defenseless members of the group — the very young, the disabled, or the very old — regardless of sex. This is another way of saying that among people, the biological dimorphism of the sexes has become institutionalized (Hrdy, 1981, p. 185).

62 See Cucchiari (1981, pp. 56ff. and note 24), who sees a process of polarisation of sexuality and 'genderisation of sexuality' at work.

Whitehead (1981) has made an interesting analysis of institutionalised homosexuality among the North-American Indians, which she also compares to the very different forms of male homosexuality in New Guinea and those of modern American culture. She concludes that in the three cases: 'We see some manifestation of the dominance of heterosexuality as the model for sexual exchange', and recalls the observations of Rubin (1975, pp. 182ff.): 'The rules of gender divisions and of obligatory heterosexuality are present even in their transformations'.

63 Although it is too broad for my purposes, the following definition of work is used in biological anthropology:

> to the biological anthropologist I think 'work' would be defined as the expenditure of energy. Any form of energy expenditure is a form of work. In this sense the only time when we stop working is when we die because it requires work just to keep alive — that is to say it requires an energy expenditure (Harrison, 1979, p. 37).

Various examples of expenditure of energy are: an adult man needs 70 kilocalories an hour to stay alive in a state of sleep or light activity; walking requires 110 kcals/hr; really heavy work, like cutting wood or clearing a forest, requires 450 kcals/hr; one day's work (8 hours) for a Quechua shepherd in the Andes takes from 685 to 982 kcals (the calorific cost of the work of a child or a man) (Harrison, ibid, pp. 37ff.).

Pregnancy demands increased expenditure of energy: (1) to synthesise the new tissues to service the foetus (the placenta) and in the maternal organs (uterus and breasts); and (2) for the metabolism of the unit of foetus and placenta, as well as for the increased respiratory and myocardial activity of the mother. According to Hytten and Leitch (1964), this involves an expenditure of around 75 000 kcals. Frisch and McArthur (1974) calculated the expenditure necessary for pregnancy and the first three months of breast-feeding at 144 000 kcals. Lactation alone needs 1000 supplementary kcals per day.

In well-fed populations there may be 'fat stocks' accumulated as a reserve by the maternal organism during pregnancy (women put on 12 kg in total, of which

3.5 kg is fat, in addition to the foetus, placenta, etc.), which may provide around 300 kcals/day. But in many Third World populations, the mother puts on only 5 kg of weight in total — that is when she doesn't actually lose weight (see Jelliffe and Jelliffe, 1978, pp. 61 ff.).

One day's breast-feeding therefore uses up as much energy as two hours' cutting wood or nine hours' walking. Pregnancy requires the same expenditure as a month (around 160 hours) of cutting wood. In most populations, moreover, women do not stop work on subsistence tasks during pregnancy and nursing, nor do they have access to supplementary food (see Howell, 1979, p. 207). Hence the exhaustion of the maternal organism, 'maternal depletion' (Jelliffe and Jelliffe, 1978, pp. 62 and 114), progressive weight loss, 'prematurely aged appearance', and high female morbidity and mortality.

Breast-feeding is also not just work that involves expenditure of energy within the maternal organism (lactation); it also takes up a considerable amount of the mother's time, especially where there is feeding on demand. Research in the Philippines calculated the mother gave the breast seven or eight times a day, and each time it took from 15 to 30 minutes (Jelliffe and Jelliffe, 1978, p. 138). In the Kivu zone of Zaire, mothers give the breast *13 to 15 times a day* (Vis, Hennart and Ruchababisha, 1981, pp. 173 ff.).

In these conditions of women's energy expenditure and reproductive work, we have a right to ask if even the most meticulous researchers, such as Lee (1979), are blind or ill-willed. Lee calculates to the second the time needed for productive activities — even the most minor (the time to construct a shelter for the dogs divided by the number of days it lasts = 0.08 minutes per day, etc.), but *he gives no estimate at all of time for breast-feeding* nor of time for the care of children. (He says only that the mother does 60–80 per cent of the work with young children.) He considers (and this was already an innovation) women's load of reproductive work *solely from the point of view of the weight of children they carry* per kilometer during gathering and when moving camp (and the consequent impossibility of a woman supporting too closely spaced births). From his very partial calculations, he concludes: (1) that *the everyday work of women is less* than that of men, and (2) that even 'adding the work of [unmeasured] child rearing does not raise women's total work-load significantly above the range of men's'.

64   This applies not only to conception but also to nursing:

> The mammary gland is an open, essentially one-way system, in which the nutrients taken up from the blood are completely or partly broken down, resynthesized, rearranged, repackaged, and exported. It differs from other secretory glands in the body in the amount of secretion produced, in its perpetual availability, and in that it is directed outside the body itself to sustain the growth and development of another being (Jelliffe and Jelliffe, 1978, pp. 52–3).

65   From this point of view, modern contraception transforms the reproductive process by achieving the separation of non-reproductive and reproductive sexuality outlined in human biological structure. This separation remains partial while the possibility of choosing or refusing conception is not integral to the coital relationship. In this sense, the transformation of the reproductive process makes possible (or even imposes) a transformation of relations of reproduction (as O'Brien maintains, 1981, p. 62).

66   I partly use here a distinction proposed by Cirese, who distinguishes nature external to the species, on which one acts by *work*, from nature internal to the species, 'on which generally one does not accomplish work in the strict sense (except in the case of doctors, surgeons, slave merchants, etc.)', but on which one

accomplishes either operations: rearing, training, etc. or 'operations of *procreation*' (Cirese, 1979, p. 113).

Cirese oscillates between these two positions, however. Sometimes he defines products of procreation, children, as

> natural production [which he elsewhere calls 'nature's "spontaneous" production'] as regards conception, pregnancy and labour; and as human products in that they are raised within the cultural framework of the group (Cirese quoted in Prestipino, 1979, p. 142, note 12 and p. 145, note 19).

Sometimes he takes account of intentionality in procreation (under its form of regulation: control of births, abortions and infanticides) and of course in the raising of children; and he defines relations with nature as a whole as the 'utilization and social elaboration of the nature internal (psychosomatic) and external (extrasomatic) to the species' (Cirese, 1979, p. 113).

I part company with Cirese's analysis in posing procreation *as work*, and the produce of procreation as an integrally social and human product.

67   It will suffice to recall the case of ancient Greek society, where there was no overall word corresponding to the modern concept of work. Here a slave (whose work allowed free men to devote themselves completely to politics or to philosophy and to mathematics) was not considered a worker but part of the natural order of things, of the natural conditions of production.

> For the Greeks, and the Romans, a slave was part of the instruments of labour, among those endowed with speech, hence with a certain state of consciousness . . . A slave was situated between man and domestic cattle, the draft cattle.

According to Roman Law, he was defined as 'an *instrumentum vocale*, an instrument endowed with speech' (Godelier, 1975, pp. 40–1; and also 1978, pp. 160ff.).

Women as signs that speak, as Lévi-Strauss conceived them, seem a singular politico-semantic echo of this Roman legal definition.

68   It would in fact be very useful to make an inventory of not only the representations ('ideal realities') about what we consider 'work' (see Godelier, 1978), but also, at the same time, the representations of women's (and men's) reproductive work, the analogies and oppositions established between productive and reproductive activities, and

> the representations which *legitimize the place and status* of individuals and groups faced with realities which are permitted, imposed or forbidden them (Godelier, 1978, pp. 160–1).

69   Willis adds: 'Clearly, abortion is by normal standards an act of self-defense' (quoted in Pollack Petchesky, 1980, p. 669, note 17). Pollack Petchesky recalls that this relation was analysed in the women's movement which took up definitions of the right to integrity of the body as part of personal rights (ibid, pp. 663–5). See, for example the Leveller text:

> To every individual in nature is given an individual property by nature, not to be invaded or usurped by any: for every one as he is himselfe, so he hathe a selfe property, else could he not be himselfe (ibid, p. 664).

70   Among the numerous representations that have reproductive *work* accomplished by men, see the frequent one where the wife is fertile ground ploughed by the husband (for ancient Greece, see Vernant, 1972); or those which reserve an active

role for men or men's semen alone, the woman being only a recipient — or even just a bag, which is what the Nyakyusa say. ('Nyakyusa ideas of physiology are those of a strongly patrilineal society', see Wilson, 1957, p. 227. For opposite representations in matrilineal societies, see Richards, 1956.)

Showing such ideological expropriation at work in Baruya thinking, Godelier wrote:

> There is an essential difference between the model of exploitation of one class by another and the Baruya model of domination of one sex by another. In the former, the producers are socially and materially separate from the conditions of production, as they are concretely expropriated of an essential part of their products. In the second, women are separated in thought, and only in thought, from their powers of procreation (Godelier, 1982, p. 228).

It would seem, however, that Baruya mythical discourse is a better interpreter of the reality of relations between the sexes in this society than Godelier.

If women are not separated from, not deprived of, their reproductive capacity, it is only in the sense that (and only because) their uteruses are not detachable. One does not cut off slaves' arms either. They are, however, certainly separated from control of the conditions of reproduction. These are imposed on them (the partner is imposed, it is impossible to refuse coitus, there is sexual violence, etc., see Godelier, ibid, passim).

This constitutes *the only possible form of material and social separation* of women from their power of procreation and conditions of reproduction, and conversely, of exploitation of reproduction by men. The only place of partial control by women is the space reserved for childbirth, where they can decide the life of the child. But we should also ask: does this liberty (whatever its extent) contradict or is it coherent with the demographic needs of Baruya society (and others like it)?

71 Much other research also contributes to this programme as a whole, such as that relating to sex predetermination, genetic malformation, etc.

72 See, Guillaumin (in Jacquard and Guillaumin, 1982–1983, pp. 97ff.); Hanmer and Allen, 1979; and Hanmer, 1981 on the dangers of genetic engineering as a 'socially applied genetic manipulation' (Guillaumin, ibid). Hence an intervention that could lead to all sorts of discrimination, including conceivably the suppression of groups considered not 'genetically' valuable (as evidenced by recent history). The central problem facing these technologies is '*Who* decides? Who decides *what* and *against whom*?' (Guillaumin, ibid, p. 100, stress in original).

73 This is an expression used by Godelier (1975, p. 41) to describe the condition of Greco-Roman slaves.

74 There can actually be an 'intermediary' stage, like the one we saw in the contracts in Florence. There, it will be recalled, the husband or the father of the nurse sold his wife's or daughter's milk, and was the real possessor of the individual woman and her capacities as a whole. Note this form of management of the work of another person derives directly from relations of bodily appropriation (of ownership), here constituted by descent or marriage (Guillaumin, this volume).

Such management of work was exercised in similar but not identical forms in regard to:

1 daughters or sons being sent away to work (see Scott and Tilly, 1975; Tilly and Scott, 1978). The children's wages were paid directly to the father. Such relations were common in Europe for centuries;

2 wives, for instance in France, where they did not have the right to receive

directly their own wages until 1907 (see the analysis in Guillaumin, this volume, pp. 96–100);

3 prostitutes where they have to hand over their earnings to their pimp or brothel (Barry, 1979); and

4 plantation slaves, who were 'loaned' or 'hired out' by their master. They had to hand over any wage they received to their master. Douglass records his consciousness of the relationship of slavery, based on the ten cents his master left him from the wage paid (Douglass, 1980). (My thanks to Colette Guillaumin for drawing my attention to Douglass's work, as well as for many other points made in the course of discussions that have accompanied my work from the start.)

In many societies it could be said that sexual rights, 'the price of love' (*prix de l'amante*) or 'the price of the fiancée', like rights '*in uxorem*', in reproductive capacities paid to the father or husband of a woman, constitute a demonstration of bodily appropriation — just like the forms of management of work mentioned above, and the fairly widespread forms of pledging or lending of children.

75 For a comparative analysis of types of adoption, see J. Goody, 1976; and for adoption in Africa, E. N. Goody, 1978. For forms of adoption controlled by men in Polynesia, see Carroll, 1970; and for the Tonga, where, on the contrary, a sister exercises rights of adoption on the children of her brother, see Gailey, 1980. On Baoule adoption practices as women's strategy, see Etienne, 1979 (and also 1981).

Lallemand (1977, pp. 189–222) shows that in Mossi adoption, wives who receive adopted children are intermediaries of a gift that profits their husband. Adoption occurs after weaning and goes from women who are younger and less well situated in the family hierarchy, to women who are older and have better links to the agnates. Adoption serves patrilateral consanguines and particularly the chief of a concession (grant of land); the children (who are brought up by the older women) being progressively integrated into his work unit.

76 Marx cites in support of this a magnificent passage by Hegel on alienation:

I may make over to another the use, for a limited time, of my particular body and mental aptitudes and capabilities; because, in consequence of this restriction, they are impressed with a character of alienation with regard to me as a whole. But by the alienation of all my labour-time and the whole of my work, I should be converting the substance itself, in other words, my general activity and reality, my person, into the property of another (Marx, 1974, p. 165, note 2).

77 Guillaumin (this volume) clearly shows this constitutive characteristic of marital relationships in modern western societies. And see Duby (1981) for the history of the installation of structures of modern marriage in feudal Europe.

Let us look swiftly at another case, that of the numerous forms of marriage with marriage payments. Here the exchange does not take place between equal individuals — self-evidently, because the girl is *given* (sometimes against her will) or exchanged. She obviously does not own herself (nor her reproductive power, nor her labour power); and the 'bride price' does not go to her. Her person and its capacities are transferred en bloc, and in principle with no determination of the time or quantity of work she will be required to do.

Procreation remains the fundamental if not obligatory prestation, whatever productive work the wife may accomplish (and its absence can be a cause for divorce, repudiation, etc., because she is exchanged as a reproducer). This exchange is sometimes explicitly defined as 'purchasing a womb' (Krige, 1974), or, as the Buka say, what they pay for are the genitals of a woman (Blackwood, 1935, p. 98).

It seems important to stress, however, that we do often find introduced — in outline — a *measure* of reproductive work. A minimum quantity of work is established: a number of children to be given to a husband to which the marriage payment gives him rights. When this work is accomplished, there is no longer a reimbursement of the bride price in the event of a divorce (or death). Another possible qualifying procedure is one where each child is the object of a particular transaction to redeem it (see Muller, 1982).

These forms of quantification — like, on a different level, the case of 'womb-renting' — lead us to reconsider the status of reproductive activity and make it necessary to envisage categorising types of relations of reproduction. Their complexity (and historical and ethnic variability) seem comparable to those of relations of production, but they have not yet been suitably analysed.

78 My thanks to Nicole-Claude Mathieu for having pointed out to me the ideological aspects of the term 'single-parent family' and for the stimulating discussions we had during the elaboration of this essay.

79 The private appropriation of women may be only one of the possible historical forms of the general relation of domination of women by men. But perhaps this private appropriation of women is beginning to be no longer 'profitable', either individually or at the level of collective organisation? In which case, male domination might even be reinforced by the disappearance (or weakening) of a contradiction 'at the heart of social appropriation itself': that between the collective appropriation of women and individual appropriation of each woman in marriage (Guillaumin, this volume, p. 100). For what is affected by the dissolution of ties of personal dependence, is, it must be stressed, not directly the generalised relation of 'material appropriation of the class of women by the class of men: sexage', but the 'restrictive ... individualized expression' of this relationship, its 'institutional (contractual) surface': marriage (Guillaumin, this volume, p. 98ff.).

80 Or, to use the marxian formulation, a transformation analogous to the passage from relations of serfdom, where 'the labourer himself, living labour power, was still counted among the objective conditions of production and appropriated as such', to relations of production specific to capitalism, where the worker is a free person and where

> it is not the labourer but labour which is a condition of production. So much the better if capital can carry out the work using machines, or even with the help of water and air. It appropriates not the labourer but his work (Marx, 1968, p. 340).

Chapter 7

Our Costs and Their Benefits

Monique Plaza[1]

For several years we have been fighting to get rape recognised as an act of violence committed by men as a class on women as a class. This struggle has been difficult because we have been up against the judicial system and, in addition, a prevalent ideological conception that rape is a 'sexual act' committed by a man *with* a woman. Non-consent by the woman supposedly constitutes the only illegal thing about rape as a practice.[2] In most cases the woman's non-consent is denied, and the Law aims to prove the sexual act was desired, invited or sought by her. Parallel to this supposed desire by women, statements are made (by the judicial system and the mass media) that affirm a particular *picture of men* — as natural predators with over-developed sexual instincts.[3]

Our denunciations seem to have been partially heard. Some (a few) members of the Left Wing intelligentsia do now recognise rape as violence, and see our struggle against it as politically legitimate. Michel Foucault and David Cooper, for instance, both of whom are well-known for their subversive interpretations of power relationships within contemporary society, have denounced the violence of rape and debated which strategies should be implemented (essentially at a legal level) to combat its effects. However, although I hold Cooper and Foucault in high esteem, I have to say their arguments do not provide a theoretical-political support for our struggle. Instead, they constitute a closure, a 'major compromise', which is all the more pernicious because they are, in some respects, and in part, *abstractly* (ideally) right. A 'new-look' ideology seems currently to be forming around rape — which is certainly more subtle than the traditional one, but which is dangerous because it could lock us into a 'double bind'[4] with terrible political consequences.

I want here to try to take this double bind apart, because it is important not to get caught up in its paradoxical logic. We must pursue our argument, and of course analyse contradictions within our struggle, but we must not take steps backward.

* * *

In October 1977, the 'Change Collective' published a volume entitled *La folie encerclée* (*Encircling Madness*). It includes transcriptions of a series of debates on topics relating to repression (particularly psychiatric repression); one of these discussions particularly caught my attention because it deals with rape. It is introduced by Michel Foucault as follows:

> There is currently a Commission considering a Reform of the Criminal Law in France. This has been in operation for several months (in the expectation of a change of government?), and so far has made a few unimportant decisions. To my surprise, they 'phoned me. They said: 'We are in the process of studying the section of the legislation on sexuality. We are at a loss and would like to know what you think about it . . . .' [T]here are two areas which I find problematic. That of rape. And that of children (Change Collective, 1977, pp. 98–9).

The question of rape is thus raised in a very pointed way. On one hand, it is considered in relation to the subject of punishment, hence *more from the standpoint of the rapist*; and on the other, it is inscribed within the general problem of 'sexuality'. This has considerable consequences for the debate.

I think Foucault himself is at a loss because he is caught in a political contradiction. Rape is an important battle cry for feminists, who have proclaimed that 'every man is a potential rapist'. But who is speaking through the voice of Foucault? He is a famous philosopher, certainly, but he is also a man. And this man, far from declaring his political incompetence to speak on the problem in the first place, provides a 'theoretical' assertion that immediately presents a hypothesis as something obvious, and as a sort of prohibition:

> One can always stick to the theoretical discourse which says: sexuality cannot, under any circumstances, be subject to punishment (Change Collective, 1977, p. 99)

At first, I thought 'That's right.' Foucault's formulation of the 'theoretical discourse' carries such conviction that you say to yourself 'That's completely justified'. So where does this immediate ideological approval come from? Apparently from two things. On the one hand, we can't really support the idea of 'punishment', which seems reactionary because it is linked to repression. And on the other, the West has bemoaned for some time the sexual repression puritan and Victorian society imposed on it. So putting 'sexuality' and 'punishment' together produces an immediate and negative response. It is a banned conjunction; an association we reject.

However, beyond this obvious wall lies a question: What *is* 'sexuality'? Since Foucault has devoted a book to this,[5] we can refer to it to understand what sexuality means for him. He says the concept of sexuality is the product of power over the body:

> ... this power had neither the form of the law, nor the effects of the taboo. On the contrary, it acted by multiplication of singular sexualities. It did not set boundaries for sexuality; it extended the various forms of sexuality, pursuing them according to lines of indefinite penetration. It did not exclude sexuality, but included it in the body as a mode of specification of individuals.... It produced and determined the sexual mosaic. Modern society is perverse, not in spite of its puritanism or as if from a backlash provoked by its hypocrisy; it is in actual fact, and directly, perverse (Foucault, 1981, p. 47).

'Sexuality' is thus *a product of power*, a power which must be defined, according to Foucault, in terms of:

> ... manifold relationships of force that take shape and come into play in the machinery of production, in families, limited groups, and institutions [and which] are the basis for wide-ranging effects of cleavage that run through the social body as a whole (ibid. p. 94).

Foucault argues that since the eighteenth century this force has developed four principal strategic elements in relation to sex: the 'hysterisation of women's bodies', the 'pedagogisation of children's sex', the 'socialisation of procreative behaviours', and the 'psychiatrisation of perverse pleasure'. What is at work in these strategies, he says, is *the very production of sexuality*.

It is this sexuality — produced by a whole apparatus of power in which women turn out to be the privileged victims (and not only through the hysterisation of their bodies!) — that should not be punished. So what does he think should be penalised?

> ... when rape is punished, it should be exclusively the physical violence that is penalized (Change Collective, 1977, p. 99).

If we understand correctly, it is an issue of finding a way for 'sexuality' to escape the criminal law, by not forbidding sexuality but only 'violence'. That is to say, of *not forbidding the deployment of power which has as its object of privileged appropriation the bodies of women*, but saying rape

> ... is nothing more, and nothing other, than an assault (Change Collective, 1977, p. 99).

This repetitive denial draws our attention. What does this 'nothing more, and nothing other' connote, if not a hollow assertion of *the specificity of the violence of rape*? But this assertion escapes and gets hidden behind the negation. So what is misunderstood here? What is at stake in this misunderstanding? M. Foucault . . . ?

> . . . there can be no misunderstanding that is not based on a fundamental relation to truth. Evading this truth, barring access to it, masking it: these were so many local tactics which, as if by superimposition and through a last-minute detour, gave a paradoxical form to a fundamental petition to know (Foucault, 1981, p. 55).

So what 'local tactic' of power is at work in this persistent denial? What actual (total) action does it stipulate? What is 'unknown' in the specificity of rape which is masked by the curious 'defence' of sexuality?

Let us look at another comment made by Foucault in the Change debate:

> . . . it makes no difference whether one is punched on the jaw by a fist or in the sex (organs) by a penis . . . (Change Collective, 1977, p. 99).

Who is the 'one' who is speaking here? I was taught at school that 'one' is a man (*on, l'homme*)! In fact the speaker is Man: the bearer of the penis which is liable to enter 'the sex (organs)'. But (to play naïve) what is 'sex'? Let us refer again to *The History of Sexuality*:

> 'sex' was defined in three ways: as that which belongs in common to men and women; as that which belongs, *par excellence*, to men, and hence is lacking in women; but at the same time, as that which by itself constitutes woman's body, ordering it wholly in terms of the functions of reproduction and keeping it in constant agitation through the effects of that very function (Foucault, 1981, p. 153).

Since the penis is defined implicitly as non-sex in the previous quotation, we must accept that 'sex' there means implicitly 'women's bodies'.

But stop a moment. Rape must not be punished as sexuality. So as what should it be punished, since it seems uniquely sexual? In describing it, Foucault in fact opposes two terms:

- 'his penis', i.e. the genital organ of a man; and
- 'the sex', i.e. following his theory, women's bodies, which have been reduced to 'sex'.

But in French 'sex' also designates women's genital organs (vulvas and vaginas), which here do not have the benefit of a name, unlike the penis. So for the moment women are not named, although men are — through the intermediary of their penises.

This differential treatment gives rise to an interesting hypothesis, since men also rape *men*. The anus of a man can socially be put into the position of 'the sex'; or again, a (biological) man can be put in the place of 'women's bodies', and appropriated as such. In *Histoires d'Elles*, Jean-Michel was raped and he says: 'I had been raped like a woman, I was treated like a hole, and I didn't want to be a woman any more, above all, worse still, I didn't want to be a homosexual . . . I wanted frankly to be almost macho.'[6]

So exactly what is rape? Is it or is it not a 'sexual' practice? We need to reach an agreed understanding of the notion of sexuality. *Rape is an oppressive act by a (social) man against a (social) woman, which can concretely take the form of a bottle held by a man being introduced into the anus of a woman*. In this case rape is not sexual, or rather it is not genital. It is very sexual in the sense that it is frequently a sexual activity, and above all in the sense that it opposes men and women. It is *social sexuation* that underlies rape. If men rape women it is precisely because they are socially women, or because they are 'the sex'. That is to say, because women are bodies which men have appropriated by exercising the 'local tactic' of nameless violence. Rape is sexual essentially because it rests on the *very social* difference between the sexes.

So, using the reversals and paradoxes so dear to Foucault, I would say: it does make a difference whether one is punched in the jaw by a fist or in the sex organ by a penis — it makes the difference between the sexes. Men rape women because women as a class belong to men as a class. Men have appropriated the bodies of women. Men rape what they have learned to consider is their property, that is to say, individuals of the other/opposite sex class, the class of women (which, I repeat, can also contain biological men).

If then, in our society, rape is sexual, what does not punishing the sexual in it mean? Foucault, who in his theoretical assertions forgets that in our society there is a class of men and a class of women and that rape must be referred to this social reality, suddenly remembers something: 'But first: I am not sure that women would agree . . .' (Change Collective, 1977, p. 99).

At last, we are named. 'Sex' is us. And what are we? Spoil-sports! Michel Foucault is not sure we would agree with him? Oh come on! He knows full well *we completely disagree*. We have shouted, written, debated and organised against rape. We have demanded court sessions against rapists. Which proves that for us rape is an assult unlike any other; that we think being punched in the face is not at all the same as being raped.

The two women present at the Change discussion (Marine Zecca and Marie-Odile Faye) did in fact make their disagreement clear, stressing the existence of very commonplace and intense oppression of women *within the sexual arena*. Foucault then supplied a piece of outside information:

> I discussed this yesterday with a magistrate from the Magistrates' Association. He said, 'There is no reason to penalize rape. Rape could be outside the criminal law. It should be made simply a matter of civil responsibility: of damages and compensation' (Change Collective, 1977, p. 100).

There is *no reason to penalise rape*. Rape could be allowed. A raped woman would 'simply' go and ask for damages. In other words, she could go and get paid for a sexual act a man has committed 'with' her but without her consent. Hence, every woman would be a sexual prize for men. Either she wouldn't say a word (and 'consent'); or she would exact recompense before the act (prostitution) or after (rape).

But let us be more precise and imagine the scene:

- Mrs Y brings charges. She says: I have been injured by Mr X (since she has not been raped — rape does not exist). She gives evidence of her injuries. And then the round of questions begins. 'But don't you have any wounds? Where is the sperm? Are you sure you didn't consent? Where are your witnesses? . . . '
- Mr Z brings charges. He received a punch in his face from Mr X (the same assailant X). He shows his black eye. Will he be asked if he is sure he did not, perhaps, consent? Will they try to take bits of skin from his fist? Certainly not. Precisely because *Mr Z and Mr X do not have the same power relationship as Mrs Y and Mr X*, and because a punch in the face is an abnormal act and generally understood as aggression, while putting a penis in 'a sex' is a normal act and *never understood as aggression*. Women belong to men; the vagina belongs naturally to the penis.

To make rape a 'simple' matter of civil responsibility would be quite simply to *permit rape* — to run counter to women, who have shown it to be one of the most violent demonstrations of the oppression they suffer.

Reporting this scandalous opinion of a magistrate from the Magistrates' Association (an organisation generally esteemed for its 'advanced' ideas), Foucault again turned to women and said:

What do you think about this? I say: you, women . . . because men have, unfortunately perhaps, much less pressing experience here (Change Collective, 1977, p. 100).

Really? I think on the contrary men have, unfortunately and *without a doubt* much *too pressing* an experience of rape — as rapists. If rape were *like any other* aggression, Michel Foucault, men would indeed have much more pressing experience of it as a reality they have undergone. But clearly it is unlike any other form of violence, and so you cannot resolve the question. From the position of potential rapist, to which your status as a man 'constrains' you, you can only hide the web of oppressive power that women are subject to. You can only defend the rights of rapists.

And, indeed, the discussion did get involved in a defence of rapists. Marine Zecca seemed troubled by the way things were presented. In order to develop a strategy against rape, the problem has to be posed from the point of view of the oppression of women, and in terms of what rape represents as an *oppressive tactic* here and now. But the whole Change discussion started from the rapist's side: from what men want to have the right to do with complete impunity, from the restraints they do not want to appear. In the context of a discussion dealing with repression, and while the problem of rape was posed by men, what else could Marine Zecca say but: 'I can't look on this as a legislative project. And as "punishment" — for that disturbs me' (Change Collective, 1977, p. 100).

Jean-Pierre Faye, however, developed a pretty unambiguous line of argument: 'On one hand, in the name of women's liberation, one is anti-rape. And, in the name of anti-repression one is — the opposite?' (ibid, p. 100). In other words, in the name of anti-repression, one is pro-rape?! But then, what repression is one talking about? If women demand 'liberation', it is also certainly from *repression: from the oppression they suffer*. So let us even-out the terms of the debate:

1   being 'anti-rape' in the name of women's liberation (I would add that a demand for liberation has meaning only in the context of suffering an oppression);
2   being 'the opposite', hence 'pro-rape', in the name of anti-repression (I would add, of men, hence for the maintenance of the oppression-repression they currently exercise over women).

What underlies the latter is surely the myth of the 'sexual misery' of men, of the repression they already suffer, which should not be increased by penalising rape.

So how come Michel Foucault did not intervene in the discussion, since he denounces the postulate of sexual repression throughout the 159 pages of his book? Probably because one of the functions of this myth escapes him: that of masking men's oppression of women. Further, not only does this dimension escape him theoretically, but he uses it politically for his own purposes. Perhaps we could say that there is here (to paraphrase the subtitle of volume 1 of *The History of Sexuality*) something of 'a will *not* to know'!

Marie-Odile Faye presented rape as being precisely *contrary* to the idea of 'freely consented, non-penalized sexuality' (Change Collective, 1977, p. 100), which seemed to bring Jean-Pierre Faye back to a slightly more contradictory view of things: 'It (rape) itself has a repressive side . . . but repression of rape — how can we imagine that?' (ibid, p. 100). Rape has a repressive side. In other words, it has a *non*-repressive side? A liberating one, perhaps? Indeed it has — for men! So it is the interests of men that are back on the table when they say that there would be a problem if a practice (which we judge to be *completely* repressive) were curbed (forbidden, and penalised if it takes place). What they are saying is that *they want to defend the freedom they currently have to repress us by rape*. They are saying that *what they call (their) Liberty is the repression of our bodies*.

Michel Foucault then returned to his question and asserted that the contradiction the two women had raised posed problems:

> Because one ends by saying: sexuality as such has a preponderant place in the body; the sex (organ) is not a hand, it is not hair, it is not the nose. It must be protected, surrounded, in any event vested with legislation which is not deserved by the rest of the body (Change Colletive, 1977, pp. 100–1).

If I understand correctly, he is saying it would be women's fault if sexuality *were to* acquire a preponderant place in the body and *were to be* specially treated. Really, Michel Foucault, you exaggerate! Have you forgotten this has *already* happened? That 'sexuality, far from being repressed in . . . society, on the contrary [is] constantly aroused' (Foucault, 1981, p. 148)? Have you forgotten that

> All along the great lines which the development of the deployment of sexuality has followed since the nineteenth century, one sees the elaboration of this idea that there exists something other than bodies, organs, somatic localizations, functions, anatomo-physiological systems, sensations, and pleasures; something else and something more, with intrinsic properties and laws of its own: 'sex' (Foucault, 1981, pp. 152–3)?

Don't you understand this deployment affects women most sharply? That we are the ones most seriously injured? And if we demand the destruction of 'sex differences', it is in order to destroy our oppression? It is certainly not women who want sex organs not to be hair [i.e. who want sex organs to have no more social significance than other parts of the body]. That *is exactly what we want*. But we cannot function in the ideal and act as if — here and now — sex (organs) were hair! That would cost us dearly, and certainly save you a lot of questions.

Foucault's reasoning is dangerous in that it risks blaming women. What men (from a position of power in patriarchal relationships) are intent on creating and perpetuating (the oppression of women, 'sex difference', the primacy of sex), he imputes to women as being something they want to create and perpetuate. He says women want to make rape something other than aggression, so they are pan-sexualists. They want to punish rapists for raping them, so they are repressive.

This culpabilisation seemed to influence the Change discussion. Marine Zecca, when speaking of children being raped, said 'I believe this is no longer a sexual act: it is really physical violence' (Change Collective, 1977, p. 101). But do we believe that when an adult woman is raped, rape is not physical violence? Or do we need to question the notion of the 'sexual act'? Do we expect an adult woman to be used to it — to be used to the violence inherent in men–women relationships? Does she, in the end, see rape in every sexual act? This would reverse the proposition: rape is a sexual act. *It is the refusal to recognise the explicit connection between sexuality today and violence that leads the discussion into an impasse*. This dissociation of violence from sexuality, which women can only make with difficulty, is accomplished by David Cooper: 'Rape is non-orgasmic. It is a sort of rapid masturbation in the body of another. It is not sexual. It is wounding' (Change Collective, 1977, p. 101).

In other words, it would be 'sexual' if it lead to an orgasm. But whose orgasm? That of the one who masturbates rapidly in the body of another. This confuses sexuality and (man's) pleasure.[7] The absence of pleasure [*jouissance*] does not mean an absence of sexuality. Furthermore, sexuality can wound; and a wound can be specifically sexual. We can of course dream of good — non-violent and orgasmic — heterosexuality. But this is just a dream, and reality shows sexuality to be a very precise and well-organised apparatus of oppression. Rape must not be cast as happening elsewhere: in a field 'other' than that of sexuality, away from everyday power relationships established between men and women. On the contrary, we need to *bring contemporary heterosexuality very close to rape* and take care not to dissociate them.

* * *

To summarise the important elements of the Change discussion and its ideological bedrock: rape should not be penalised insofar as it constitutes one of men's existing rights, and penalising it would restrict their freedom — it would 'repress' them. That their current freedom is our repression matters little, since in the antagonism between the sex classes that is clearly revealed here, it is men who must *preserve their privileges* and not women who should *win the right to struggle against a form of appropriation of our bodies*.

Up to now, the ideology governing approaches to the issue of rape has pictured man as a sort of rutting billy-goat, whose ardour cannot bear to be shackled: as an unrestrained beast. This naturalist discourse defines men with unequalled violence and horror, but it allows the injustice of contemporary social relationships to remain unquestioned. The male rapist has to arise from nature, never from an oppressive society. It has been preferable to offer him a lobotomy[8] to lessen his 'instinct to rape', than to make him recognise the oppression of women — which he, as a (social) man, participates in. To combat this naturalist ideology, feminists have asserted that rape does not arise from sexuality. But we must also simultaneously assert that rape *is* sexual — insofar as it refers to social sexuation, to the social differentiation of the sexes — so as to be certain not to dissociate heterosexual sexuality from violence.[9]

The 'new' ideology of rape, which co-exists with the older one, does not refer to the image of the man-goat. It is based instead on a much more contradictory thematic. On the one hand, we are told there is nothing natural about 'sexuality': that it is not a given, not an object in itself, but that on the contrary it is produced by social modalities of power over the body. Further, it is conceded *theoretically* that this sexuality is particularly oppressive for women. On the other hand, we are asked to make a *special condition* for this social practice (at the level of legal rules) by excluding it. Further, we are reproached for considering it to be something special, for not pushing it aside when we consider it oppressive, and for wanting *in practice* to defend ourselves against it.

We are thus subject to contradictory statements, for if sexuality is a particularly privileged oppressive social practice in contemporary society, we *cannot* ignore it or push it aside.

This 'double bind' is explained by the fact that *the debate counterposes antagonistic interests*: those of rapists and those of victims, of men and women. 'Revolutionary' thinkers cannot now refuse to recognise this antagonism completely. They cannot use naturalist ideology to explain/justify rape. They have therefore enunciated a new one, which again starts from the position of the male rapist. They do not deny rape is violence, but they set themselves up as the defence counsel and say first: 'men rape because they live in a repressive society'. However, this is not a serious argument, because why do women not rape if they live in the same society? So our thinkers then propose a second argument, which is clearly superior since it does not seem to defend rapists. It says basically: 'rape is like any other "individual" violence carried out "at random"'. In their view we should no longer talk about rape as sexuality. Obviously, since reference to sexuality risks it being seen that what happens in rape has something to do with the existence of antagonisms between men as a class and women as a class; with men's oppression of women.

Women have therefore had to constitute the public prosecutor before finally becoming the real counsel for the defence: *that is, before defending the victims of oppression — raped women.*

Michel Foucault, you have not clearly analysed the 'enunciative modality'[10] you adopt when you talk about rape. If you had, when the Magistrates' Association asked you to give your views on rape, you would not have launched directly into a completely pre-emptive 'theoretical' explanation. You would first have 'turned to the women' who are currently politically active around rape. And you would never for a moment have tried to convince us that *we* are playing false. You would not have lost a certain political memory and would have recalled that insofar as we are exposed in the front line of the strategic field of patriarchal power relations, it is women who are best able to structure

a plurality of resistances, each of them a special case: resistances that are possible, necessary, improbable; others that are spontaneous, savage, solitary, concerted, rampant, or violent[11] (Foucault, 1981, p. 96).

Notes

1 'Nos dommages et leurs intérêts' was originally published in *Questions féministes*, no. 3, in 1978, and a translation was provided in *Feminist Issues*, vol. 1, no. 3, Summer 1981, pp. 25–35 ('Our Damages and Their Compensation. Rape: The Will Not To Know of Michel Foucault'). The version here is a new translation by Diana Leonard.

2 I say 'only' because for me the illegality does not only lie there (I'd even say, not *there* at all). For what does 'to consent' mean if not to acquiesce in, to permit, a situation imposed by another, a situation which is *an act by another*? In the case of rape, 'consent' would be acceptance of objectification, of the violence another inflicts on you. The notion of 'non-consent' may be the only recognised illegality in rape, but it is *the possibility of deploying rape that should be outlawed*. However, we must remember such deployment is legal:

> Marriage, by virtue of the obligations it places on the spouses, authorizes the husband to fulfil on the wife, even despite her and by violence, the act which conforms to the purposes of marriage. It does not, however, permit the obtaining of 'unnatural' relations by violence (Extract from the Dalloz *Répertoire pratique*, p. 13, cited in Halimi, 1978, p. 205).

3 See Péron (1978) and Fournier and Reynaud (1978).

4 A process described in Anglo-Saxon psychology and central to English anti-psychiatry accounting for the paradoxical character of a message. The message is structured in such a way as to affirm something, and to affirm something else about this affirmation — the two affirmations being mutually exclusive. In parent–child relations, this process can lead to madness.

5 Foucault (1981), originally published in French in 1976.

6 See 'Un trou . . . rien qu'un trou' ['A hole . . . just a hole'], included in a collection of 'Remarks' produced by Dominique Pujebet (1978).

7 Rather a certain form of pleasure [*jouissance*] that men sometimes dream about — an ideal pleasure which would produce a 'good', 'equal' relationship with a women. In fact rape doubtless gives the rapist a great deal of pleasure, which 'liberated' men reject. Other men, on the contrary, insist upon it, and boast about it exaltantly (see the songs of Michel Sardou).

8 A psycho-surgical technique that seeks to sever that part of the brain held responsible for a behavioural disorder. The fact that, during a television programme on rape, a rapist was shown who had been normalised by a lobotomy demonstrates the extreme ascendancy of the naturalist ideology. It was probably just a sample case: doubtless few men have to submit to a lobotomy. But ideologically the 'explanation' and its practical implications are to hand. It is interesting to note that when it is a question of rape, a man gets treated as a biological entity (something ordinarily reserved for women), and that one can even think of applying to him a 'curative' (mutilating) technique usually 'reserved' for women. See for example, Breggin (1973).

9 The definition I give to heterosexuality is sociological and not biological. I refer not to the meeting of a vulva and a penis, but to a sexual practice structured on the existence of a difference between the sexes — on the existence of 'men' and 'women'. In this sense the rape of Jean-Michel by men can be said to be sociologically ascribable to heterosexuality, since he was appropriated as 'a woman' by men ('machos').

10 See Foucault (1976a). The idea of an 'enunciative modality' integrates the place from which the author of a discourse speaks: his or her statutorily defined personage; and the institutional sites from which he or she utters the discourse. To

this should be added all the diverse strategies that organise power relations in the social formation.

11   I have omitted 'still others that are quick to compromise, interested, or sacrificial', since this phrase tastes too much of defeat and death.

References

ACKER, C.L. and TOWNSEND, P.K. (1975) 'Demographic Models of Female Infanticide', *Man*, vol. 10, pp. 469–70.

ACKER, J. (1989) 'The Problem with Patriarchy', *Sociology*, vol. 23, no. 2, pp. 235–40.

ACSADI, G. and NEMESKERI, J. (1970) *History of Human Life Span and Mortality*, Budapest, Akademiai Kaido.

ADKINS, L. (1995) *Gendered Work: sexuality, family and the labour market*, Buckingham, Open University Press.

ADKINS, L. and LURY, C. (1992) 'Gender and the Labour Market: old theory for new?', in HINDS, H., PHOENIX, A. and STACEY, J. (Eds) *Working Out: new directions for women's studies*, London, Falmer.

ADKINS, L. and LURY, C. (1996) 'The Sexual, the Cultural and the Gendering of the Labour Market', in ADKINS, L. and MERCHANT, V. (Eds) *Sexualizing the Social: power and the organization of sexuality*, Basingstoke, Macmillan.

ALTERNATIVES (1977) 'Justice patriarcale et peine de viol', *Alternatives*, no. 1, Face-à-femmes, June.

AMADIUME, I. (1987) *Male Daughters, Female Husbands. Gender and Sex in an African Society*, London, Zed Books.

ANGEL, J.L. (1975) 'Paleoecology, Paleodemography and Health', in POLGAR, S. (Ed.) *Population, Ecology and Social Evolution*, Paris and The Hague, Mouton.

Annales de Démographie historique (1981) *Démographie historique et condition féminine*, Paris, Editions de l'EHESS.

ARCHER, J. and LLOYD, B. (1985 revised edn.) *Sex and Gender*, Cambridge, Cambridge University Press.

ARDENER, S. (1973) 'Sexual Insult and Female Militancy', *Man*, vol. 8, no. 3, pp. 422–40. Reprinted in ARDENER (1975) pp. 29–53.

ARDENER, S. (Ed.) (1975) *Perceiving Women*, London, Malaby Press.

ARDENER, S. (Ed.) (1978) *Defining Females. The nature of women in society*, London, Croom Helm.

ASSOCIATION POUR LES LUTTES FÉMINISTES (1981) *Chronique d'une imposture: du mouvement de libération des femmes á une marque commerciale*, Paris: Association pour les Luttes Féministes.

ASTUTI, R. (1988) '"Cattle Beget Children" — But women must bear them. Fertility, sterility and belonging among women in Swaziland', in TIELEMAN, H.J. (Ed.) *Scenes of Change: visions on developments in Swaziland*, African Studies Centre, Research Report no. 33.

ATKINSON, T. (1974) 'The Older Woman: a stockpile of losses', in ATKINSON, T. (Ed.) *Amazon Odyssey*, New York, Links, pp. 223–6.

AZARA, F. (1809) *Voyages dans l'Amérique méridionale*, Paris, 4 vols.

BALIKCI, A. (1967) 'Female Infanticide on the Arctic Coast', *Man*, vol. 2, no. 4, pp. 615–25.

References

BALIKCI, A. (1970) *The Netsilik Eskimo*, Garden City, New York, The Natural History Press.

BARRAU, J. (1978) 'Domesticamento', in *Enciclopedia*, vol. 5, Torino, Einaudi.

BARRETT, M. (1992) 'Words and Things: materialism and method in contemporary feminist analysis', in BARRETT, M. and PHILLIPS, A. (Eds) *Destabilizing Theory: contemporary feminist debates*, Cambridge, Polity.

BARRETT, M. and MCINTOSH, M. (1979) 'Christine Delphy: towards a materialist feminism?' *Feminist Review*, no. 1, pp. 229–35.

BARRY, K. (1979) *Female Sexual Slavery*, Englewood Cliffs, New Jersey, Prentice-Hall.

BATESON, G. (1936) *Naven. A survey of the problems suggested by a composite picture of the culture of a New Guinea tribe drawn from three points of view*, London, Cambridge University Press [2nd edn. 1958, Stanford University Press].

BEACH, F. A. (1974) 'Human Sexuality and Evolution', in MONTAGMA, W. and SADLER, W. A. (Eds) *Reproductive Behavior*, New York, Plenum.

BEAGLEHOLE, P. and BEAGLEHOLE, E. (1938) *Ethnology of Pukapuka*, Honolulu, Hawaii, Bernice P. Bishop Museum Bulletin, no. 150.

BEAUVOIR, S. DE (1949) *Le Deuxième Sexe*, 2 vols, Paris, Gallimard.

BEAUVOIR, S. DE (1953) *The Second Sex*, trans. H. M. Parshley, New York, Alfred A. Knopf; Reprinted Harmondsworth, Penguin 1986.

BEAUVOIR, S. DE (1984) 'France: feminism alive, well and in constant danger', in MORGAN, R. (Ed.) *Sisterhood is Global*, New York, Anchor Press, Doubleday, pp. 229–35.

BERNDT, R. M. (1962) *Excess and Restraint*, Chicago, University of Chicago Press.

BLACKWOOD, B. (1935) *Both Sides of Buka Passage*, Oxford, Clarendon Press.

BLACKWOOD, E. (1984) 'Sexuality and Gender in Certain Native American Tribes: the Case of Cross-Gender Females', *Signs: Journal of Women in Culture and Society*, vol. 10, no. 1, pp. 27–42.

BLACKWOOD, E. (Ed.) (1986) *The Many Faces of Homosexuality. Anthropological Approaches to Homosexual Behavior*, New York, Harrington Park Press. Republication of *Journal of Homosexuality*, vol. 11, nos 3/4, 1985 and *Anthropology and Homosexual Behavior*, New York, The Haworth Press, 1986.

BLEIBTREU-EHRENBERG, G. (1987) 'New Research into the Greek Institution of Pederasty', in *Homosexuality, Which Homosexuality?* (History, vol. 2, pp. 50–8). Papers of the International Scientific Conference on Gay and Lesbian Studies, Free University/Schorer Foundation, Amsterdam.

BOGGIANI, G. (1895) *Viaggi d'un artista nell'America Meridionale. I Caduvei (Mbayà o Guaycurù)*, con prefazione ed uno studio storico ed etnografico del dott. G. A. Colini, Roma, Loescher.

BOIGEOL, A. (1977) 'A propos du nom', *Actes*, no. 16, *Femmes, droit et justice*.

BOISSON, J. (1987) *Le Triangle rose. La déportation des homosexuels (1933–1945)*, Paris, Laffont.

BONTE, P. (1976) 'A propos de la circulation des femmes', in *Cahiers du CERM*, no. 128, *Le problème des formes et des fondements de la domination masculine*.

BORRIE, W. D., FIRTH, R. and SPILLIUS, J. (1957) 'The Population of Tikopia 1929 and 1952', *Population Studies*, vol. 10, pp. 229–52.

BOURDIEU, P. (1984) *Distinction: a social critique of the judgement of taste*, London, RKP.

BOURGEOIS-PICHAT, J. (1965) 'Les Facteurs de la fécondité non dirigée', *Population*, May-June, pp. 383–424.

BOURNE, G. H. (1972) 'Breeding Chimpanzees and Other Apes', in BEVERIDGE, W. J. B. (Ed.) *Breeding Primates*, Basel, S. Karger.

BREGGIN, P. (1973) 'La lobotomie revient', *Les temps modernes*, no. 321, April, pp. 1773–92.

BRETON, A. (1924) *Le Premier Manifeste du Surréalisme*.

BROWN, P. and TUZIN, D. (Eds) (1983) *The Ethnography of Cannibalism*, Washington, DC, Society for Psychological Anthropology.

BUJRA, J. M. (1977) 'Production, Property, Prostitution. "Sexual Politics" in Atu', *Cahiers d'Études africaines*, vol. 65, no. XVII(1) special issue, *Des femmes sur l'Afrique des femmes*, pp. 13–39.

BUTLER, H. (1974) 'Evolutionary Trends in Primate Sex Cycles', *Contributions to Primatology*, vol. 3, pp. 2–35.

BUTLER, J. (1990) *Gender Trouble: feminism and the subversion of identity*, New York, Routledge.

BUTLER, J. (1993) *Bodies That Matter: on the discursive limits of 'sex'*, London, Routledge.

CALLENDER, C. and KOCHEMS, L. M. (1983) 'The North American Berdache', *Current Anthropology*, vol. 24, no. 4, pp. 443–70.

CALLENDER, C. and KOCHEMS, L. M. (1986) 'Men and Not-Men: male gender-mixing statuses and homosexuality', in BLACKWOOD, E. (Ed.) *The Many Faces of Homosexuality. Anthropological Approaches to Homosexual Behavior*, New York, Harrington Park Press, pp. 165–78.

CANTRELLE, P. and LÉRIDON, H. (1971) 'Breast Feeding, Child Mortality and Fertility in a Rural Zone of Senegal', *Population Studies*, vol. 25, no. 3, pp. 505–33.

CAPLAN, P. (Ed.) (1987) *The Cultural Construction of Sexuality*, London, Tavistock.

CAPLAN, P. and BUJRA, J. M. (Eds) (1978) *Women United, Women Divided. Cross-Cultural Perspectives on Female Solidarity*, London, Tavistock.

CARROLL, V. (Ed.) (1970) *Adoption in Eastern Oceania.* Honolulu, University of Hawaii Press (ASAO Monographs, no. 1).

CHAGNON, N. A. (1974) *Studying the Yanomamo*, New York, Holt, Rinehart and Winston.

CHAGNON, N. A. (1979) 'Is Reproductive Success Equal in Egalitarian Societies?', in CHAGNON, N. A. and IRONS, W. (Eds) *Evolutionary Biology and Human Social Behavior: an anthropological perspective*, North Scituate, MA, Duxbury Press, pp. 374–401.

CHANGE COLLECTIVE (1977) *La folie encerclée*, no. 32–33, October, Paris: Seghers/Laffont.

CHAPMAN, M. (1980) 'Infanticide and Fertility among Eskimos: a computer simulation', *American Journal of Physical Anthropology*, vol. 53, pp. 317–27.

CIRESE, A. M. (1979) 'Note provvisorie su segnicità, fabrilità, procreazione e primato delle infrastrutture', *Problemi del Socialismo*, vol. 20, no. 4(15), pp. 93–126.

COCKBURN, C. (1981) 'The Material of Male Power', *Feminist Review*, no. 9, pp. 41–58.

COCKBURN, C. (1991) *In the Way of Women: men's resistance to sex equality in organizations*, Basingstoke, Macmillan.

COHEN, M. N. (1980) 'Speculations on the Evolution of Density Measurement and Population Regulation in *Homo Sapiens*', in COHEN, M. N., MALPASS, R. S. and KLEIN, H. G. (Eds) *Biosocial Mechanisms of Population Regulation*, New Haven and London, Yale University Press, pp. 275–303.

COLLARD, C. (1979) 'Mariage "à petits pas" et mariage "par vol": pouvoir des hommes, des femmes et des chefs chez les Guidars', *Anthropologie et Sociétés*, vol. 3, no. 1, pp. 41–73.

COLLARD, C. (1981) 'Echangés, échangistes: structures dominées et structures dominantes d'échange matrimonial — Le cas guidar', *Culture*, vol. I, no. 1, pp. 3–11.

COLLIER, J. F. and ROSALDO, M. Z. (1981) 'Politics and Gender in Simple Societies', in ORTNER, S. and WHITEHEAD, H. (Eds) *Sexual Meanings*, Cambridge and London, Cambridge University Press.

COLSON, E. (1958) *Marriage and the Family Among the Plateau Tonga*, Manchester, Manchester University Press.

COMMUNICATIONS 35 (1982) *Sexualités occidentales: contribution à l'histoire et à la sociologie de la sexualité*, Paris, Seuil.

CORBIN, A. (1982) *Les filles de noce: misère sexuelle et prostitution (19ᵉ siècle)*, Paris, Flammarion (first edition 1978). English edition *Women for Hire*.

COUNIHAN, C.M. (1985) 'Transvestism and Gender in a Sardinian Carnival', *Anthropology*, vol. 9, no. 1–2 (Special issue 3: Sex and Gender in Southern Europe: Problems and Prospects), pp. 11–24.

COWLISHAW, G. (1978) 'Infanticide in Aboriginal Australia', *Oceania*, vol. 48, no. 4, pp. 262–83.

COWLISHAW, G. (1981) 'The Determinants of Fertility Among Australian Aborigines', *Mankind*, vol. 13, no. 1, pp. 37–55.

CROWDER, D.G. (1994) 'Monique Wittig', in SARTORI, E. and ZIMMERMAN, D. (Eds) (1994) *French Women Writers*, Lincoln and London, University of Nebraska Press.

CUCCHIARI, S. (1981) 'The Gender Revolution and the Transition from Bisexual Horde to Patrilocal Band: the origin of gender hierarchy', in ORTNER, S. and WHITEHEAD, H. (Eds) *Sexual Meanings: the cultural construction of gender and sexuality*. Cambridge and London, Cambridge University Press.

DALLA COSTA, M. and JAMES, S. (1975) *The Power of Women and the Subversion of the Community*, Bristol, Falling Wall Press.

DANDURAND, R.B. (1981) 'Famille du capitalisme et production des êtres humains', *Sociologie et Sociétés*, vol. 13, no. 2 special issue, *Les femmes dans la sociologie/Women in Sociology*, pp. 95–111.

DAUNE-RICHARD, A-M., HURTIG, M-C. and PICHEVIN, M-F. (Eds) (1989) *Catégorisation de sexe et Constructions scientifiques*, Aix-en-Provence, Université de Provence (Petite Collection CEFUP).

DAVENPORT, W.H. (1977) 'Sex in Cross-Culture Perspective', in BEACH, F.A. (Ed.) *Human Sexuality in Four Perspectives*, Baltimore, Johns Hopkins University Press, pp. 115–63.

DELPHY, C. (1970) 'L'ennemi principal', *Partisans* (trans Delphy, 1977).

DELPHY, C. (1975) 'Pour un matérialisme féministe', *L'Arc*, no. 61, pp. 61–7.

DELPHY, C. (1976) 'Continuities and Discontinuities in Marriage and Divorce', in LEONARD BARKER, D. and ALLEN, S. (Eds) *Sexual Divisions and Society: process and change*, London, Tavistock.

DELPHY, C. (1977) *The Main Enemy*, London: Women's Research and Resources Centre, pamphlet. Reprinted in Delphy, 1984.

DELPHY, C. (1978) 'Le mariage et le travail non-rémunére', *Le Monde Diplomatique*, 286, January.

DELPHY, C. (1979) 'Sharing the Same Table: consumption and the family', in HARRIS, C.C. et al. (Eds) *The Sociology of the Family*, Keele, Sociological Review Monograph.

DELPHY, C. (1980) 'A Materialist Feminism *is* Possible', *Feminist Review*, no. 4, pp. 79–104.

DELPHY, C. (1984) *Close to Home: a materialist analysis of women's oppression*, London, Hutchinson.

DELPHY, C. (1993) 'Rethinking Sex and Gender', *Women's Studies International Forum*, vol. 16, no. 1, pp. 1–9.

DELPHY, C. (1995) 'The Invention of French Feminism: an essential move', *Yale French Studies*, no. 87, Special Issue: Another Look, Another Woman: Retranslations of French Feminism, pp. 190–221.

DELPHY, C. and LEONARD, D. (1992) *Familiar Exploitation: a new analysis of marriage in western societies*, Cambridge, Polity.

DERRIDA, J. (1976) *Of Grammatology* (translated Gayatri Spivak), Baltimore, Johns Hopkins University Press.

References

DESCARRIES-BÉLANGER, F. and ROY, S. (1988) 'Le mouvement des femmes et ses courants de pensée: essai de typologie', *The CRIAW Papers/Les Documents de l'ICREF 19*, Ottawa, Institut Canadien de Recherches sur les Femmes.

DÉSY, P. (1978) 'L'homme-femme (les berdaches en Amérique du Nord)', *Libre*, vol. 3, pp. 57–102 (Petite Bibliothèque Payot, 340).

DETIENNE, M. (1972) *Les jardins d'Adonis*, Paris, Gallimard.

DEVEREUX, G. (1937) 'Institutionalized homosexuality of the Mohave Indians', *Human Biology*, vol. 9, pp. 498–527. Reprinted in Ruitenbeek, 1963, pp. 183–226.

DEVEREUX, G. (1976) *A Study of Abortion in Primitive Societies*, New York, International Universities Press (first edn. 1955).

DOUGLAS, C. A. (1980) Interview with Christine Delphy and Monique Wittig, *Off Our Backs*, vol. 10, no. 1, p. 6.

DOUGLASS, F. (1980) *Mémoires d'un esclave américain*, Paris, Maspero. (Originally published (1849) as *Narrative of the Life of Frederick Douglass, an American Slave, Written by Himself*, Boston, Anti-slavery Office.)

DUBY, G. (1981) *Le Chevalier, la femme et le prêtre: le mariage dans la France féodale*, Paris, Hachette.

DUCHEN, C. (1984) 'What's the French for "political lesbian"?', in *Trouble and Strife*, no. 2. pp. 24–34.

DUCHEN, C. (1986) *Feminism in France: from May '68 to Mitterand*, London, Routledge.

DUCHEN, C. (Ed.) (1987) *French Connections: voices from the women's movement in France*, Hutchinson, London.

DUFOUR, R. (1977) *Les noms de personne chez les Inuit d'Iglulik*, thèse de maîtrise en sciences sociales (anthropologie), Université de Laval, Québec, mimeo.

DUKAS, H. and HOFFMAN, B. (1972) *Albert Einstein: creator and rebel*, New York, Viking.

EATON, J. W. and MAYER, A. J. (1954) *Man's Capacity to Reproduce: the demography of a unique population*, Glencoe, IL, Free Press.

ECHARD, N. (1985) 'Même la viande est vendue avec le sang. De la sexualité des femmes, un exemple', in MATHIEU, N-C. (Ed.) *L'Arraisonnement des femmes: essais en anthropologie des sexes*, Paris, Éditions de l'École des Hautes Études en Sciences Sociales (Cahiers de L'Homme), pp. 37–60.

ECHARD, N., JOURNET, O. and LALLEMAND, S. (1981) 'L'Afrique de l'Ouest. De l'Obligation à la prohibition: sens et non-sens de la virginité des filles', *La Première fois ou le roman de la virginité perdue à travers les siècles et les continents*, Paris, Ramsay, pp. 337–95.

EDHOLM, F., HARRIS, O. and YOUNG, K. (1977) 'Conceptualising Women', *Critique of Anthropology*, vol. 3, no. 9–10 (Women's Issue), pp. 101–30.

ELAM, Y. (1973) *The Social and Sexual Roles of Hima Women: a study of nomadic cattle breeders in Nyabushozi County, Ankole, Uganda*, Manchester, Manchester University Press.

ELWIN, V. (1959) *Maisons des jeunes chez les Muria*, Paris, Gallimard.

ETIENNE, M. (1979) 'Maternité sociale, rapports d'adoption et pouvoir des femmes chez les Baoulé (Côte d'Ivoire)', *L'Homme*, vol. 19, no. 3–4, pp. 63–107.

ETIENNE, M. (1981) 'Gender Relations and Conjugality among the Baule (Ivory Coast)', *Culture*, vol. 1, no. 1, pp. 21–30.

ETIENNE, M. and LEACOCK, E. (Eds) (1980) *Women and Colonization*, New York, Praeger.

ETIENNE, R. (1973) 'La Conscience médicale antique et la vie des enfants', *Annales de Démographie historique*, pp. 15–46 (*Enfant et sociétés*).

EVANS, M. (1991) 'The Problem of Gender for Women's Studies', in AARON, J. and WALBY, S. (Eds) *Out of the Margins: women's studies in the nineties*, London, Falmer Press.

EVANS-PRITCHARD, E. E. (1970) 'Sexual Inversion Among the Azande', *American Anthropologist*, vol. 72, pp. 1428–34.

EZEKIEL, J. (1992) 'Radical in Theory: organized women's studies in France, the women's movement and the state', *Women's Studies Quarterly*, vol. 20, nos 3 and 4, Fall/Winter, pp. 75–84.

FALLAIZE, E. (1993) *French Women's Writing: recent fiction*, Macmillan, Basingstoke.

FINCH, J. (1983) *Married to the Job: wives incorporation in men's work*, London, George Allen and Unwin.

FINE, A. and LALANNE, M. (1980) 'Les Femmes et l'évolution récente de la nuptialité', *Annales*, revue de l'Université de Toulouse-Le Mirail, vol. 16, pp. 85–101. Numéro spécial du Group de Recherches Interdisciplinaire d'Études des Femmes (GRIEF).

FIRTH, R. (1963) *We, the Tikopia*, Boston, Beacon Press (first edition, London, Allen and Unwin, 1936).

FLANDRIN, J. L. (1976) *Familles: parenté, maison, sexualité dans l'ancienne société*, Paris, Hachette.

FLANDRIN, J. L. (1981) *Le Sexe et l'Occident: évolution des attitudes et des comportements*, Paris, Seuil.

FLANDRIN, J. L. (1982) 'La Vie sexuelle des gens mariés dans l'ancienne société: de la doctrine de l'Église à la réalité des comportements', *Communications*, vol. 35, pp. 102–15 (*Sexualités occidentales*).

FLANDRIN, J. L. (1983) *Un Temps pour embrasser: aux origines de la morale sexuelle occidentale (VIᵉ–XIᵉ siècles)*, Paris, Seuil.

FOUCAULT, M. (1969) *L'archéologie du savoir*, Paris, Ed. Gallimard. Translated as Foucault, M. (1976a).

FOUCAULT, M. (1976a) *The Archaeology of Knowledge*, New York, Harper Colophon Books.

FOUCAULT, M. (1976b) *Histoire de la sexualité I, La volonté de savoir*, Paris, Editions Gallimard, 1976. Translated as Foucault, M. (1981).

FOUCAULT, M. (1981) *The History of Sexuality, Volume 1: An Introduction*, trans. Robert Hurley, Harmondsworth: Penguin. First published in English, New York, Random House, 1978.

FOURNIER, G. and REYNAUD, E. (1978) 'La Sainte Virilité', *Questions féministes*, no. 3, May, pp. 31–62.

FRASER, N. (1992) 'Introduction', to FRASER, N. and LEE BARTKY, S. (Eds), *Revaluing French Feminism: Critical essays on difference, agency and culture*, Bloomington and Indianapolis, Indiana University Press.

FRASER, N. and LEE BARTKY, S. (Eds) (1992) *Revaluing French Feminism: Critical essays on difference, agency and culture*, Bloomington and Indianapolis, Indiana University Press.

FREEMAN, D. (1983) *Margaret Mead and Samoa: the making and unmaking of an anthropological myth*, Cambridge, MA and London, Harvard University Press.

FREEMAN, M. (1971) 'A Social and Ecological Analysis of Systematic Female Infanticide among the Netsilik Eskimo', *American Anthropologist*, vol. 73, pp. 1011–18.

FRISCH, R. E. (1975) 'Demographic Implications of the Biological Determinants of Female Fecundity', *Social Biology*, vol. 22, no. 1, pp. 17–22.

FRISCH, R. E. (1978) 'Population, Food Intake and Fertility', *Science*, vol. 199, pp. 20–30.

FRISCH, R. E. and McARTHUR, J. W. (1974) 'Menstrual cycles: fatness as a determinant of minimum weight for height necessary for their maintenance or onset', *Science*, vol. 185, pp. 949–51.

GAILEY, C. W. (1980) 'Putting Down Sisters and Wives: Tongan Women and Colonization', in ETIENNE, M. and LEACOCK, E. (Eds) *Women and Colonization*, New York, Praeger.

References

GARCIA, S. (1994) 'Project for a Symbolic Revolution: the rise and fall of the women's movement in France', *The South Atlantic Quarterly*, vol. 93, no. 4, Fall, pp. 825–69. Special Issue on Materialist Feminism, edited by MOI, T. and RADWAY, J.

GARDEN, M. (1975) *Lyon et les Lyonnais au XVIIIᵉ siècle*, Paris, Flammarion.

GATENS, M. (1983) 'A Critique of the Sex/Gender Distinction', in ALLEN, J. and PATTON, P. (Eds) *Beyond Marxism? Interventions after Marx*, New South Wales, Intervention Publications. Republished in GUNEW, S. (Ed.) (1991) *A Reader in Feminist Knowledge*, London, Routledge.

GELIS, J. (1977) 'Sages-femmes et accouchées: l'obstétrique populaire aux XVIIᵉ et XVIIIᵉ siècles', *Annales E.S.C.*, vol. 32, no. 5, pp. 927–57.

GELIS, J., LAGET, M. and MOREL, M.-F. (presenters) (1978) *Entrer dans la vie: naissances et enfances dans la France traditionelle*, Paris, Gallimard/Julliard (Archives).

GESSAIN, R. (1969) *Ammassalik ou la civilisation obligatoire*, Paris, Flammarion.

GIBBS, A., BRAIDOTTI, R., WEINSTOCK, J. and HUSTON, N. (1980) 'Round and round the looking glass: responses to Elaine Marks and Isabelle de Courtivron, New French Feminisms . . .', *Hecate*, pp. 23–45.

GILLISON, G. (1980) 'Images of Nature in Gimi Thought', in MACCORMACK, C. P. and STRATHERN, M. (Eds) (1980) *Nature, Culture and Gender*, Cambridge, Cambridge University Press, pp. 143–73.

GILLISON, G. (1983) 'Cannibalism Among Women in the Eastern Highlands of Papua New Guinea', in BROWN, P. and TUZIN, D. (Eds) (1983) *The Ethnography of Cannibalism*, Washington, DC, Society for Psychological Anthropology, pp. 33–50.

GILLISON, G. (1986) 'Le pénis géant. Le frère de la mère dans les Hautes Terres de Nouvelle-Guinée', *L'Homme*, vol. 99, XXVI, 3, pp. 41–69.

GILLISON, G. (1989) 'L'horreur de l'inceste et le père caché: mythe et saignées rituelles chez les Gimi de Nouvelle-Guinée', in *Le Père. Métaphore paternelle et fonctions du père: l'Interdit, la Filiation, la Transmission*, Paris, Denoël, pp. 197–216.

GLADWIN, T. and SARASON, S. B. (1953) *Truk: man in paradise*, New York, Wenner-Gren Foundation for Anthropological Research (The Viking Publications in Anthropology, 20).

GODELIER, M. (1975) 'Perspectives ethnologiques et questions actuelles sur le travail', *Lumière et vie*, vol. 124, pp. 35–58.

GODELIER, M. (1976) 'Le Sexe comme fondement ultime de l'orde social et cosmique chez les Baruya de Nouvelle-Guinée', in *Cahiers du CERM*, 128, *Le problème des formes et des fondements de la domination masculine*.

GODELIER, M. (1977) 'Modes de production, rapports de parenté et structures démographiques', in *Horizon, trajets marxistes en anthropologie*, I, Paris, Maspero.

GODELIER, M. (1978) 'La Part idéelle du réel: essai sur l'idéologique', *L'Homme*, vol. 18, nos 3–4, pp. 155–88.

GODELIER, M. (1982) *La Production des Grands Hommes: pouvoir et domination masculine chez les Baruya de Nouvelle-Guinée*, Paris, Fayard.

GOODY, E. N. (1978) 'Some Theoretical and Empirical Aspects of Parenthood in West Africa', in OPPONG, C., ADABA, G. *et al.* (Eds) *Mariage, fécondité et rôle des parents en Afrique de l'Ouest*, Canberra, The Australian National University, pp. 222–72.

GOODY, J. (1976) *Production and Reproduction: a comparative study of the domestic domain*, Cambridge, Cambridge University Press.

GROSZ, E. (1989) *Sexual Subversions: three French feminists*, London, Allen and Unwin.

GUILLAUMIN, C. (1972) 'Les caractères spécifiques de l'idéologie raciste', *Cahiers Internationaux de Sociologie*, LIII. Reprinted in Guillaumin (1995), chapter 1.

GUILLAUMIN, C. (1977) 'Race et nature: système de marques, idée de groupe naturel et rapports sociaux', *Pluriel*, vol. 11, pp. 39–55. Reprinted in Guillaumin (1995), chapter 6.

GUILLAUMIN, C. (1978a) 'Pratique du pouvoir et idée de Nature. (I) L'Appropriation des femmes', *Questions féministes*, no. 2, pp. 5–30. Translated Guillaumin (1981a). Abridged in this volume.

GUILLAUMIN, C. (1978b) 'Pratique du pouvoir et idée de Nature. (II) Le Discours de la Nature, *Questions féministes*, no. 3, pp. 5–28. Translated Guillaumin (1981b). Abridged in this volume. Reprinted in Guillaumin (1995), chapter 10.

GUILLAUMIN, C. (1978c) 'Les Harengs et les tigres. Remarques sur l'éthologie', *Critique*, nos 375–6, pp. 748–63. Reprinted in Guillaumin (1995), chapter 11.

GUILLAUMIN, C. (1979) 'Question de différence', *Questions féministes*, no. 6, Sept, pp. 3–21. Translated Guillaumin (1982).

GUILLAUMIN, C. (1980) 'The Idea of Race and its Elevation to Autonomous Scientific and Legal Status', in *Sociological Theories: race and colonialism*, Paris, UNESCO. Reprinted in Guillaumin (1995), chapter 2.

GUILLAUMIN, C. (1981a) 'The Practice of Power and Belief in Nature, Part 1, The Appropriation of Women', *Feminist Issues*, vol. 1, no. 2, pp. 3–28. Abridged in this volume. Reprinted in Guillaumin (1995), chapter 9.

GUILLAUMIN, C. (1981b) 'The Practice of Power and Belief in Nature, Part 2, The Discourse of Nature', *Feminist Issues*, vol. 1, no. 3, pp. 87–109. Abridged in this volume. Reprinted in Guillaumin (1995), chapter 10.

GUILLAUMIN, C. (1981c) 'Femmes et théories de la société', *Sociologie et Sociétés*, vol. 13, no. 2, pp. 19–31. Translated Guillaumin (1984).

GUILLAUMIN, C. (1982) 'The Question of Difference', *Feminist Issues*, vol. 2, no. 1, pp. 33–52. Reprinted in Guillaumin (1995), chapter 11.

GUILLAUMIN, C. (1982) 'The Question of Difference', *Feminist Issues*, vol. 2, no. 1, pp. 33–52

GUILLAUMIN, C. (1984) 'Women and Theories about Society: the effects on theory of the anger of the oppressed, *Feminist Issues*, vol. 4, no. 1, pp. 23–39. Reprinted in Guillaumin (1995), chapter 7.

GUILLAUMIN, C. (1985) 'The Masculine: Denotations/Connotations', *Feminist Issues*, vol. 5, no. 1.

GUILLAUMIN, C. (1995) *Racism, Sexism, Power and Ideology*, London and New York, Routledge.

GUTMANN, B. (1926) *Das Recht der Dschagga*, München, C. H. Beck. [Chagga Law. English translation for the HRAF (Human Relations Area Files), New Haven, CN.]

GUTMANN, B. (1932) *Die Stammeslehren der Dschagga*, vol. I, München, C. H. Beck. [The Tribal Teaching of the Chagga. English translation for the HRAF, New Haven, CN.]

HALIMI, G. (presenter) (1978) *Le programme commun des femmes*, Paris, Grasset.

HANMER, J. (1978) 'Violence and the Social Control of Women', in LITTLEJOHN, G. SMART, B., WAKEFORD, J. and YUVAL-DAVIS, N. (Eds) *Power and the State*, London, Croom Helm.

HANMER, J. (1981) 'Sex Predetermination, Artificial Insemination and the Maintenance of Male Dominated Culture', in ROBERTS, H. (Ed.) *Women, Health and Reproduction*, London, Routledge and Kegan Paul.

HANMER, J. and ALLEN, P. (1979) 'La Science de la reproduction — solution finale?', *Questions féministes*, vol. 5, pp. 29–51.

HARAWAY, D. (1978) 'Animal Sociology and a Natural Economy of the Body Politic. Part I: A Political Physiology of Dominance; Part II: The Past is the Contested Zone: human nature and theories of production and reproduction in primate behavior studies', *Signs: Journal of Women in Culture and Society*, vol. 4, no. 1, pp. 21–60.

References

HARAWAY, D. (1981) 'In the Beginning was the Word: the genesis of biological theory', *Signs: Journal of Women in Culture and Society*, vol. 6, no. 3, pp. 469–81.

HARRELL, B. (1981) 'Lactation and Menstruation in Cultural Perspective', *American Anthropologist*, vol. 83, pp. 796–823.

HARRISON, G. A. (1979) 'Biological Anthropology', in WALLMAN, S. (Ed.) *Social Anthropology of Work*, London and New York, Academic Press (ASA Monograph no. 19).

HARTMANN, H. (1979) 'Capitalism, patriarchy and job segregation by sex' in EISENSTEIN, Z. R. (Ed.) *Capitalist Patriarchy and the Case for Socialist Feminism*, New York, Monthly Review Press.

HARTMANN, H. (1981) 'The unhappy marriage of Marxism and feminism: towards a more progressive union' in SARGENT, L. (Ed.) *The Unhappy Marriage of Marxism and Feminism: a debate on class and patriarchy*, London, Pluto.

HASSAN, F. (1980) 'The Growth and Regulation of Human Population in Prehistoric Times', in COHEN, M., MALPASS, R. and KLEIN, H. (Eds) *Biosocial Mechanisms of Population Regulation*, New Haven and London, Yale University Press, pp. 305–19.

HASSAN, F. (1981) *Demographic Archaeology*, New York, London, Toronto, Academic Press.

HASTRUP, K. (1978) 'The Semantics of Biology: Virginity', in ARDENER, S. (Ed.) (1978) *Defining Females. The nature of women in society*, London, Croom Helm, pp. 49–65.

HAYDEN, B. (1972) 'Population Control Among Hunter/Gatherers', *World Archaeology*, vol. 4, pp. 205–21.

HENRY, L. (1961) 'La Fécondité naturelle: observations, théorie, résultats', *Population*, vol. 16, no. 4, pp. 625–36.

HENRY, L. (1964) 'Mesure du temps mort en fécondité naturelle', *Population*, vol. 19, no. 3, pp. 485–514.

HERDT, G. H. (Ed.) (1984) *Ritualized Homosexuality in Melanesia*, Berkeley and Los Angeles, University of California Press.

HÉRITIER, F. (1976) 'Adolescence et sexualité', *Le Groupe familial*, Revue de l'École des parents et des éducateurs, no. 73 (*Adolescent et monde contemporain*), pp. 3–12.

HÉRITIER, F. (1979a) 'Famiglia', in *Enciclopedia*, vol. 6, Torino, Einaudi.

HÉRITIER, F. (1979b) 'Maschile-Femminile', in *Enciclopedia*, vol. 8, Torino, Einaudi.

HILLEL, M. (with HENRY, C.) (1975) *Au Nom de la race*, Paris, Fayard (Le Livre de Poche).

HIMES, N. (1963) *Medical History of Contraception*, New York, Gamut Press (first edition 1936).

HOSKEN, F. (1979) *The Hosken Report: genital/sexual mutilation of females*. Lexington, MA, WIN News.

HOSKEN, F. (1980) 'Les Mutilations sexuelles en Afrique', *Questions féministes*, vol. 8, pp. 43–67.

HOWELL, N. (1979) *The Demography of the Dobe !Kung*, New York, San Francisco, London, Academic Press.

HRDY, S. B. (1981) *The Woman That Never Evolved*, Cambridge, MA and London, Harvard University Press.

HUBER, H. (1968/69) '"Woman-Marriage" in some East African Societies', *Anthropos*, vol. 63/64, nos 5/6, pp. 745–52.

HUNT, E. E., SCNEIDER, D., KIDDER, N. R. and STEVENS, W. S. (1949) *The Micronesians of Yap and their Repopulation: report of the Peabody Museum expedition to Yap Island, Micronesia 1947–1948*, Cambridge, MA, Peabody Museum — Harvard Museum.

HURTIG, M.-C. and PICHEVIN, M.-F. (1985) 'La variable sexe en psychologie: Donne ou construct?', *Cahiers de Psychologie Cognitive*, vol. 5, no. 2, pp. 187–228.

HURTIG, M.-C. and PICHEVIN, M.-F. (1986) *La différence des sexes*, Paris, Tierce.

HUSTON, N. (1978) 'French feminism', *Camera Obscura*, nos 3–4, pp. 237–244.

HYTTEN, F. E. and LEITCH, I. (1964) *The Physiology of Human Pregnancy*, Oxford, Blackwell.

IFEKA-MOLLER, C. (1975) 'Female Militancy and Colonial Revolt: the Women's War of 1929, Eastern Nigeria', in ARDENER, S. (Ed.) (1975) *Perceiving Women*, London, Malaby Press, pp. 127–57.

JACKSON, S. (1996) *Christine Delphy*, London, Sage.

JACQUARD, A. and GUILLAUMIN, C. (1982–1983) 'Un Débat: espoirs et craintes', *Le Genre humain*, vol. 6 (*Les manipulations*), pp. 94–101.

JELLIFFE, D. B. and JELLIFFE, E. F. P. (1978) *Human Milk in the Modern World: psychosocial, nutritional and economic significance*, Oxford, Oxford University Press.

JOURNET, O. (1981) in ECHARD, N., JOURNET, O. and LALLEMAND, S. 'L'Afrique de l'Ouest. De l'Obligation à la prohibition: sens et non-sens de la virginité des filles', in *La Première fois ou le roman de la virginité perdue à travers les siècles et les continents*, Paris, Ramsay, pp. 337–395.

JOURNET, O. (1985) 'Les hyper-mères n'ont plus d'enfants. Maternité et ordre social chez les Joola de Basse-Casamance', in MATHIEU, N-C. (Ed.) *L'Arraisonnement des femmes: essais en anthropologie des sexes*, Paris, Éditions de l'École des Hautes Études en Sciences Sociales (Cahiers de L'Homme), pp. 17–36.

JUTEAU-LEE, D. (1995) '(Re)constructing the categories of "race" and "sex": the work of a precursor', Introduction to GUILLAUMIN, C. *Racism, Sexism, Power and Ideology*, London, Routledge.

KAPLAN, G. (1992) *Contemporary European Feminism*, London: UCL Press.

KITZINGER, S. (1978) *Women as Mothers*, New York, Random House.

KLAPISCH-ZUBER, C. (1980) 'Genitori naturali e genitori di latte nella Firenze del Quattrocento', *Quaderni Storici*, vol. 44, pp. 543–63.

KNIBIEHLER, Y. and FOUQUET, C. (1983) *La Femme et les médicins: analyse historique*, Paris, Hachette.

KOMAROVSKY, M. (1950) 'Functional Analysis of Sex Roles', *American Sociological Review*, vol. 15, no. 4.

KRIGE, E. JENSEN (1974) 'Woman-Marriage, with Special Reference to the Lovedu — Its Significance for the Definition of Marriage', *Africa*, vol. 44, pp. 11–36.

KRUKS, S. (1992) 'Gender and Subjectivity: Simone de Beauvoir and contemporary feminism', *Signs*, vol. 18, no. 1, pp. 89–111.

LABBY, D. (1976) *The Demystification of Yap: culture on a Micronesian Island*, Chicago and London, University of Chicago Press.

LAGET, M. (1977) 'La Naissance aux siècles classiques: pratique des accouchements et attitudes collectives en France aux XVIIe et XVIIIe siècles', *Annales E.S.C.*, vol. 32, no. 5, pp. 958–92.

LALLEMAND, S. (1977) *Une Famille mossi*, Paris and Ouagadougou, CNRS, CVRS (Recherches Voltaïques, 17).

LANDRY, D. and MACLEAN, G. (1993) *Materialist Feminisms*, Oxford, Blackwell.

LAQUEUR, T. (1990) *Making Sex: body and gender from the Greeks to Freud*, Cambridge, MA, Harvard.

LAURIN-FRENNETTE, N. (1981) 'Féminisme et anarchisme: quelques éléments théoriques et historiques pour une analyse de la relation entre le Mouvement des femmes et l'État', in COHEN, Y. (Ed.) *Femmes et politique*, Canada, Le Jour Editeur, pp. 147–91.

LE BRAS, H. (1981) 'Histoire secrète de la fécondité', *Le Débat*, vol. 8, pp. 77–101.

LE PÉRON, M. (1978) 'Priorité aux violées', *Questions féministes*, no. 3, May, pp. 83–92.

LEACOCK, E. (1978) 'Women's Status in Egalitarian Society: implications for social evolution', *Current Anthropology*, vol. 19, no. 2, pp. 247–75.

LEAKEY, L. S. B. (1930) 'Some Notes on the Masai of Kenya Colony', *Journal of the Royal Anthropological Institute*, vol. 60, pp. 185–209.

LEE, R. B. (1972) 'Population Growth and the Beginning of Sedentary Life Among the !Kung Bushmen', in SPOONER, B. (Ed.) *Population Growth: anthropological implications*, Philadelphia, University of Pennsylvania Press.

LEE, R. B. (1979) *The !Kung San: men, women and work in a foraging society*, Cambridge and London, Cambridge University Press.

LEE, R. B. (1980) 'Lactation, Ovulation, Infanticide and Women's Work: a study of hunter-gatherer population regulation', in COHEN, M. N., MALPASS, R. S. and KLEIN, H. G. (Eds) *Biosocial Mechanisms of Population Regulation*, New Haven and London, Yale University Press, pp. 321–48.

LÉRIDON, H. (1971) 'Les Facteurs de la fécondité en Martinique', *Population*, vol. 26, no. 2, pp. 277–300.

LÉRIDON, H. (1973) *Aspects biométriques de la fécondité humaine*, Paris, PUF (INED, Travaux et Documents, Cahier 65).

LÉRIDON, H. (1977) *Human Fertility: the basic components*, Chicago, University of Chicago Press.

LÉRIDON, H., ZUCKER, E. and CAZENAVE, M. (1970) *Fécondité et famille en Martinique: faits, attitudes, opinions*, Paris, PUF (INED, Travaux et Documents, 56).

LEROI-GOURHAN, A. (1965) *Le Geste et la parole: la mémoire et les rythmes*, Paris, Albin Michel.

LESSEPS, E. DE (1981) 'Female Reality: biology or society?', *Feminist Issues*, vol. 1, no. 2.

LESSEPS, E. DE (1973) *Le divorce comme révélateur et garant d'une fonction économique de la famille*, Mémoire de Maîtrise, Université de Vincennes.

LÉVI-STRAUSS, C. (1956) 'The Family', in SHAPIRO, H. L. (Ed.) *Man, Culture and Society*, New York, Oxford University Press, pp. 261–85.

LÉVI-STRAUSS, C. (1962) *Tristes Tropiques*, Paris, Union Générale d'Editions (10/18). First edition, Plon, 1955.

LÉVI-STRAUSS, C. (1969) *The Elementary Structures of Kinship*, London, Eyre and Spottiswoode.

LÉVI-STRAUSS, C. (1975) Compte rendu du cours 1974–1975 sur 'Cannibalisme et travestissement rituel', *Annuaire du Collège de France*. Reprinted in *Paroles données*, Paris, Plon, 1984, pp. 141–9.

LEVINE, R. A. (1959) 'Gusii Sex Offenses: a study in social control', *American Anthropologist*, vol. 61, pp. 965–90.

LEWIS, J. (1981) 'The Registration of "MLF" in France', *Spare Rib*, no. 108.

LINDBLOM, M. (1969) *The Akamba in British East Africa: an ethnological monograph*, New York, Negro Universities Press (first edition 1920).

LURY, C. (1996) *Consumer Culture*, Cambridge, Polity Press.

MACCORMACK, C. P. and STRATHERN, M. (Eds) (1980) *Nature, Culture and Gender*, Cambridge, Cambridge University Press.

MARKS, E. and COURTIVRON, I. DE (Eds) (1981) *New French Feminisms: an anthology*, Brighton, Harvester.

MARSHALL, D. S. (1971) 'Sexual Behavior on Mangaia', in MARSHALL, D. S. and SUGGS, R. C. (Eds) *Human Sexual Behavior*, New York, Basic Books.

MARX, K. (1887/1974) *Capital, Volume 1*, London, Lawrence and Wishart.

MARX, K. (1968) 'Les Principes d'une critique de l'Economie Politique', in *Oeuvres*, t. 2, Paris, Gallimard (Bibl. de la Pléiade).

MARX, K. and ENGELS, F. (1845–6) *The German Ideology*, republished (1964) London, Lawrence and Wishart.

MATHIEU, N.-C. (1971) 'Notes pour une définition sociologique des catégories de sexe', *Epistémologie sociologique*, no. 11, pp. 19–39. Translated Mathieu (1974). Reprinted in Mathieu (1991).

MATHIEU, N.-C. (1973) 'Homme-culture et femme-nature?', *L'Homme*, vol. 13, no. 3, pp. 101–13. Translated Mathieu (1978). Reprinted in Mathieu (1991).

MATHIEU, N.-C. (1974) 'Notes Towards a Sociological Definition of Sex Categories', *The Human Context*, vol. 6, no. 2, pp. 345–61.

MATHIEU, N.-C. (1977) 'Paternité biologique, maternité sociale...', in MICHEL, A. (Ed.) (1977) *Femmes, sexisme et sociétés*, Paris, PUF, pp. 39–48. Translated Mathieu (1979). Reprinted in Mathieu (1991).

MATHIEU, N.-C. (1978) 'Man-Culture and Woman-Nature?', *Women's Studies International Quarterly*, vol. 1, no. 1, pp. 55–65.

MATHIEU, N.-C. (1979) 'Biological Paternity, Social Maternity: on abortion and infanticide as unrecognised indicators of the cultural character of maternity', in HARRIS, C. C. *et al.* (Eds) *The Sociology of the Family: new directions for Britain*, University of Keele: Sociological Review Monographs, no. 28, pp. 232–40.

MATHIEU, N.-C. (1980) 'Masculinity/femininity', *Feminist Issues*, vol. 1, no. 1, pp. 51–69.

MATHIEU, N.-C. (1981) 'Les Idéologies du sexe: anthropologie, sociologie et politique', communication à l'Atelier 'Anthropologie des femmes et femmes anthropologues', Colloque CNRS/AFA, Sèvres, 19-20-21 November 1981.

MATHIEU, N.-C. (Ed.) (1985) *L'Arraisonnement des femmes. Essais en anthropologie des sexes*, Paris, Editions de l'École des Hautes Études en Sciences Sociales.

MATHIEU, N.-C. (1985a) 'Quand céder n'est pas consentir. Des déterminants matériels et psychiques de la conscience dominée des femmes, et de quelques-unes de leurs interprétations en ethnologie', in MATHIEU, N.-C. (Ed.), pp. 169–245. Translated Mathieu (1989 and 1990). Reprinted in Mathieu (1991).

MATHIEU, N.-C. (1985b) 'Critiques épistémologiques de la problématique des sexes dans le discours ethno-anthropologique', rapport pour la Réunion internationale d'experts: *Réflexion sur la problématique féminine dans la recherche et l'enseignement supérieur*, Paris: UNESCO, SHS-85/Conf. 612/6. Published in Mathieu (1991), pp. 75–127.

MATHIEU, N.-C. (1989 and 1990) 'When Yielding is Not Consenting. Material and psychic determinants of women's dominated consciousness, and some of their interpretations in Ethnology', *Feminist Issues*, 1989, vol. 9, no. 2, pp. 3–49; and 1990, vol. 10, no. 1, pp. 51–90.

MATHIEU, N.-C. (1991) *L'Anatomie politique. Catégorisations et idéologies du sexe*, Paris, Côté-femmes.

MEAD, M. (1935) *Sex and Temperament in Three Primitive Societies*, New York: William Morrow.

MEAD, M. (1956) *New Lives for Old*, New York, William Morrow.

MEAD, M. (1975) *Coming of Age in Samoa*, Harmondsworth, Penguin Books (first edition 1928).

MEILLASSOUX, C. (1975) *Femmes, greniers et capitaux*, Paris, Maspero, translated Meillassoux (1981).

MEILLASSOUX, C. (1981) *Maidens, Meal and Money: capitalism and the domestic community*, Cambridge, Cambridge University Press.

MERKER, M. (1910) *Die Masai: ethnographische Monographie eines ostafricanischen Semitenvolkes*, second edition, Berlin, Dietrich Reimer (Ernst Vohsen). [The Masai. Ethnographic Monograph of an East African Semite People. English translation for the HRAF Human Relations Area Files, New Haven, CN.]

MICHARD-MARCHAL, C. and RIBÉRY, C. (1982) *Sexisme et Sciences Humaines: pratique linguistique du rapport de sexage*, Lille, Presses Universitaires de Lille.

MICHEL, A. (1959) *Famille, industrialisation, logement*, Paris, Centre National de Recherche Scientifique.

MICHEL, A. (1960) 'La femme dans la famille française', *Cahiers Internationaux de Sociologie*, 111.

MICHEL, A. (Ed.) (1977) *Femmes, sexisme et sociétés*, Paris, PUF.

MIES, M. (1983) 'Gesellschaftliche Ursprünge der geschlechtlichen Arbeitsteilung', in VON WERLHOF, C., MIES, M. and BENNHOLDT-THOMSEN, V. (Eds) *Frauen, die letzte Kolonie*, Reinbek bei Hamburg, Rowohlt Taschenbuch Verlag, pp. 164–93. [Orig. in *Beiträge zur feministischen Theorie und Praxis*, vol. 3, 1980.]

MIES, M. (1986) *Patriarchy and Accumulation on a World Scale*, London, Zed.

MINORITY RIGHTS GROUP (1980) *Female Circumcision, Excision and Infibulation: the facts and proposals for change* (Ed. S. McLean) London, Minority Rights Group, Report 47.

MOI, T. (Ed.) (1987) *French Feminist Thought*, Oxford, Blackwell.

MOIA, M. (1981) *La Saumone*, Paris, Mercure de France.

MONEY, J. and EHRHARDT, A. (1972) *Man and Woman, Boy and Girl*, Baltimore, Johns Hopkins University Press.

MOORE, H. (1994) *A Passion for Difference: Essays in Anthropology and Gender*, Cambridge, Polity.

MOREAU-BISSERET, N. (1982) 'La Démographie, science de la reproduction des classes de sexe', communication au Xe Congrès Mondial de Sociologie, Mexico, August (Symposium 33).

MOSES, C. (1987) 'French Feminism's Fortunes', *The Women's Review of Books*, vol. 5, no. 1, October, pp. 16–17.

MOSES, C. (1992) 'French Feminism in U.S. Academic Discourse', a paper presented at the Berkshire Conference on Women's History, 12 June.

MULLER, J.-C. (1976) *Parenté et mariage chez les Rukuba* (*Etat Benue-Plateau, Nigeria*), Paris and The Hague, Mouton (Cahiers de l'Homme XVII).

MULLER, J.-C. (1981) 'M.L.F. Rukuba: l'ancien et le nouveau', *Culture*, vol. 1, no. 1, pp. 12–20.

MULLER, J.-C. (1982) *Du bon usage du sexe et du mariage: structures matrimoniales du haut plateau nigérian*, Paris and Québec, L'Harmattan/Serge Fleury Ed.

MURDOCK, G. (1949) *Social Structure*, New York, Macmillan.

MURPHY, Y. and MURPHY, R. (1974) *Women of the Forest*. New York and London, Columbia University Press.

MYRDAL, A. and KLEIN, V. (1956) *Women's Two Roles: Home and Work*, London, Routledge and Kegan Paul.

NAG, M. (1962) *Factors Affecting Human Fertility in Non-Industrial Societies: a cross-cultural study*, New Haven, Yale University Press (Yale University Publications in Anthropology, 66).

NAG, M. (1971) 'The Influence of Conjugal Behavior, Migration and Contraception on Natality in Barbados', in POLGAR, S. (Ed.) *Culture and Population*, Cambridge, Schenkman.

NAG, M. (1972) 'Sex, Culture, and Human Fertility: India and the United States', *Current Anthropology*, vol. 13, no. 2, pp. 231–7.

NANDA, S. (1986) 'The Hijras of India: cultural and individual dimensions of an institutionalized third gender role', in BLACKWOOD, E. (Ed.) (1986) *The Many Faces of Homosexuality. Anthropological Approaches to Homosexual Behavior*, New York, Harrington Park Press, pp. 35–54.

NAVA, M. (1983) 'From Utopian to Scientific Feminism? Early Feminist Critiques of the Family', in SEGAL, L. (Ed.) *What is to be Done About the Family?*, Harmondsworth: Penguin.

NEWTON, E. (1979) *Mother Camp: Female Impersonators in America*, Chicago, University of Chicago Press. [First edn. 1972.]

O'BRIEN, D. (1972) 'Female Husbands in African Societies', paper presented at the 71st annual meeting of the American Anthropological Association, Toronto.

O'BRIEN, D. (1977) 'Female Husbands in Southern Bantu Societies', in SCHLEGEL, A.

(Ed.) (1977) *Sexual Stratification: a Cross-Cultural View*, New York, Columbia University Press, pp. 109–26.

O'BRIEN, M. (1981) *The Politics of Reproduction*, London, Routledge and Kegan Paul.

OAKLEY, A. (1972/1985) *Sex, Gender and Society*, London, Temple Smith (revised edition, 1985, Gower).

OAKLEY, A. (1976) 'Wisewoman and Medicine Man: changes in the management of childbirth', in MITCHELL, J. and OAKLEY, A. (Eds) *The Rights and Wrongs of Women*, Harmondsworth, Penguin.

OBBO, C. (1976) 'Dominant Male Ideology and Female Options: three East African case studies', *Africa*, vol. 46, no. 4, pp. 371–89.

OBOLER, R. SMITH (1980) 'Is the Female Husband a Man? Woman/woman marriage among the Nandi of Kenya', *Ethnology*, vol. 19, no. 1, pp. 69–88.

OROBIO DE CASTRO, I. (1987) 'How Lesbian is a Female Trans-Sexual', in *Homosexuality, which Homosexuality?* (Social Science, vol. 2, pp. 210–15), Papers of the International Scientific Conference on Gay and Lesbian Studies (December 15–18, 1987), Free University/Schorer Foundation, Amsterdam, September 1987.

ORTNER, S. (1981) 'Gender and Sexuality in Hierarchical Societies: the case of Polynesia and some comparative implications', in ORTNER, S. and WHITEHEAD, H. (Eds) *Sexual Meanings: the cultural construction of gender and sexuality*, Cambridge and London, Cambridge University Press.

ORTNER, S. B. and WHITEHEAD, H. (Eds) (1981) *Sexual Meanings. The Cultural Construction of Gender and Sexuality*, Cambridge and London, Cambridge University Press.

PARSONS, T. (1954) *Essays in Sociological Theory*, Illinois, Free Press.

PATEMAN, C. (1988) *The Sexual Contract*, Cambridge, Polity.

PATTERSON, Y. A. (1994) 'Simone de Beauvoir', in SARTORI, E. and ZIMMERMAN, D. (Eds) (1994) *French Women Writers*, Lincoln and London, University of Nebraska Press.

PÉRON, M. LE (1978) 'Priorité aux violées', Questions féministes, no. 3, May, pp. 83–92.

PHETERSON, G. (Ed.) (1989) *A Vindication of the Rights of Whores*, Seattle, Seal Press.

PHETERSON, G. (1994) 'Group Identity and Social Relations: divergent theoretical conceptions in the United States, the Netherlands and France', *European Journal of Women's Studies*, vol. 1, no. 2, Autumn, pp. 257–64.

PLAZA, M. (1977) 'Pouvoir "phallomorphique" et psychologie de "la femme": un bouclage patriarcal', *Questions féministes*, no. 1, pp. 91–119. Translated Plaza (1978).

PLAZA, M. (1978) '"Phallomorphic power" and the psychology of "woman": a patriarchal chain', *Ideology and Consciousness*, no. 4, Autumn, pp. 4–36.

PLAZA, M. (1984) 'Psychoanalysis: subtleties and other obfuscations', *Feminist Issues*, vol. 4, no. 2, Fall, pp. 51–8, first published in *Penelope*, Spring, 1981.

PLAZA, M. (1986) *Ecriture et Folie*, Paris, Press Universitaires de France.

POLGAR, S. (1972) 'Population History and Population Policies from an Anthropological Perspective', *Current Anthropology*, vol. 13, no. 2, pp. 203–11.

POLLACK PETCHESKY, R. (1980) 'Reproductive Freedom: beyond "a woman's right to choose"', *Signs: Journal of Women in Culture and Society*, vol. 5, no. 4, pp. 661–85.

PRESSAT, R. (1979) *Dictionnaire de Démographie*, Paris, PUF.

PRESTIPINO, G. (1979) *Da Gramsci a Marx: il blocco logico storico*, Roma, Editori Riuniti.

PUJEBET, D. (1978) '"Un trou... rien qu'un trou". Propos recueillis', *Histoires d'elles*, no. 3, 8 Feb–8 Mar, p. 22.

RAPHAEL, D. (1972) 'Anthropology and Population Problems: comment', *Current Anthropology*, vol. 13, no. 2, pp. 253–4.

References

RASMUSSEN, K. (1931) *The Netsilik Eskimos: social life and spiritual culture. Report of the Fifth Thule Expedition 1921-24*, vol. 8 (1-2), Copenhagen, Gyldendalske Boghandel, Nordisk Forlag.

RAUM, O. (1940) *Chaga Childhood: a description of indigenous education in an East African tribe*, London, and New York, Oxford University Press (for the International Institute of African Languages and Cultures).

RECHY, J. (1979) *Rushes*, New York, Grove Press.

REITER, R. R. (Ed.) (1975) *Toward an Anthropology of Women*, New York, Monthly Review Press.

RICH, A. (1976) *Of Woman Born*, New York, W. W. Norton and Co.

RICH, A. (1980) 'Compulsory Heterosexuality and Lesbian Existence', *Signs: Journal of Women in Culture and Society*, vol. 5, no. 4, pp. 631-60.

RICHARDS, A. I. (1956) *Chisungu: a girl's initiation ceremony among the Bemba of Northern Rhodesia*, London, Faber and Faber.

ROHEIM, G. (1933) 'Women and their Life in Central Australia', *Journal of the Royal Anthropological Institute*, vol. 63, pp. 207-65.

ROSCOE, J. (1911) *The Baganda: an account of their native customs and beliefs*, London, Macmillan.

ROSCOE, J. (1923) *The Banyankole*, Cambridge, Cambridge University Press.

ROSEN, D. M. (1983) 'The Peasant Context of Feminist Revolt in West Africa', *Anthropological Quarterly*, vol. 56, no. 1, pp. 35-43.

ROSSIAUD, J. (1982) 'Prostitution, sexualité, société dans les villes françaises du XVe siècle', *Communications*, vol. 35 (*Sexualités occidentales*), pp. 68-84.

ROTH, W. E. (1897) *Ethnological Studies among the North-West-Central Queensland Aborigines*, Brisbane.

RUBIN, G. (1975) 'The Traffic in Women: notes on the "political economy" of sex', in REITER, R. R. (Ed.) *Toward an Anthopology of Women*, London and New York, Monthly Review Press, pp. 157-210.

RUITENBEEK, H. M. (Ed.) (1963) *The Problem of Homosexuality in Modern Society*, New York, E. P. Dutton.

RUNTE, A. (1987) 'Male Identity as a Phantasm: the Difficult Border-Line between Lesbianism and Female Trans-Sexualism in Autobiographical Literature', in *Homosexuality, which Homosexuality?* (Social Science, vol. 2, pp. 216-29), Free University, Amsterdam, September 1987.

RUNTE, A. (1988) 'Récits (auto)biographiques de transsexuel(le)s', Paris, June 1988, mimeo.

SAHLINS, M. (1976) *The Use and Abuse of Biology: an anthropological critique of sociobiology*. Ann Arbor, Michigan, University of Michigan Press.

SALADIN D'ANGLURE, B. (1977) 'Mythe de la femme et pouvoir de l'homme chez les Inuit del'Arctique central (Canada)', *Anthropologie et Sociétés*, vol. 1, no. 3, pp. 79-98.

SALADIN D'ANGLURE, B. (1985) 'Du projet "PAR.AD.I" au sexe des anges: notes et débats autour d'un "troisième sexe"', *Anthropologie et Sociétés*, vol. 9, no. 3, pp. 139-76.

SALADIN D'ANGLURE, B. (1986) 'Du foetus au chamane: la construction d'un "troisième sexe" inuit', *Études/Inuit/Studies*, vol. 10, nos 1-2, pp. 25-113.

SALADIN D'ANGLURE, B. (1988) 'Penser le "féminin" chamanique, ou le "tiers-sexe" des chamanes inuit', *Recherches amérindiennes au Québec*, vol. 18, nos 2-3, pp. 19-50.

SANKAR, A. (1986) 'Sisters and Brothers, Lovers and Enemies: Marriage Resistance in Southern Kwangtung', in BLACKWOOD, E. (Ed.) (1986) *The Many Faces of Homosexuality. Anthropological Approaches to Homosexual Behavior*, New York, Harrington Park Press, pp. 69-81.

SARTORI, E. M. and ZIMMERMAN, D. W. (Eds) (1994) *French Women Writers*, Lincoln and London, University of Nebraska Press.

SAUCIER, J. C. (1972) 'Correlations of the Long Post-Partum Taboo: a cross-cultural study', *Current Anthropology*, vol. 13, no. 2, pp. 238–49.

SAUSSURE, F. DE (1959) *Course in General Linguistics* (trans. W. Baskin), London, The Philosophical Library.

SCHAPERA, I. (1971) *Married Life in an African Tribe*, Harmondsworth, Penguin Books (first edition, London, Faber and Faber).

SCHLEGEL, A. (Ed.) (1977) *Sexual Stratification: a cross-cultural view*, New York, Columbia University Press.

SCHNEIDER, D. M. (1955) 'Abortion and Depopulation on a Pacific Island', in PAUL, B. D. (Ed.) *Health, Culture and Community*, New York, Russell Sage Foundation.

SCHRIRE, C. and STEIGER, W. L. (1974) 'A Matter of Life and Death: an investigation into the practice of female infanticide in the Arctic', *Man*, vol. 9, no. 2, pp. 161–84.

SCHWARZER, A. (1984) *Simone de Beauvoir Today: Conversations 1972–1982*, London, Chatto & Windus.

SCOTT, J. W. and TILLY, L. A. (1975) 'Women's Work and Family in Nineteenth Century Europe', *Comparative Studies in Society and History*, vol. 17, pp. 36–64.

SHAPIRO, H. L. (Ed.) (1956) *Man, Culture and Society*, New York, Oxford University Press.

SHEPHERD, G. (1978) 'Transsexualism in Oman?' *Man*, vol. 13, no. 1, pp. 133–4.

SHEPHERD, G. (1987) 'Rank, Gender and Homosexuality: Mombasa as a key to understanding sexual options', in CAPLAN, P. (Ed.) (1987) *The Cultural Construction of Sexuality*, London, Tavistock, pp. 240–70.

SHEPS, M. C. (1965) 'An Analysis of Reproductive Patterns in an American Isolate', *Population Studies*, vol. 19, no. 1, pp. 65–80.

SHERFEY, M. J. (1973) *The Nature and Evolution of Female Sexuality*, New York, Vintage Books (first edition, 1966).

SHORT, R. V. (1978) 'L'Evolution de la reproduction humaine', in SULLEROT, E. (Ed.) *Le Fait féminin*, Paris, Fayard.

SHOSTAK, M. (1983) *Nisa: the life and words of a !Kung woman*, New York, Vintage Books, Random House (first edition, Harvard University Press, 1981).

SILBERBAUER, G. B. (1972) 'The G/Wi Bushmen', in BICCHIERI, G. (Ed.) *Hunters and Gatherers Today*, New York, Holt, Rinehart and Winston.

SILBERBAUER, G. B. (1981) *Hunter and Habitat in the Central Kalahari Desert*, Cambridge and London, Cambridge University Press.

SINDZINGRE, N. (1977) 'Le Plus et le moins: à propos de l'excision', *Cahiers d'Études africaines*, 65, vol. 17, no. 1, special issue, *Des femmes sur l'Afrique des femmes*, pp. 65–75.

SINDZINGRE, N. (1979) 'Un Excès par défaut: excision et représentations de la féminité', *L'Homme*, vol. 19, nos 3–4, pp. 171–87.

SKEGG, B. (1996) *Becoming Respectable: an ethnography of white working class women*, London, Sage.

SPENCER, B. and GILLEN, F. J. (1927) *The Arunta: a study of a stone-age people*, London, Macmillan.

SPENCER, P. (1965) *The Samburu: a study of gerontocracy in a nomadic Masai tribe*, Berkeley and Los Angeles, University of California Press; London, Routledge and Kegan Paul.

SPENCER, P. (1973) *Nomads in Alliance: symbiosis and growth among the Rendille and the Samburu of Kenya*, London, Oxford University Press.

SULLEROT, E. (1968) *Histoire et sociologie du travail féminin*, Paris, Gonthier.

SULLEROT, E. (Ed.) (1978) *Le fait féminin*, Paris, Fayard.

SYMONS. D. (1979) *The Evolution of Human Sexuality*, New York and London, Oxford University Press.

References

TABET, P. (1979) 'Les Mains, les outils, les armes', *L'Homme*, vol. 19, nos 3–4, special issue, *Les catégories de sexe en anthropologie sociale*, pp. 5–61. Translated Tabet (1982).

TABET, P. (1982) 'Hands, Tools, Weapons', *Feminist Issues*, vol. 2, no. 2, pp. 3–62.

TABET, P. (1985) 'Fertilité naturelle, reproduction forcée', in MATHIEU, N-C. (Ed.), Sexual, Sexed and Sex-Class Identities: Three Ways of Conceptualising the Relationship Between Sex and Gender, pp. 61–146. Translated in this volume.

TABET, P. (1987) 'Du don au tarif. Les relations sexuelles impliquant une compensation', *Les Temps modernes*, vol. 490, pp. 1–53.

TABET, P. (1989) '"I'm the meat, I'm the knife". Sexual service, migration and repression in some African societies', in PHETERSON, G. (Ed.) *A Vindication of the Rights of Whores*, Seattle, Seal Press.

TABET, P. (1991) 'Les dents de la prostituée: échange, negotiation, choix dans les rapports économico sexuels', in HURTIG, M-C., KAIL, M. and ROUCH, H. (Eds) *Sexe et Genre. De la hiéarchive entre les sexes*, Paris, Editions du CNRS.

TELEKI, G., HUNT, E. E. and PFIFFERLING, J. H. (1976) 'Demographic Observations (1963–1973) on the Chimpanzees of Gombe National Park, Tanzania', *Journal of Human Evolution*, vol. 6, pp. 559–98.

THALMANN, R. (1982) *Etre femme sous le IIIᵉ Reich*, Paris, Robert Laffont.

The Petit Robert dictionary (1973 edition).

TILLY, L. A. and SCOTT, J. W. (1978) *Women, Work, and Family*, New York, Holt, Rinehart and Winston.

TINDALE, N. (1972) 'The Pitjandjara', in BICCHIERI, G. (Ed.) *Hunters and Gatherers Today*, New York, Holt, Rinehart and Winston.

TOPLEY, M. (1975) 'Marriage Resistance in Rural Kwangtung', in WOLF, M. and WITKE, R. (Eds) *Women in Chinese Society*, Stanford, Stanford University Press.

VANDELAC, L. (1981a) 'Contraception autoroute pour sexualité bolide', *Le Temps fou*, vol. 13 (February–March), Montréal.

VANDELAC, L. (1981b) ' "... Et si le travail tombait enceinte???": essai féministe sur le concept travail', *Sociologie et Sociétés*, vol. 13, no. 2, pp. 67–82.

VANDERSYPEN, M. (1977) 'Femmes libres de Kigali', *Cahiers d'Études africaines*, 65, XVII, no. 1, special issue, *Des femmes sur l'Afrique des femmes*, pp. 95–120.

VAN DE VELDE, F. (1954) 'L'Infanticide chez les Esquimaux', *Eskimo*, vol. 34, pp. 6–8.

VARIKAS, E. (1987) 'Droit naturel, nature féminine et égalité de sexes', *L'Homme et la Société*, vol. 21, nos 85–86, pp. 98–112.

VERNANT, J.-P. (1972) 'Introduction', in DETIENNE, M. (Ed.) *Les Jardins d'Adonis*, Paris, Gallimard.

VERNANT, J.-P. (1974) *Mythe et société en Grèce ancienne*, Paris, Maspero.

VEYNE, P. (1982) 'L'Homosexualité à Rome', *Communications*, vol. 35 (Sexualités occidentales), pp. 26–33.

VIDAL, C. (1977) 'Guerre des sexes à Abidjan: masculin, féminin, CFA', *Cahiers d'Études africaines*, 65, XVII, no. 1, numéro spécial, *Des femmes sur l'Afrique des femmes*, pp. 121–53.

VIS, H. L., HENNART, Ph. and RUCHABABISHA, M. (1981) 'L'Allaitement en zone rurale pauvre: l'alimentation maternelle et l'allaitement au Kivu, Zaire', *Les Carnets de l'Enfance* (2: 'Allaitement maternel et santé'), pp. 55–6.

WALBY, S. (1986) *Patriarchy at Work: patriarchal and capitalist relations in employment*, Cambridge, Polity.

WARD-JOUVE, N. (1991) *White Woman Speaks with Forked Tongue: criticism as autobiography*, London and New York, Routledge.

WARNER, W. L. (1937) *A Black Civilisation: a social study of an Australian tribe*, New York, Harper.

WERLHOF, C. VON, MIES, M. and BENNHOLDT-THOMSEN, V. (Eds) (1983) *Frauen, die letzte Kolonie*, Reinbek bei Hamburg, Rowohlt Taschenbuch Verlag.

WHITE, L. (1990) *The Comforts of Home: Prostitution in Colonial Nairobi*, Chicago and London, University of Chicago Press.

WHITEHEAD, H. (1981) 'The Bow and the Burden Strap: a new look at institutionalized homosexuality in native North America', in ORTNER, S. and WHITEHEAD, H. (Eds) *Sexual Meanings: the cultural construction of gender and sexuality*, Cambridge and London, Cambridge University Press, pp. 80–115.

WILLIAMS, F. E. (1969) *Papuans of the Trans-Fly*, Oxford, Clarendon Press (first edition 1936).

WILSON, M. (1951) *Good Company: a study of Nyakyusa age-villages*, London and New York, International African Institute, Oxford University Press.

WILSON, M. (1957) *Rituals of Kinship among the Nyakyusa*, London and New York, International African Institute, Oxford University Press.

WILSON, M. (1977) *For Men and Elders: change in the relations of generations and of men and women among the Nyakyusa-Ngonde people, 1875–1971*, London, International African Institute.

WITTIG, M. (1980a) 'On ne naît pas femme', *Questions féministes*, no. 8, pp. 75–84. Translated Wittig (1981).

WITTIG, M. (1980b) 'The Straight Mind', *Feminist Issues*, vol. 1, no. 1, summer. Reprinted in Wittig (1992).

WITTIG, M. (1981) 'One is Not Born a Woman', *Feminist Issues*, vol. 1, no. 2, summer. Reprinted in Wittig (1992).

WITTIG, M. (1992) *The Straight Mind and Other Essays*, Boston, Beacon Press/Hemel Hempstead, Harvester Wheatsheaf.

WOLF, M. and WITKE, R. (Eds) (1975) *Women in Chinese Society*, Stanford, Stanford University Press.

Notes on Contributors

Lisa Adkins is a Lecturer in Sociology at the University of Kent at Canterbury. She has recently published *Gendered Work: sexuality, family and the labour market* (Open University Press, 1995) and is the co-editor of two collections from the 1994 British Sociological Association conference: (with Janet Holland) *Sex, Sensibility and the Gendered Body* and (with Vicki Merchant) *Sexualizing the Social* (both Macmillan, in press).

Christine Delphy is a Chargée de recherche on the staff of the Centre National de Recherche Scientifiques (CNRS), IRESCO, Paris and Editor of *Nouvelles Questions Féministes*. A collection of her papers was published as *Close to Home: a materialist analysis of women's oppression* (Hutchinson, 1984) and she is the author (with Diana Leonard) of *Familiar Exploitation: a new analysis of marriage in contemporary western society* (Polity Press, 1992).

Colette Guillaumin is a Chargée de recherche with the CNRS, Paris. She is the author of *L'Idéologie raciste. Genèse et langage actuel* (Mouton, 1972). A collection of her papers was published as *Sexe, race et pratique du pouvoir. L'idée de Nature* (Côté-femmes, 1992) and another as *Racism, Sexism, Power and Ideology* (Routledge, 1995).

Diana Leonard is a Senior Lecturer in Sociology and Head of the Centre for Research and Education on Gender at the Institute of Education, University of London. Her most recent publications have been an edited collection (with Sheila Allen) of *Sexual Divisions Revisited* (Macmillan, 1991) and a book (with Christine Delphy) *Familiar Exploitation* (Polity Press, 1992).

Nicole-Claude Mathieu is Maître de conférences at the École des Hautes Études en Sciences Sociales in Paris, and a member of the Laboratoire d'Anthropologie sociale. She is the editor of the very influential collection *L'Arraisonnement des femmes: essais en anthropologie des sexes* (Éditions de l'École des Hautes Études en Sciences Sociales, 1985) and a collection of her papers was published as *L'Anatomie politique: catégorisations et idéologies du sexe* (Côté-femmes, 1991).

Monique Plaza has a doctorate in psychology and is a Chargée de recherche with the CNRS in Paris. She is the author of *Ecriture et folie* (Presses Universitaires de France, 1986) and co-author of *La démarche clinique en sciences humaines* (Revault d'Allones ed, Dunod, 1989). Her current research is on childhood neuropsychology.

Paola Tabet is Professor of Anthropology at the University of Calabria. From 1976–1991 she conducted research on the anthropology of the sexes and published articles on gender differentiated access to tools, reproduction and sexual-economic exchange. Her current research is on children and racism in contemporary Italy. A collection of her main essays is forthcoming (Paris, L'Harmattan).

Monique Wittig is a writer and Professor in the Department of French and Italian at the University of Arizona. She is the author of several plays and novels, including *Les Guérillères* and *The Lesbian Body* and winner of the Prix Medicis. A collection of her essays was published in 1992 as *The Straight Mind and other essays* (Harvester Wheatsheaf).

Other publications by the contributors can be found in the bibliography.

Index

Note: 'n.' after a page reference indicates the number of a note on that page.